ANSWERING SODOM

RALPH OVADAL

Heart of the Matter Publications
Monroe, Wisconsin

Unless otherwise noted, all Scripture quotations are from the King James Version.

Answering Sodom

ISBN 0-9665251-0-8

Library of Congress Catalog Card Number 98-093183

Heart of the Matter Publications
P.O. Box 621
Monroe, Wisconsin 53566

Table of Contents

Acknowledgments

Cover design by Michael J. Foht.

Cover photo by Richard Bergum.

Special thanks to Janet and Joy Ovadal for their dedication and hard work which helped make this book possible.

Author's Note

In September of 1996, I received a phone call from the Dane County, Wisconsin District Attorney's office. That one phone call, as much as any other experience I have ever had, demonstrates the urgent need for Christians to stand up against the homosexual movement before it is too late.

On May 1, 1996, I had been attacked from behind and knocked unconscious as I had stood, Bible in hand, handing out "anti-gay" literature in front of a public (government) elementary school in Madison, Wisconsin which was hosting a pictorial display of "gay and lesbian families." The person who had assaulted me had not appreciated my ministry and made his opinion plain by leaving me with a swollen ear, cuts and contusions to the side of my head, a pounding headache, and a badly wrenched knee and ankle. Police arriving on the scene had arrested the man and charged him with substantial battery for what they had called a life-threatening act.

The call I referred to earlier came one day before my assailant was due to go on trial. An assistant district attorney cheerfully informed me that my presence would not be needed at the trial because it had been called off! Indeed, I was told that since my attacker "does not want a criminal record," the charge against him would be dropped to an ordinance violation as long as he was willing to pay my medical bills! The sad part of the whole episode is that I was not the least bit surprised by the sordid affair.

While much of the body of Christ has slept, sodomites and their supporters have inched their way into positions of influence in virtually every American institution. We have now arrived at a place where a man who responds with any measure of force to the lewd advances of a sodomite may well be charged not only with battery, but also with a hate crime in many states. Meanwhile, a champion of homosexuality can brutally attack a Christian pastor and get off with the equivalent of a traffic ticket. What this tells us is that there is a form of fascism afoot in America, a form of fascism which threatens the well-being and liberty of every moral man, woman, and child in this nation—especially those who love the Lord and His eternal precepts. A fascist beast is on the loose, a beast which must be met head-on and pushed back into the dark lair from whence it came before it gains so much strength that it will completely overwhelm all opposition.

Over the years, I have felt the fury of the homosexual movement, via both physical attacks and hundreds of threats. I have seen the rage that a simple gospel message of repentance and rebirth can kindle in the hard-core sodomite's heart. My testimony to those with ears to hear is that a fascist heart beats in the bosom of America's very dangerous homosexual movement. Yet this is no excuse to draw back or to mute the gospel in the face of the "gay" brown shirts. Quite the opposite. Though the sodomites may rage and gnash their teeth, this is no time to be timid. Winston Churchill captured the folly of co-existing with tyranny in the vain hope that somehow the wicked will all see the error of their ways or perhaps will be willing to live peacefully side-by-side with the righteous. Churchill wrote: *"If you will not fight when you can easily win without blood shed, and if you will not fight when your victory will be sure and not so costly, then you may come to the time when you will have to fight with all of the odds against you and only a slight chance for survival. There may be a worse case though. You may have to fight when there is no chance of victory because it is better to perish than to live as slaves."*

I have written *Answering Sodom* for the same reason that I dedicate a great deal of my time to fighting the homosexual movement: I perceived an urgent need and felt a clear call from the Lord. I pray this book will contribute to the cause of Christ. I pray it will be a great asset to His people by equipping them to fight the good fight against a movement from hell, even as they pray and work to snatch members of that movement from a fiery eternity and see them brought into God's heavenly kingdom.

The author and Dr. Tony Campolo debating on the public sidewalk in Madison, Wisconsin.

Shedding light on a dark subject with a prophetic picket.

Television debate between Pastor Ralph Ovadal and one of Sodom's clergymen champions. ("Citizens Comments," WHKE-TV 55, June 7, 1995)

Ralph Ovadal versus homosexual State Representative Tammy Baldwin on Wisconsin Public Television. ("Weekend," May 24, 1996)

CHAPTER ONE

Harbingers of Hell in the Halls of the Church

Just who's making the rules here?
—"Gay" United Church of Christ Pastor

The evening of April 12, 1996 was beautiful and calm in Madison, Wisconsin. Well, at least the weather was calm. By seven o'clock, the night air in front of Trinity Evangelical Fellowship Church was rent with curses, blasphemous invectives, and chants such as "Crush the Christians! Bring back the lions!" and "Queer mob rule!" The event inside the church, which had touched off the raucous demonstration outside, was a joint speaking appearance by Scott Lively and me. Scott is the author of *The Pink Swastika: Homosexuality in the Nazi Party.* The protesters, who numbered over four hundred strong, were representatives of that most tolerant of all groups, the homosexual community. While sodomites outside the church trespassed en masse on church property, blocked off a city street, cursed, screamed, waved signs, threw stones at the church, and even ate fire, one hundred of their comrades who had gained entrance to the small sanctuary mocked and spat epithets at Lively and me as we took advantage of the opportunity to preach to them. Several of the sodomites, apparently wishing to express their utter disdain for Scott, me, and the eternal truths upon which our messages were based, urinated on the basement floor of the church. At the end of the evening, Madison police officers escorted Mr. Lively out of the front of the church, while insisting that I be taken out of the building's darkened rear into an unmarked squad car in which I was then whisked away to a rendezvous point with the Christian brother who had originally driven me to the meeting. At two subsequent meetings in Plover and Janesville, Wisconsin, homosexual activists, organized and led by the Lesbian Avengers, also greeted Lively and me with similar antics. However, thanks to much better police work in those two cities, the sodomites were kept under control.

Two incidents from that Wisconsin Christians United Truth Tour have been deeply etched into my mind—incidents which speak volumes concerning the dangerous and perverse state to which America has degenerated. At the end of the evening in Madison, police would not allow me to leave the church on my own by the way in which I had entered. One told me, "You'll never make it." When it was time to exit Trinity Evangelical, four police officers escorted me to the rear of the now empty, darkened church and took up positions in the front, the back, and on each side of me, the ones on the sides grasping my arms. Earlier, their commanding officer had asked me to call off our meeting due to his assessment that he could not guarantee Lively's or my safety. I had, of course, turned down his request. As we waited for the radio signal to rush out of the church door and into the waiting unmarked squad car, I sensed that the officers surrounding me were nervous about their pending mission! These men who had faced all manner of volatile, dangerous situations were actually uneasy at the prospect of having the howling sodomites in the front of the church spot us as we secreted out of the back. I have seen many things in my years of ministry, but as I stood surrounded by four tense police officers in a darkened church, listening to the screams emanating from the mob of homosexuals outside, I felt deeply grieved in my heart that such a thing could be happening in America. I must say, at that moment, I felt an eerie kinship with Lot.

The second episode which was indelibly etched into my mind happened in both Madison and Plover. At both stops on the Truth Tour, I went out to speak with the homosexual mobs and did so until I was ordered by the police to go back inside for safety's sake. In both instances, a number of homosexuals, upon seeing me, began to scream, "You are the antichrist!" The antichrist? I—a Christian broadcaster and missionary; the shepherd of a Bible-believing, non-denominational church—the antichrist? Such is the demented mind of the homosexual community. Evil is good; good is evil; light is darkness; and darkness is light. A perverse reformation is sweeping our land; a perverted gospel is being preached; doctrines of devils are being promoted as holy writ—all for the advancement and glorification of a behavior which God has pronounced to be an abomination.

On March 6, 1975, leaders of the National Council of Churches adopted what they called "A Resolution on Civil Rights Without Discrimination as to Affectional or Sexual Preference." That resolution reads in part:

> The National Council of the Churches of Christ has always held that, as a child of God, every person is endowed with worth and dignity that human judgment cannot set aside. Therefore every person is entitled to equal treatment under the law.
>
> For this reason the National Council of the Churches of Christ has endeavored to insure for all persons regardless of race, class, sex, creed, or place of national origin their full civil rights. To this list the Governing Board now adds affectional or sexual preference. Discrimination based on any of those criteria is morally wrong.[1]

What the National Council of Churches was in essence claiming, way back in 1975, was that God has granted man complete autonomy regarding sexual relations and that every person's "sexual preference" should be respected and protected. That cutting-edge statement espoused the concept that each person may legitimately engage in any sexual act which is right in his own eyes. The writers of the resolution also took the position that it is morally wrong to discriminate against homosexuals in any way and called for the force of civil law to be used to ensure that such discrimination not take place. Seven years later, Wisconsin became the first of a dozen states to codify that tenet of the homosexual agenda into state law.

Twenty-two years and many pro-"gay" proclamations after the National Council of Churches issued its resolution, another pro-homosexual manifesto was published by seventy-six Wisconsin pastors and eighteen religious leaders representing a variety of mainline Protestant denominations as well as a Jewish synagogue and several Unitarian and Roman Catholic churches. The widely publicized statement was titled "On Homosexuality and Christian Faith: A Madison Affirmation" and contained this amazing and, might I add, demonic statement:

> Jesus Christ calls us to love God and our neighbor as ourselves. As Christian clergy we embrace gay and lesbian persons as our neighbors. From our reading of scripture and from our pastoral experiences, we believe there is sufficient evidence to conclude that homosexuality is neither sickness nor sin.[2]

The Madison Affirmation identified homosexuals as "a unique, holy, and precious gift" to the church of Jesus Christ and called upon us Christians who are against homosexual behavior to "acknowledge our sin and be forgiven for our ignorance, fear, arrogance and self-righteousness." Addressing those who defend scriptural passages which condemn homosexual behavior, the pastors haughtily instructed, "[T]he Bible has been misused in support of this condemnation. This abuse of scripture must end."[3]

In 1975, a rogue, ostensibly Christian organization proclaimed that homosexual people have the "right" to practice the perverted sexual acts they prefer or choose and that no one, including presumably God, has the right to discriminate against such persons in any case for any reason. In 1997 in yet another stunning display of how far America has fallen, seventy-six pastors and eighteen representatives of eleven religious and "Christian" denominations publicly portrayed homosexuality as a wonderful gift from God, an inherent trait defining the very personhood of certain individuals. The lie which those false shepherds foisted upon a Biblically illiterate world was that God Himself specifically creates certain individuals to perform homosexual acts. In other words, the message to the masses was this: God is pro-homosexual; the Creator Himself blesses sodomy and other related perversions central to the homosexual life. This is a message many are working hard to spread under the color of Christianity in hopes of gaining credibility for an incredible lie.

In 1994, before I had become quite as well-known among homosexual leaders, I attended a day-long seminar at the Catholic St. Benedict Center in Middleton, Wisconsin. The conference was dubbed "Opening the Doors: Inclusive Ministry with Gays, Lesbians, and Bisexuals." The doors which were so in need of opening were the doors to the church of Jesus Christ—not just one denominational church, but all Christian churches, all denominations.

The keynote speaker was Chris Glaser, a "gay" author with a Master's degree in Divinity from Yale Divinity School. Glaser is also the former director of the Lazarus Project, "a ministry reconciling the church and the lesbian and gay community." Mr. Glaser opened and closed his presentation with prayer. Throughout his lengthy remarks he denigrated the "religious right" and, at one point, said that "fundamentalists are bizarre" for being against same-sex marriages. The enthusiastically-received keynoter also called for "more explicit sexuality and more explicit spirituality in the church" as he spoke of tearing down "old church structures." Glaser informed his listeners, "The church will feel less threatened as they see our coming out as a sacred offering; we sacrificially offer ourselves to the church. Our coming out of the closet is similar to God coming out of the closet of heaven in the person of Jesus." He also portrayed the covenant between David and Jonathan in I Samuel 18 as a homosexual covenant. During his talk, Mr. Glaser compared homosexuals to the prophets of the Old Testament, saying both "live on the margins of society, and are, therefore, better able to critique it."

By the grace of God, I was able to sit through nearly the entire Opening the Doors seminar before being recognized. During the course of the day, religious authors, pastors, elders, and activists (most of them homosexual) spoke and took part in workshops. One openly homosexual United Church of Christ pastor, who pronounced homosexuality to be the "call and claim of God on my life," began his message by proclaiming, "I'm on with the Holy Spirit today." The wolf in sheep's clothing then proceeded to call for "God's church to admit their mistake" for condemning homosexuality and angrily posed the question, "Just who's making the rules here?"

A non-homosexual pastor who confessed to once being a "homo-phobe" was received by his listeners with much appreciation as he spoke of how to become an advocate of homosexuality in the church. "I cannot be silent," the Lutheran (ELCA) pastor exhorted his rapt audi-ence. "This [homosexuality] is a gospel issue!"

Another interesting speaker at the conference was the mother of a homosexual man who said that she had grown up in the church and had been devastated upon learning of her son's "orientation." After having a pastor assure her that her son was heaven-bound because "it does not make sense that God would abandon some of His children [to hell]," the woman had not only accepted her son's homosexuality, but had gone to work with the homosexual advocacy group Parents and Friends of Lesbians and Gays.

Other speakers also related how clergymen had encouraged them to accept homosexuality as being approved of by God. Meg Gaines, a lesbian Episcopalian church leader and author spoke of struggling with her sexuality in college and finally going to a campus chaplain for counsel. She shared how he had told her, "Your sexuality, whatever it is, is a gift from God." Smiling broadly, the lesbian exclaimed that she had then realized that it "is my duty to God to be who I am as a lesbian. . . . I never looked back."

Throughout the Opening the Doors conference, there was one theme to which every speaker constantly returned and to which all strategy was directed; it was the unbroken thread which ran through every presentation. That theme was summed up by Meg Gaines. Articulating a truth which many in the true Bible-believing church have not yet grasped, Gaines said, "The church is the place this issue must be addressed; churches set tone and policy [in the nation]. The church is so important because the church is seen as authority."

The Opening the Doors gathering in Madison that spring day in 1994 was no aberration, but rather part and parcel of a concerted, on-going effort by the homosexual movement to enlist as many churches and denominations as possible to openly assist in the homosexualization of America. Many homosexuals view the church as an institution which must be converted to their perverted doctrine and, in turn, used to advance the "gay" agenda by legitimizing it in the minds of as many Americans as possible. Still, other homosexuals desperately desire God to vicariously bless their perverted lifestyle through ministers who claim to speak for Him.

All unsaved people have an inborn fear of death and of, what is for them, the unknown which lies beyond the grave. At some point, all human beings search for some assurance of life after death. Because no person has the power to grant eternal life to himself, this search inevitably leads to God. People, even incredibly evil people, want to believe in God, or at least in a god who can save them from death and the grave. At the same time, many want to be their own god, answerable to no higher power in this life other than their own warped concept of right and wrong.

In a recent survey, it was revealed that over 70% of all Americans never doubt the existence of God.[4] To see the wickedness and rebellion of American society today is to realize what that survey really means. The majority of Americans who profess faith in God do so because they believe in a god whom they have created in their own image! The cheap-grace-without-law, my-God-is-loving-and-never-judgmental Christians envision a God Who sent His Son to die on a cross so that man might have a license to sin. The "Christian" feminists believe in mother god. The New Agers see themselves as gods. The pro-abortionists trust in a god who is pro-death. And of course, the homosexuals are enthusiastically embracing a god who is pro-sodomy. As one lesbian told me, "I am a lesbian and proud of it. I am at peace with God, my Creator, who made me exactly the way I am!"

The god that many American "Christians" acknowledge is a universalist, utilitarian god devoid of moral absolutes, wrath, and judgment. If he is angry with anyone, he is angry with those bigots who insist on "forcing their religious beliefs on others." This is the god of America in the waning days of the twentieth century. This is a god who can be embraced even by those who are in extreme rebellion against the immutable law and eternal truth of the Bible. Quite frankly, this is a god with whom over 70% of an extremely hedonistic, rebellious nation can live. Most tragically, it is a god who is being preached to a whole generation of American youth.

I have spent many hours on public sidewalks in front of state high schools and middle schools sharing information on homosexuality and preaching the gospel to young people. Because the civil government, at least in part, has justified homosexual activity in the minds of many Americans by protecting such activity instead of punishing it, many of the youth I meet have relatives who are "out and proud." Often times, the impressionable young people react with disbelief and predictable fury against anyone who would dare to suggest that their favorite "gay" uncle or "lesbian" aunt is headed for hell short of repentance. Such are the results of removing the fear and stigma once connected to homosexual acts.

Whenever I minister with others from Wisconsin Christians United on the public sidewalk in front of a state school, we are inevitably confronted by young people who are outraged that the word *repent* could be connected to homosexuality. Countless times I have been told, "God loves everyone; there is nothing wrong with homosexuality. Judge not lest you be judged. You're the one who needs to repent. You're going to hell for your hatred and judgmentalism."

Sadly enough, but not surprisingly, I have heard the same perverted gospel from pastors. I will never forget the United Methodist clergyman who stopped to confront me during a Wisconsin Christians United prophetic picket along a busy street during rush hour in Wausau, Wisconsin. Pointing to one of our large signs which read, "Homosexuals:

Repent or Perish—I Cor. 6:9-11" (and ignoring the next sign which said, "Christ Can Set You Free"), the pastor demanded to know how I dared to display such a "hateful, unbiblical message." He stood with a red face, clenched-teeth, and doubled-up fists, apparently ignoring every Scripture verse I presented to him, and finally left after darkly warning me that I was headed for an eternity in hell as a result of my lack of "Christian love."

Yet another of many memorable events which comes to my mind when speaking of pro-homosexual church leaders concerns a confrontation with a woman youth group leader from a liberal Lutheran church in Stoughton, Wisconsin. During a WCU picket and literature distribution in that town, the woman pulled her van to the curb and confronted me for my "homophobia." As her young charges from the local church mocked me, I debated her on the Word of God regarding homosexuality and shared the gospel with her. By the grace of God, several of the youth finally agreed to take some literature on the subject. Their lady leader, however, apparently deciding that she could not debate the issue of homosexuality on Biblical grounds and not wanting to yield to the truth, blurted out, "Go to hell!" and squealed away from the curb!

The sad fact is that the homosexual movement has been fabulously successful in commandeering much of the American church for its own use, to one extent or another. Time after time, during public witnessing, radio or television talk shows, and formal debates, I have met scorn and downright hatred from self-identified Christians for simply stating the obvious: *Homosexual acts are acts of extreme sexual perversion and rebellion against God. Homosexuals are sexual outlaws who will spend eternity in the torment of the lake of fire unless they repent and give their lives to Jesus Christ. Those who are willing to repent can be washed, sanctified, and justified in the name of the Lord Jesus and in the Spirit of our God.* I can confidently relate from personal experience that a great many of those 70% of Americans who say they believe in God find such a Biblically-based message to be judgmental, hateful, and very unchristian!

There is a great struggle over homosexuality in progress in America. This is a battle for the heart, mind, and soul of our nation. Those who support homosexuality are desperate to convince the American people that God also condones such activity. The homosexualists (all who promote homosexuality) are literally terrified of Christians who, armed with Christ's righteousness and Biblical truth, are not afraid or ashamed to attack the flawed presuppositions, distorted doctrines, and outright lies of the homosexual movement. Liars have no effective defensive weapons with which to respond when the artillery of truth is aggressively and repeatedly brought to bear on their flimsy breastwork of falsehoods. This explains why the homosexualists so often resort to mockery, more deception, and character assassination when they are faced with irrefutable truth.

It is time that Christians understood that the homosexual movement is, at heart, a fascist movement which uses fascist tactics to silence its opponents. Those Americans who dissent from pro-homosexual doctrine are demonized, marginalized, and eventually isolated in hopes of destroying their credibility and, at times, even their humanity. Such tactics were honed to a fine edge by Adolf Hitler and his Nazi friends. Just ask any Jew or dissenting Christian who lived in Germany during the 1930s and '40s. Ironically, those dissenting Christians who speak out against homosexuality in America today are portrayed as operating on the same moral plane as Adolf Hitler and as being very nearly as dangerous to public safety and welfare. The strategy is simple, tried, and true: link an honestly-held moral position to an immoral, illogical, even violent philosophy or group of people in hopes that the reputation and credibility of the targeted person will be destroyed. This is a classic fascist maneuver. As the Führer is credited with once saying, "Tell a lie, tell it often, and soon the people will believe it."

In recent years, this strategy has been used in the growing push to enact civil laws to punish those who speak out against homosexuality, calling such dissent "hate speech." Typical evidence of this trend appeared in the Winter 1998 issue of the Parents and Friends of Lesbians and Gays newsletter which carried a report on PFLAG President Nancy

McDonald's attendance of the White House Conference on Hate Crimes in the fall of 1997. Summarizing the conference, the article ended with this revealing statement:

> "Hopefully this summit will bring much more attention to the high rise in hate crimes against gays and lesbians," McDonald added. In addition, other areas needing attention include tracking hate crimes, supporting strategies to prevent such acts of violence and ending hate speech, she said.[5]

As an enemy of the homosexual agenda, I have many times experienced first-hand the pro-homosexuals' fascist tactic of public mischaracterization and demonization. Allow me to share just one case-in-point. As part of my ministry with Wisconsin Christians United, I often lead fellow Christians to the sidewalks in front of pro-homosexual church events to take a stand against homosexuality and to witness on behalf of Biblical truth while sharing the gospel. On March 3, 1996, WCU was present on the public sidewalk in front of University United Methodist Church in Madison in order to be a prophetic witness at a service of "remembrance, healing and hope." The event had been called to mourn the loss of the Hotel Washington, a local gay night club complex pandering to the various perverted activities which make such establishments so popular with the homosexual community. The Hotel Washington had burned down on February 18, 1996, perhaps as a result of many fervent prayers by a number of Christians, including, quite frankly, myself. At the UUMC that night, we stood on the public sidewalk holding signs with Biblical messages, passing out salvation tracts, and engaging in the hallowed and constitutionally-protected tradition of street preaching. That was all.

Several days later, the leaders of UUMC, along with a number of other pro-homosexual clergy people, held a press conference. The Reverend Dianne Reistroffer, leader of the group and pastor of UUMC, read an amazing statement accusing WCU of conducting an "escalating campaign of harassment, intimidation, and disorderly conduct."[6] The statement also asserted as fact that WCU had engaged in a variety of unlawful activities at Reistroffer's church, activities which never took place as police officers who were on the scene that night agreed. As if it were not enough to cast concerned Christians exposing the unfruitful works of darkness and sharing the gospel of Jesus Christ to be some sort of brown-shirted storm troopers, the document issued at the press conference included this libelous, baseless statement:

> As Jews, Catholics, Unitarian Universalists, and Protestants, we are deeply disturbed by the anti-gay and anti-Semitic rhetoric and activity in our city by a group calling itself Wisconsin Christians United ...
> We from the Christian community are particularly grieved and embarrassed by Wisconsin Christians United's blatant anti-Semitism ...[7]

In a subsequent interview during the local CBS news broadcast in Madison, the Reverend Dianne Reistroffer repeated charges of anti-Semitism against WCU and made wild claims that we had blocked her church driveways, video taped license plates of her congregation, and harassed her parishioners to the point that they were afraid to come to the church.[8]

Of course, we should not be surprised that those who praise activity which God condemns would also so easily engage in false witness. That is how the homosexualists work. The only hope that they have of countering a no-compromise message based on immutable truth is to kill the messenger by destroying his credibility with the general population. What better way is there to accomplish that task than to equate "anti-gays" to violent, racist bigots? As I pointed out in a newspaper article following the Reistroffer group's press conference, those who are determined to mainstream homosexual activity are not above capitalizing on the horrible suffering of the Jews at the hands of Hitler in order to advance their own perverse agenda.[9]

In this particular case, a quick call from me to the manager of the television station which aired the story caused it to be scratched from subsequent news reports that day.

I do not share these things with you to frighten you. The Scriptures are clear that we are to trust in the Lord and not be frightened by any fear. We can indeed do all things through Him who strengthens us—all things, even winning victories over the homosexual lobby and snatching individual homosexuals from the flames of hell. Such victories are, of course, predicated on our willingness to suffer reproach and sometimes even physical danger for the cause of Christ. I have seen great victories won over the purveyors of perversion. I have seen political victories won, minds educated, hearts changed, and souls saved.

Here in Wisconsin, we have seen some of the very enemies of righteousness spoken of in this chapter routed and silenced because Christians were willing to hold their ground under withering fire and then boldly counterattack using the homosexualists' own eccentric behavior and blatant lies to discredit them and expose the true heart of the homosexual movement. By the grace of God, I fully expect to see many more such victories in the future.

Raising up God's righteous standard in the face of the growing sodomite nation in our midst is not optional. To hate evil, warn the wicked, reprove the ruthless, establish justice, and earnestly contend for the faith are all commands of Scripture. Beyond that, a battle is raging. The enemy is relentlessly attacking, and every single family, every child, all of our treasured institutions and civil structures, as well as our nation's very future, are faced with a real and present danger. America truly stands on the brink of a great yawning precipice from which there may be no return once she has slid over the edge and into the black pit of total anarchy. This is no time for timidity, compromise, or equivocation on the part of the body of Christ. Those Christians who cower before the sodomite juggernaut in hopes of clinging to peace a bit longer may well end up swept away by the judgment of God which is most certainly coming upon America. We must equip ourselves and take a pro-active, Biblically-correct stand against the homosexual movement. To do otherwise is to ensure that America will indeed go into a long, dark night of depravity and slavery under the heavy hand of the God-haters.

On March 23, 1775, Patrick Henry rose to answer certain gentlemen in the Virginia Second Convention who felt that compromise and appeasement with British tyranny was an option. To those well-meaning dreamers Henry retorted:

The battle, sir, is not to the strong alone; it is to the vigilant, the active, the brave. Besides, sir, we have no election. If we were base enough to desire it, it is now too late to retire from the contest. There is no retreat but in submission and slavery! . . .

It is in vain, sir, to extenuate the matter. Gentlemen may cry peace, peace—but there is no peace. . . . Our brethren are already in the field! Why stand we here idle? What is it that gentlemen wish? What would they have? Is life so dear, or peace so sweet, as to be purchased at the price of chains and slavery? Forbid it, Almighty God! I know not what course others may take; but as for me, give me liberty or give me death![10]

The serpent of homosexuality has slithered into every American institution. The secular media has been only too happy to act as a mouthpiece for the advancement of perversion. The two major political parties are heavily influenced by the "gay" community. The government school system has become an advocate for the sodomite cause. Many social action organizations include homosexuals and their supporters at the highest levels. The medical community has been, in many cases, a virtual handmaiden of the queer nation. Last, but not least, the American church has been extensively used, in various ways, to advance a cause which can only be described as originating from the pit of hell.

The sodomite nation in our midst has declared war on all who have not willingly acquiesced to their deranged agenda. For the sake of Christ and His gospel, the weak and the vulnerable, our nation and our families, for the sake of the homosexuals themselves, the true church of Jesus Christ must rise up and take a righteous, public stand against homosexuality. Yes, there is a price to be paid, a cross to be borne by those who stand against the sodomite nation which has grown up in our midst. We will be misunderstood, threatened, slandered, and mocked. Some of us will be the recipients of physical violence. Some of us already have been. Yet did not our Master warn us that the wicked will hate us just as they hated Him?

The disciple is not above his master, nor the servant above his lord. It is enough for the disciple that he be as his master, and the servant as his lord. If they have called the master of the house Beelzebub, how much more shall they call them of his household? (Matthew 10:24-25)

No, it is not the place of a Christian to sit idly by as a perverse, anti-God sodomite culture assaults eternal truth and deceives and steals vulnerable hearts and minds. There truly is no retreat from this struggle which has been thrust upon us except at the price of submission, shame, and slavery. Besides, to retire from this contest now or to fail to fight the battle at all would be nothing less than base, very base indeed. As to those Christians, especially Christian leaders, who have not taken a public stand against homosexuality, I can only ask: *Your brethren are already in the field. Why stand you idle?*

CHAPTER TWO

Homosexuality: America's Sacred Sin

These things hast thou done, and I kept silence;
thou thoughtest that I was altogether such an one as thyself:
but I will reprove thee, and set them in order before thine eyes.
Psalm 50:21

I f there is one sin which many American Christians seem to almost treat as sacred, a sin which the body of Christ as a whole seems determined to approach with deference, it is the sin of homosexuality. The verbiage used and the patronage shown by Christians when discussing homosexuality is a case study of the effects of allowing the world and the devil to dictate rules of engagement to the church. The truth is that God's people are more influenced, or perhaps polluted would be more accurate, by the world than we sometimes realize or admit. This seems to be especially true concerning the sin of homosexuality. For whatever reason, that particular sin seems to hold an almost mystical sway over many in the body of Christ. Christian leaders, pastors, politicians, and lay people all make fawning concessions, both in word and deed, to the sodomite nation in our midst, accommodations which they would never make relative to other sexual sins such as pedophilia, rape, or adultery. Could it be that, with regard to sexual morality, many Christians have consciously or unconsciously signed onto the humanist credo "do no harm"? Pedophilia, rape, and adultery, all sexual crimes or sins with obvious victims, trigger outrage among Christians and elicit loud condemnation in no uncertain terms. On the other hand, the proliferation of homosexual acts comes nowhere near evoking similar righteous indignation from the same people. Is it possible that many Christians are increasingly viewing homosexuality as a victimless sin, surmising that such acts, while certainly not commendable, are really not all that bad and that the persons perpetrating them should even be treated with respect?

Certain high profile Christian leaders such as Ralph Reed, the former executive director of the Christian Coalition, have even made it a point to condemn Christians who take an aggressive Biblical stance against homosexuality. In his book *Active Faith,* Reed rebukes fellow Christians for "announcing that AIDS is 'God's judgment' on the gay community" and condemns the use of such words as "'perverts'" pertaining to homosexuality. According to Mr. Reed, this is "rhetoric that is inconsistent with our Christian call to mercy."[1] Reed and other Christian leaders of like theological mindset lead American Christians to believe that while we "disagree with these moral choices,"[2] we should honor and respect homosexuals as people. So much for rendering honor to whom honor is due.[3] Reed also insists that the civil government should "tolerate . . . homosexual conduct"[4] and that homosexuals should have all the rights of other citizens, including the right to "affect the public policy process."[5]

These days many Christian leaders, including pastors, often portray the sin of homosexuality in a manner which is far from Scriptural. Those Christians who strive to simply define the sin in a Biblically accurate manner are told that they are being too harsh, too condemning, too unloving. Besides, as has been pointed out to me numerous times, are we not just turning homosexuals away from the gospel by using condemning language? After all, many homosexuals seem so nice and they only appear to be hurting themselves. So why not do our best to avoid sounding too harsh or condemning when discussing homosexuality? Of course, the truth is that homosexuals are hurting many people other than themselves, and their "niceness" lasts only as long as things are going their way. Some of us can certainly testify that homosexual civility is a very thin veneer that evaporates like summer snow when the sodomite agenda is resisted.

But far more importantly, God's Word is very clear and concise regarding this issue. Those Christians who take the nicer-than-God approach when dealing with homosexuality are laying the groundwork for the judgment and destruction of our nation. It is a sad truth that many twentieth century Christians act and speak as if the immutable Word of God is just not appropriate as written to address one of the most crucial moral issues of our day. In this, they ape the world's subjective evolutionary approach to God, law, and morality. In so doing, they minimize the sin, thus causing others to stumble. They also denigrate the steadfast love of the Lord and the mercy which He has shown to even the vilest of sinners and the most blatant of lawbreakers by making the way of salvation available to them through His Son. But before we delve any further into that subject, let us take a quick look at what some of the blatantly pro-homosexual "Christian" leaders of our day have said about the sin of homosexuality.

The enemy has become extremely bold regarding this sin. He has planted his colors and set up his standards as far from eternal truth as possible so as to delude many true Christians into taking a stand which seems quite righteous by comparison. That is all too often the problem with modern Christianity. Rather than simply discovering God's eternal standard by the careful study of His revealed Word and then objectively speaking and applying those unchanging truths as they were written, many Christians simply reconnoiter the immediate theological and cultural landscape and then judge the rightness and strength of their own position by the distance it is from the enemy's lines.

Such subjective Christianity serves only to draw the army of God onto ground which is ultimately indefensible, much as Sickles's position in the Peach Orchard was at Gettysburg and with the same result. General Daniel Sickles felt confident of his ability to defend the position which he had taken up, contrary to his commander's orders, opposite to the Confederate lines some distance away. The Union position of strength, the line to which he and his men were supposed to cleave, was behind him from Culp's Hill to the Round Tops. Sickles's position was exposed, and when the enemy attacked in strength, he and his men were crushed and suffered humiliating defeat. Sickles's debacle almost cost the Union the battle and could have cost the war.

I have seen much the same thing happen far too many times when well-meaning Christians set up their colors, contrary to their Commander's wishes, far from His protective perimeter of immutable truth. I have seen those same Christians routed and humiliated when the enemy attacks with fury, thus further jeopardizing the prospects for the Christian army to turn back the onslaught of the pro-sodomite host which the church now faces.

By contrast, the ecclesiastical champions of homosexuality do not compromise or equivocate on the issue; they leave that to the more conservative brethren we spoke of earlier and will speak of again. No, the preachers of perversion take an uncompromised position on the subject of homosexuality, and that is one reason why their perverted tenets have gained so much ground in the last several decades. The sad truth is that few Americans read the Bible; fewer still actually study it. Consequently, most Americans look to those who claim to have spent time in the Word to define it. As many Bible-believing pastors and Christian leaders agonizingly approach the subject of homosexuality in the most sensitive, inoffensive, patronizing, inane way possible, the workers of iniquity gather their forces together, boldly plant their nefarious colors, set up a united front, and vigorously defend their position. The sons of Satan have most decisively framed the argument; consequently, they are winning the debate.

In 1992, the group Parents and Friends of Lesbians and Gays (PFLAG) published a booklet entitled *Is Homosexuality a Sin?* The stated purposes of the booklet are:

- To learn how religious experts in the field answer questions frequently asked by families and friends of gays and lesbians.

- To share these answers with gays and lesbians, their parents and friends, with religious leaders, policy makers, teachers, counselors, judges, physicians, and with all those who interact with our gay and lesbian family members.
- To serve as a resource for those who would like to read more about this topic or wish to join a religious group for gays and lesbians in their area.[6]

PFLAG's booklet features nineteen theologians, each with an educational, theological résumé "as long as your arm." After perusing the impressive educational accomplishments of PFLAG's panel and then looking at how they answered the questions asked of them in the booklet, I could not help but think of something my father used to say when I was young and long before he was a Christian. My father viewed with a certain amount of disdain those men who were highly educated yet lacked discernment, wisdom, and yes, even simple common sense. *Educated idiots* is the term he used to describe the same type of individuals who the Bible says are "ever learning, and never able to come to the knowledge of the truth."[7] The Scriptures tell us, "The fear of the Lord is the beginning of knowledge."[8] Without the fear of the Lord, without a holy reverence for His Word, even the most educated man reasons and speaks as a fool, an educated idiot, if you will. "Professing themselves to be wise, they became fools."[9]

The first question asked of PFLAG's learned panel was this: "In your opinion, does God regard homosexuality as a sin?"[10] Listen to some of the typical responses from the panelists and remember that these are influential individuals. Some are prolific authors; many hold Master's degrees of Divinity; and many have Doctorate of Divinity degrees. Some currently pastor churches or are in high leadership positions within their denominations; others are in teaching positions or lead powerful religious organizations. Some have won prestigious awards for their teaching and humanitarian activities. All wield considerable influence in the name of Christ. While the PFLAG panel also included Roman Catholics, Jews, a Unitarian, and a Mormon, the excerpts I have chosen are from Protestant leaders.

As you read, also keep in mind the stated purposes of the PFLAG booklet. Again, the question being asked is whether or not God regards homosexual acts as sin. Listen to the answers. Listen and hear the enemy of our souls speak.

Rev. Dr. William R. Stayton, Baptist: Absolutely not! There is nothing in the Bible or in my own theology that would lead me to believe that God regards homosexuality as sin. God is interested in our relationships with ourselves, others, the things in our lives, and with God. (Matt. 23:36-40). There is nothing in the mind of God that could be against a loving, sexual relationship, freely entered into, without coercion, among sincere adults whether gay, bisexual, or straight.[11]

Bishop John S. Spong, Episcopalian: Some argue that since homosexual behavior is "unnatural," it is contrary to the order of creation. Behind this pronouncement are stereotypic definitions of masculinity and femininity that reflect the rigid gender categories of patriarchal society. There is nothing unnatural about any shared love, even between two of the same gender, if that experience calls both partners into a fuller state of being. . . .

Our prejudice rejects people or things outside our understanding. But the God of creation speaks and declares, "I have looked out on *everything* I have made and 'behold it (is) very good'." (Gen. 1:31) The word of God in Christ says that we are loved, valued, redeemed, and counted as precious no matter how we might be valued by a prejudiced world.[12]

Bishop R. Stewart Wood, Jr., Episcopalian: No. Our sexual orientation is a given, something we discover about ourselves—some might say "a gift from God." How one relates to others—caring or exploiting—is the source of sin.[13]

Bishop Stanley E. Olson, Lutheran (ELCA): Of course not. God could (not?) care less about humanly devised categories that label and demean those who do not somehow fit into the norm of those in control. God made all of us and did not make all of us alike. Diversity is beautiful in creation. . . .

The New Testament is full of verses that speak of the work of Jesus Christ in creating a new unity beyond our divisions....The Gospel is vastly more inclusive than we often imagine or have been taught.[14]

Rev. Dr. George Edwards, Presbyterian: God does not regard homosexuality as a sin any more than heterosexuality. Sin is lack of respect or love for God; it is lack of love or respect for other persons.... [15]

Dr. Karen Lebacqz, United Church of Christ: What God DOES regard as a sin is oppression, injustice, persecution, disrespect for persons. This sin, then, is homophobia, gay-bashing, discriminatory legislation toward lesbians and gays, refusal to include lesbian/gay/bisexual people into our churches and communities....[16]

Rev. Dr. James B. Nelson, United Church of Christ: I am convinced that our sexuality and our sexual orientations, whatever they may be, are a gift from God. Sexual sin does not reside in our orientations... When we express ourselves sexually in ways that are loving and just, faithful and responsible, then I am convinced that God celebrates our sexuality, whatever our orientation may be.[17]

Bishop Melvin Wheatley, Jr., United Methodist: Of course not! ... Homosexuality is an authentic condition of being with which some persons are endowed (a gift of God, if you please), not an optional sexual life-style which they have willfully, whimsically or sinfully chosen. Certainly one's sexuality—heterosexual or homosexual—may be acted out in behaviors that are sinful: brutal, exploitative, selfish, superficial. But just as surely, one's homosexual orientation as well as another's heterosexual orientation may be acted out in ways that are beautiful: tender, considerate, mutual, responsible, loyal, profound.[18]

Such are the pathologies of a sick pro-homosexual theology which revolves around human feelings and politically correct philosophy, coupled with an expansive illusory concept of God and His Holy Scriptures. It is a theology of self-deluded fools with no fear of God, fools tragically intent on teaching others to be twice the sons of hell as themselves. But enough of such wolves in sheep's clothing for now. In future chapters we will turn back to some of the general as well as the specific teachings of those who so flippantly call good evil and evil good. We will also be taking a look at some of the specific ways well-meaning, Bible-believing, but compromising, Christians often wound the cause of righteousness to the advantage of the sodomite nation in our midst.

At least in part because the true church of Jesus Christ has not taken an aggressive, Biblical stand against the abomination of homosexuality, we have now reached a point in time where heretical clergymen are boldly proclaiming that homosexual acts are not sin! If homosexuality is not sin, then nothing is sin. Any person who can read can easily ascertain that the Bible clearly and repeatedly condemns homosexual acts and that such acts are therefore sin (see chapter four).

From time to time, even members of the homosexual community come clean and admit the obvious: the Bible, the Word of God, condemns homosexual acts. Consider this excerpt from an editorial in the homosexual newspaper the *Wisconsin Light:*

> It is quite pathetic to see the apologists in action. There is no doubt that the Bible does condemn homosexuality, repeatedly and in violent and intemperate terms. The Fundamentalists who are leading the battle against church acceptance of homosexuality, have got the interpretation absolutely right. And they are correct to say that if they make an exception for homosexuality, they're going to have to tolerate an awful lot of other "sins" too. . . .[19]

To give credit where credit is due, at least the sodomite writer of that editorial was honest, which is much more than can be said for many folks calling themselves Christians today.

The real question central to the debate over homosexuality is not whether or not the Bible condemns homosexual activity; the question is whether or not the Bible will be accepted as God's eternal, immutable truth. The case concerning the status of homosexuality in God's eyes is an easy one. As we will document in subsequent chapters, there is more than a preponderance of evidence which proves that God holds homosexual acts to be wicked and sinful; that case has been proven even beyond any reasonable doubt. Still, Sodom's apologists are working hard to convince the unwary and Biblically illiterate that the Lord really does not see such acts as gross violations of His law. Outrageous as it may be, these dreamers are basing their arguments on Scripture, or rather, the misrepresentation of Scripture.

As one who has been involved in many structured debates, as well as in much street ministry and prophetic public witness against homosexuality, I can assure you that those who would justify such acts in the name of the Lord have made great strides over the years, and not just among the unsaved. Earlier, I mentioned that many Christians have adopted a nicer-than-God approach on the issue of homosexuality. Allow me to explain myself. It is very presumptuous, to say the least, to change the meaning of God's eternal Word by reshaping it into terms more palatable to the sensibilities of our post-Christian American culture. Beyond that, when Christians misrepresent the Scriptures by downplaying the extent to which certain sins provoke God's wrath, they are also downplaying the extent of His mercy and love which is available to those involved in such sins if they are willing to repent and be "washed . . . sanctified . . . and justified in the name of the Lord Jesus, and by the Spirit of our God."[20] What a testimony of the love of the Lord, that He stands willing to forgive a sin which He has called an "abomination"[21] and "vile"![22] "Come now, and let us reason together, saith the LORD: though your sins be as scarlet, they shall be as white as snow; though they be red like crimson, they shall be as wool" (Isaiah 1:18).

The sin of homosexuality is a direct assault upon the created order of God and His righteous law. It is rebellion of the first rank, yet our merciful Lord is willing to forgive and forget that sin if the sinner will truly repent and submit his life to Christ. When we minimize the depth of such a sin, we minimize God's grace. This brings us back to a previous point, that it is presumptuous, and I might add dangerous, to represent a sin in terms different from those used in the Scriptures:

> The words of the LORD are pure words: as silver tried in a furnace of earth, purified seven times (Psalm 12:6).

For ever, O LORD, thy word is settled in heaven (Psalm 119:89).

Every word of God is pure: he is a shield unto them that put their trust in him. Add thou not unto his words, lest he reprove thee, and thou be found a liar (Proverbs 30:5-6).

For I am the LORD, I change not . . . (Malachi 3:6).

Every good gift and every perfect gift is from above, and cometh down from the Father of lights, with whom is no variableness, neither shadow of turning (James 1:17).

For all flesh is as grass, and all the glory of man as the flower of grass. The grass withereth, and the flower thereof falleth away: But the word of the Lord endureth for ever. And this is the word which by the gospel is preached unto you (I Peter 1:24-25).

In my various ministries, in the media, and through pamphlets on homosexuality which I have written, I have always tried to maintain certain basic core precepts that, if summarized, would go something like this: *Homosexual acts are acts of gross sexual perversion which are an abomination to God. Homosexuals are sexual outlaws who, short of repentance and rebirth through Christ, will spend eternity in the lake of fire. On the other hand, those homosexuals who are willing to repent and submit themselves to their Creator's law can be washed, sanctified, and justified in the name of the Lord Jesus and by the Spirit of our God and adopted into the family of God by the merits of Christ, just as promised in I Corinthians 6:11.*

That is the crux of my message, the foundation upon which I base all of my positions with respect to homosexuality, including matters of law and the Constitution. Yet even many supposedly Bible-believing individuals find such Biblical terms as *abomination* and *repent* to be offensive. Allow me to give you several typical examples of what I am talking about.

After a distribution of my brochure "Homosexuality: The Truth" to students on the University of Wisconsin—Eau Claire campus, I received a letter from a female Christian student who informed me:

Along with you, I believe homosexuality is a sin. However, I believe your pamphlet "Homosexuality: The Truth" is inappropriate. God wants us to show his love for people through our love for them, and distributing this pamphlet completely defeats our mission as Christians. The article I've enclosed is from *Campus Life*. It says how I feel much better than I can. I encourage you to take the time to read it.

The article the young lady enclosed was titled "A Gift of Grace" and contained this subtitle: "When our friends are doing something wrong, it's tempting to judge them. But the Bible points to a better way."[23] The story is written by a young woman who has a friend, Dan, who is homosexual. Early on in the article, the writer bemoans the friendships she lost because she became "judgmental" when her high school friends began to drink and party. She goes on to say:

Jesus is very clear that it's *God's* job to judge, not ours. He says, "Do not judge, or you too will be judged. For in the same way you judge others, you will be judged, and with the measure you use, it will be measured to you" (Matthew 7:1-2).[24]

The young lady, like so many today, takes this verse out of context, thinking that Christ is commanding Christians to make no judgment between good and evil. Of course, Matthew 7:1-2, along with the verses following it, is written to the body of Christ and deals with the human tendency to severely judge the smallest failings of another, the mote in our brother's eye, while ignoring much more serious offenses in which we are involved. Obviously, homosexual behavior is more than a mote, and this passage in no way instructs Christians to ignore numerous Biblical commands which mandate taking a strong stand against outright evils such as homosexuality. Christians are clearly told to "judge righteous judgment"[25] and "to warn the wicked."[26] We are commanded to "hate the evil, and love the good."[27] We are instructed to "have no fellowship with the unfruitful works of darkness, but rather reprove them."[28] The church's calling is to be the "pillar and ground of the truth."[29] The Great Commission of the body of Christ is to "go ye therefore, and teach all nations, baptizing them in the name of the Father, and of the Son, and of the Holy Ghost: Teaching them to observe all things whatsoever I have commanded you . . ."[30] To claim that Christians are to refrain from making any moral judgments regarding human activity is to deny the very mission of the church on earth. To even tell a lost sinner that he is lost and in need of a Savior is to make a judgment.

The writer in *Campus Life* goes on to quote Romans 3:23, "For all have sinned, and come short of the glory of God," and decides, based on that verse, that the best way for her to deal with Dan is to just be his friend. After all, she is a sinner herself and she doesn't want to lose any more friends like she did in high school. Besides, she reasons, her sodomite friend Dan is "a person who cared for me, a person who had always shown me real, unconditional friendship. He had never let me down. 'I love you,' I said. 'And I will always be your friend, no matter what.'"[31]

Of course, if the young lady really wants to be a friend, she will get out the Bible, warn the young man of the eternal peril that he is in, and share with him the only way out of his situation. At that point, he will probably either repent and be saved or despise her. In fact, he may even call her judgmental or hateful. But at least she will have shown him true love and real mercy, not to mention having faithfully represented God's position on the issue.

If we measure the faithfulness of our Christian walk by how many friends we are making in the world, we are using a perverse, unbiblical standard of measure. The gospel, God's Word, often separates us from others. Jesus warned:

> Think not that I am come to send peace on earth: I came not to send peace, but a sword. For I am come to set a man at variance against his father, and the daughter against her mother, and the daughter in law against her mother in law. And a man's foes shall be they of his own household. He that loveth father or mother more than me is not worthy of me: and he that loveth son or daughter more than me is not worthy of me. And he that taketh not his cross, and followeth after me, is not worthy of me (Matthew 10:34-38).

Jesus also warned, "If the world hate you, ye know that it hated me before it hated you" (John 15:18). The truth is, friendship with God—not friendship with the world—must be the goal of the Christian. "[W]hosoever therefore will be a friend of the world is the enemy of God" (James 4:4). Concealing or even minimizing the extent of God's condemnation of a certain sin may win worldly friends; but it is certainly no way to endear oneself to the Lord, and it is most certainly not an act of kindness to the sinner.

As for Romans 3:23 which was alluded to in the *Campus Life* article, it is most certainly true that no human being alive is perfect. "Wherefore, as by one man sin entered into the world, and death by sin; and so death passed upon all men, for that all have sinned" (Romans 5:12). Individuals receive the gift of salvation from God by repenting of their sins and appropriating for themselves the sacrifice Christ made at Calvary. Christians are kept right with God by repenting of sins and confessing them to Him who "is faithful and just to forgive us our sins, and to cleanse us from all unrighteousness."[32] The Lord expects us to live a sanctified life in accordance with His law. He holds us accountable to that law, and Christians should likewise hold each other accountable to His immutable precepts. Although we may fall short of God's perfect standard at various times, we are not to live in rebellion.

However, if only perfect people should share the gospel with others, then the prophets and apostles, including Paul, should have kept silent. It is one thing for a Christian who is living a clearly rebellious life to attempt to call others to repentance with the very law he is so openly violating (see Romans 2). It is obviously less than desirable, and not very effective, for an open adulterer to confront a homosexual and call him to repentance. The problem is not that the law of God loses any of its authority in such a situation or that the homosexual cannot possibly be saved through such a scenario. "[W]ith God all things are possible" (Matthew 19:26). The problem is that such a situation causes the name of God to be blasphemed[33] due to the hypocrisy of the renegade preacher. Certainly an open rebel preaching against open rebellion is a situation which does not please God and which, in fact, kindles His wrath toward the preacher.[34] It is yet another matter for a less-than-perfect Christian to hold up God's Word as the only authoritative standard for human behavior. If we wait until we are perfect to preach, our only hearers will be in heaven, and they have no need of a preacher.

As another example of an unbiblical mindset concerning homosexuality which is increasing in popularity among many Christians, here are some excerpts from a letter which I received from a Christian student from Lawrence University in Appleton, Wisconsin after witnessing and passing out tracts on that campus along with others from Wisconsin Christians United. These excerpts once again reflect a basic misunderstanding concerning the handling of God's eternal truths:

> As a student on the Lawrence University campus I am writing to say how absolutely appalled I am at your distribution of hate information that you distributed on the Lawrence Campus today. . . .
>
> There is quite a large homosexual community on this campus which is both vocal and active. . . .
>
> I am telling you now that when Christ died for our sins, he died for all of our sins. Not just for the homosexuals, but also for the heterosexuals. He died for *all* of us. . . .
>
> I am a Christian . . . I have friends who are homosexuals and I can tell you that Jesus loves them as much as he loves you and me. Because of your actions today many homosexuals on this campus have heard exactly what they expected. . . .
>
> Please, I beg you, stop this spread of hatred. Show the world a side to Christianity that they don't expect...love and forgiveness. Not judgment and elitism.

The presupposition of this Christian woman appears to be that Jesus' death on the cross granted a license for man to live in abject sin. It is interesting to note the depth to which this person has been polluted by the world. It would appear that her homosexual friends have convinced her that a strong Biblical message against their chosen perversion is tantamount to the "distribution of hate." Such is the universalist doctrine which reduces Christianity down to a psychological discipline consisting of temporal peace, licentious love, forgiveness without repentance, and God without holiness. Those who hold to such dogmas naturally excoriate any reminder that the way of the cross is straight and narrow as being selfish elitism and wickedly judgmental.

Many of the rebukes which I, and no doubt others, receive from fellow Christians for taking a Biblical stand on homosexuality come from women. Perhaps this is a plain indication of how deeply the feminist movement has sunk its roots into the American church. Occasionally, when I speak strongly on the subject of homosexuality on my morning radio program "The Heart of the Matter," I receive chiding letters from Christians, often Christian women, who are upset over the use of Biblical terminology relating to homosexual acts. Here are a few excerpts from a typical letter which, quite frankly, shows that we have a real problem in the church today:

> Regarding your message this morning, Friday, September 20th. Your harsh words made me sad. I agree that homosexuality is indeed a lifestyle that is directly against the will of God. However, I would hardly call these people depraved, nor would I call their life an abomination. . . .
>
> Harassing homosexuals is not going to do one bit of good. In fact it will drive them away. . . .
>
> I pray that Jesus will soften your heart. I also pray that He will help you to love others in their sins just as He loves you in yours.
>
> Perhaps we can learn to motivate others with love, and not guilt or fear.

Christians such as this woman would do well to consider that it does not really matter what they, I, or any other human being does or says about homosexuality and the preaching of God's Word. What matters is what God says and what He wants us to say and do. He certainly desires us to relate to the world His Word as He wrote it, complete with grace and law, mercy and judgment, salvation and damnation, heaven and hell. What He calls an abomination, He certainly expects us to call an abomination. We are, after all, only His vessels, His preachers. He is the Author of the message we preach. Yet many Christians find God's Word too harsh as written, even when applied to situations crying out for the strongest of Biblical rebukes.

I am often involved in confrontations with pro-homosexual pastors, the sort of men and women whom Jesus called "ravening wolves" in sheep's clothing.[35] From time to time, I have been chastened for calling them what Jesus called them. Once after I called a sodomite preacher, who also holds the position that God is a woman, a son of hell based on Matthew 23:15, I was told by a well-meaning Christian lady that my words were too "harsh" and "could cause the unsaved to have hatred instead of conviction for their sin." While I admit that we must use the type of speech mentioned in a judicious manner at the proper time, I hold that if Christians are not willing to identify sodomite pastors as the sons of hell that they are, what message are we sending to the unsaved and the gullible? What should Christians call a pastor who literally engages in sodomy with another man and then preaches that God is a woman who approves of such acts? The Bible calls such men children of hell,[36] liars,[37] false prophets,[38] serpents,[39] vipers,[40] and ravening wolves.[41] Who are we to do otherwise?

In light of the effeminate Christianity so popular these days in America, one cannot but wonder what sort of reception Jonathan Edwards would receive today with his famous sermon "Sinners in the Hands of an Angry God."

> The God that holds you over the pit of hell, much as one holds a spider, or some loathsome insect, over the fire, abhors you, and is dreadfully provoked: his wrath towards you burns like fire; he looks upon you as worthy of nothing else, but to be cast into the fire; he is of purer eyes than to bear to have you in his sight; you are ten thousand times more abominable in his eyes, than the most hateful venomous serpent is in ours. You have offended him infinitely more than ever a stubborn rebel did his prince.[42]

Praise God that Pastor Edwards and other preachers of his caliber cared more for God's Word and lost souls than they did for the opinions of men! It was sermons such as "Sinners in the Hands of an Angry God" which fueled America's much-needed First Great Awakening in the eighteenth century. It will take similar preaching to lay the groundwork for the great spiritual awakening which is desperately needed in America today.

It has been my experience, especially among young Christians, that any gospel message which contains such words as *sin, repent, judgment,* or *damnation* is seen as hate even when combined with *forgiveness, mercy, grace,* and *salvation.* To many modern itching ears, the latter concepts are acceptable; the former are reprehensible. But of course, if one desires to be spoken well of by all men, then concessions certainly must be made.

How many Christians today understand the importance of what Paul was saying in Acts 20:26-27? "Wherefore I take you to record this day, that I am pure from the blood of all men. For I have not shunned to declare unto you all the counsel of God." Paul realized that it was not his place to edit the Word of God and that, in fact, to do so would have made him at least partially culpable for the destruction of those who, because of his words or lack of them, would be emboldened to live in such a way as to bring God's judgment upon themselves. Many other Scripture verses repeat this theme of accountability. Paul understood well what many contemporary Christians do not: namely, we are answerable to God for how we handle His Word! When we downplay the seriousness of sin and the wrath which God has against those who are in rebellion against Him, we are encouraging rebels to continue in their destructive behavior. We literally help them on their way to judgment and hell. In this way, we then become guilty of their blood. If one is not willing to preach the whole counsel of the Word of God, the way God wrote it, it would be better to say nothing at all. Yet all Christians, especially Christian pastors and leaders, have a holy commission to share and preach the Word of God. There really is no choice. So then, we must relate the Word as written, no matter how unpopular such a "harsh" message may be to the world. This is God's clear command. We dare not preach a lopsided gospel. It is just as wrong to leave out the wrath of God as it is to omit the grace of God. It may sound redundant, but we must preach the Word of God using the literal Word of God. We must include such words as *damnation, hell, abomination, wrath,* and *judgment.*

What Christian strives to minimize the love of Christ or the mercy and grace of God? Why then are so many willing to denigrate the Lord's holiness by glossing over His wrath which is kindled by such vile sins as homosexuality? Why is there such an urgency to wrongfully cast homosexual activity as simply being a hurtful behavior which harms individuals and makes God sad rather than to tell the truth that it is an abominable rebellion against God's law which kindles His wrath and triggers His judgment? And why do so many attempt to strip Christ of His deity by portraying Him as some cosmic social worker bereft of one shred of righteous anger over acts of gross rebellion such as those which define homosexuality? That is not the Christ of the Bible!

> ...the Lord Jesus shall be revealed from heaven with his mighty angels, in flaming fire taking vengeance on them that know not God, and that obey not the gospel of our Lord Jesus Christ (II Thessalonians 1:7-8).

Why is it that so many Christians are so willing to take artistic license with certain portions of the Bible? When God says that He hates a certain act and finds it to be an abomination, that is exactly what He expects us to tell the world. Anything less and we are misrepresenting Him and His holiness. So we must preach the Word as written, no matter how much grief and misunderstanding this may earn us from the world. We must do this because to do otherwise is disobedient, dishonorable, a misrepresentation of God, and an incentive for sinners to continue on in their rebellion.

There is yet another reason why we must preach the whole counsel of the Word of God. II Corinthians 7:10 tells us, "For godly sorrow worketh repentance to salvation not to be repented of: but the sorrow of the world worketh death." The truth being related here is simply that sorrow is the companion of sin, and sin is the companion of death. Homosexuals are not inherently happy people no matter what sort of facade they maintain. They are living a destructive lifestyle, and they know it. Yet such worldly sorrow will not bring about repentance but only anger, frustration, hatred, self-pity, and often violence. The homosexual needs to know that he has deeply offended his Maker. He needs to understand that the disgusting acts of gross rebellion in which he engages are an affront to God and a stench in His nostrils. The homosexual must be warned that he is standing on the precipice of hell and that at any moment he could go over the edge into an eternity of torment. All of this he must be told in hopes that he will come to the end of his excuses to a state of godly sorrow leading to repentance in which he cries out, "What must I do to be saved?"

The men to whom Peter preached on Pentecost reached that point of godly sorrow after Peter "harshly" told them:

> Ye men of Israel, hear these words; Jesus of Nazareth, a man approved of God among you by miracles and wonders and signs, which God did by him in the midst of you, as ye yourselves also know: Him, being delivered by the determinate counsel and foreknowledge of God, ye have taken, and by wicked hands have crucified and slain . . . that God hath made that same Jesus, whom ye have crucified, both Lord and Christ (Acts 2:22-23, 36).

Our prayers and our preaching must all be done with the hope that the lost, including homosexuals, will come to a realization of their peril and cry out, "What shall we do?" Our answer, of course, must then be Peter's answer: *"Repent, and be baptized every one of you in the name of Jesus Christ for the remission of sins"* (Acts 2:38). The twentieth century has seen more than its share of false conversions due to the "nice," worldly, seeker-sensitive gospel which has all too often been preached. It can only do good for sinners, homosexuals included, to be confronted with the reality of how deeply they have offended and angered the Lord by their actions. Today, however, it is a sad fact that many Christians downplay the wickedness and vileness of homosexual activity, an activity which is illustrated in chapter one of Romans as the very epitome of rebellion against God. One can only wonder how this suppression of the truth has adversely affected the eternal destination of many sodomites.

While I have often been encouraged by Christians in my work with Wisconsin Christians United, I have also been rebuked countless times by people who I do not doubt are Christians, but who, nevertheless, feel that it is wrong to use Biblical words and precepts when confronting homosexuality. Those same people never feel so protective of adulterers or rapists or pedophiles, pornographers or men who visit prostitutes. But homosexuality is different. Christians are to be nice and sweet and walk on eggshells when talking about the sin of homosexuality almost as if it somehow were a sacred sin compared to other sins of similar magnitude. After all, we are told by our kinder, gentler brethren that many homosexuals have been molested as children or have come from bad homes; and besides, it is very hard to give up the homosexual lifestyle. Certainly some homosexuals do come from bad homes; yet many others are simply sexual libertines who went a step further than their "heterosexual" peers. A troubled childhood past may be a reason which helps explain a certain individual's choice and which should elicit a measure of sympathetic insight. Nevertheless, a person's past is not an acceptable excuse for the perpetration or continuation of vile behavior which God has forbidden. But here again, much deference is shown to the homosexual.

How many Christians are willing to trivialize, even defend, the sins of a child molester, an adulterer, or a rapist based on environmental factors in the person's past or on the fact that he feels a strong compulsion to continue on in such behavior? Yet so many Christians fall over themselves to do just that when it comes to homosexuals, thus conveying the message "You can't help it." A person who cannot help what he is doing cannot be held responsible for his actions. So it is that some Christians offer encouragement to homosexuals to continue in their vile sin.

Another way in which many Christians, and even some modern-day Bible commentators, pay deference to the sin of homosexuality is by portraying God's sanctions against such activities as being put in place primarily out of concern for the individual rather than as an image of God's holy nature and as a mechanism which honors and protects His created order. Such a Biblical exegesis, which propagates a man-centered rather than a God-centered gospel, is tragically becoming increasingly popular among many Christians today.

As an example of this often well-meaning, but always wrong, approach to the Scriptures, read how Leviticus 18:22-23 is illustrated in William MacDonald's *Believer's Bible Commentary:*

Sodomy or homosexuality was forbidden, as well as sexual intercourse with an animal. In legislating against homosexuality, God may also have been anticipating the modern AIDS epidemic and seeking to save people from it.[43]

That statement regarding AIDS is a classic example of "putting the cart before the horse." There can be no doubt that the many sexual diseases common to our day, including AIDS, are a result of God's judgment of flagrant violations of His law. That law was not put in place to protect the individual from judgment; judgment comes as a result of the violation of the law. If there were no law, there would be no judgment! William MacDonald, like so many Christians, seems to have searched for a way to avoid having God cast as a hateful homophobe. One must ask, Is the reason God has forbidden homosexual activity due simply to health concerns; and if so, is that the same reason He forbade bestiality in the same passage along with incest and adultery in the surrounding verses? Or do these prohibitions have to do with God's holiness and His justice? Of course they have everything to do with God's holiness and justice.

God's teachers and preachers of the past did not quail from portraying sin as the Bible portrays it. Certainly our forefathers in the faith did not take a lackadaisical, unbiblical approach to homosexual acts, a sin which God so soundly condemns. Matthew Henry (1662-1714) was a Puritan pastor and a great Bible exegete. Concerning Henry's *Commentary on the Whole Bible,* which is still in wide use today, the great preacher and Bible teacher Charles Spurgeon (1834-1892) said this: "First among the mighty [commentaries] for general usefulness we are bound to mention the man whose name is a household word, Matthew Henry."[44] Spurgeon testified that he found Henry and his commentary to be "pious and pithy, sound and sensible, suggestive and sober, terse and trustworthy. . . . deeply spiritual, heavenly, and profitable . . . instructive to all."[45]

When we consider Matthew Henry's reputation as a great Bible teacher and pastor along with the historical significance of the era in which he lived, the prominent role he played in shaping the great Christian teachers who came after him, and the durability of his work, it would seem more than profitable to examine how he approached the subject of homosexuality. The following are excerpts from Matthew Henry's *Commentary on the Whole Bible.* The verses being expounded on are identified. For the sake of brevity, the excerpts are only very partial regarding the whole of what Henry wrote with reference to each verse.

It is important that you keep in mind that the comments from Mr. Henry, as well as those from Matthew Poole, who will be quoted later, were selected to document the honest Biblical approach to homosexuality, an approach which was once common to God's teachers and preachers; and, by comparison, to document how far the modern church as a whole and many of her preachers have strayed from Biblical absolutes. Please understand that both Henry and Poole also made it abundantly clear that God's wonderful and gracious gift of salvation and a new life through Christ is available to all those, including the vilest sodomite, who will repent of their sins and submit their lives to Christ. Here, then, are a few excerpts from Matthew Henry's *Commentary on the Whole Bible:*

Genesis 18:20: . . . Some sins, and the sins of some sinners, cry aloud to heaven for vengeance. The iniquity of Sodom was crying iniquity, that is, it was so very provoking that it even urged God to punish. . . .[46]

Genesis 19:4-11: . . . . It was the most unnatural and abominable wickedness that they were now set upon, a sin that still bears their name, and is called *Sodomy.* They were carried headlong by those vile affections (Rom. 1:26, 27), which are worse than brutish, and the eternal reproach of the human nature, and which cannot be thought of without horror by those that have the least spark of virtue and any remains of natural light and conscience. Note, Those that allow themselves in unnatural uncleanness are marked for the vengeance of eternal fire. See Jude 7. They were not ashamed to own it, and to prosecute their design by force and arms. The practice would have been bad enough if it had been carried on by intrigue and wheedling; but they proclaimed war with virtue, and bade open defiance to it. Hence daring sinners are said to *declare their sin as Sodom,* Isa. 3:9. . . .[47]

Leviticus 18:22: A law against unnatural lusts, sodomy and bestiality, sins not to be named nor thought of without the utmost abhorrence imaginable, *v.* 22, 23. Other sins level men with the beasts, but these sink them much lower. . . .[48]

Leviticus 20:13: The unnatural lusts of sodomy and bestiality (sins not to be mentioned without horror) . . .[49]

Judges 19:22-30: They designed in the most filthy and abominable manner (not to be thought of without horror and detestation) to abuse the Levite . . . they designed the gratification of that most unnatural and worse than brutish lust which was expressly forbidden by the law of Moses, and called an *abomination,* Lev. 18:22. Those that are guilty of it are ranked in the New Testament among the worst and vilest of sinners . . . This was the sin of Sodom, and is thence called *Sodomy.* . . .[50]

I Corinthians 6:9-11: Here he takes occasion to warn them against many heinous evils, to which they had been formerly addicted. . . . . Those who knew any thing of religion must know that heaven could never be intended for these. The scum of the earth are no ways fit to fill the heavenly mansions. Those who do the devil's work can never receive God's wages, at least no other than *death, the just wages of sin,* Rom. 6:23. . . .[51]

Jude 7: The apostle here calls to our remembrance the destruction of Sodom and Gomorrah . . . they were guilty of abominable wickedness, not to be named or thought of but with the utmost abhorrence and detestation; their ruin is a particular warning to all people to take heed of, and *fly from, fleshly lusts that war against the soul,* 1 Pt. 2:11 . . . God is the same holy, just, pure Being now as then; and can the beastly pleasures of a moment make amends for your suffering the vengeance of eternal fire? . . .[52]

Matthew Henry obviously feared God more than he feared being known as harsh or hateful by misled Christians. He truly was "approved unto God, a workman that needeth not to be ashamed, rightly dividing the word of truth."[53] Henry loved and revered the Lord and the Holy Scriptures too much to do anything less than preach and teach the stark truths of God's Word as He wrote them. In doing so, Matthew Henry showed true love for the lost as well. May God raise up many men like him today! How desperately we need them!

Matthew Poole (1624-1679) was another great Bible teacher whose *Commentary on the Holy Bible* is widely respected and read to this day. Poole's commentaries have been endorsed by many great preachers and teachers down through the centuries including, once again, Charles Spurgeon. Of Poole, Spurgeon said:

> [I]f I must have only one commentary, and had read Matthew Henry as I have, I do not know but what I should choose Poole. He is a very prudent and judicious commentator . . . not so pithy and witty by far as Matthew Henry, but he is perhaps more accurate, less a commentator, and more an expositor.[54]

In various places in his commentary, Poole referred to homosexuals as being "barbarous"[55] and "like brute beasts."[56] Poole described homosexual acts as "outrages,"[57] "beastly lusts,"[58] "filthy lusts,"[59] and, "pollution."[60] Commenting on the practice of lesbianism as defined by Romans 1:26-27, Poole called such acts "unnatural uncleanness" and a "filthy practice not to be named."[61] Here is a further sampling of Poole's comments on some of the Bible verses which deal with homosexual acts:

> **Deuteronomy 23:18:** . . . *Both these,* i.e. the *whore* and the *dog,* and therefore the price of either of them cannot be acceptable. And this may seem to favour the latter opinion, that the *dog* is here taken metaphorically rather than properly, because there is no mention in the law (save in this place which is in question) of any abominableness of a dog unto God, more than of an ass, or any other unclean

creature; but how abominable *sodomites* are to God is sufficiently evident from other scriptures, and from undeniable reasons.[62]

Romans 1:27: This was the sin of the Sodomites of old, for which they were destroyed, Gen. xix. 5: see Lev. xviii. 22. How meet was it that they who had forsaken the Author of nature, should be given up not to keep the order of nature; that they who had changed the glory of God into the similitude of beasts, should be left to do those things which beasts themselves abhorred! God only concurred as a just judge in punishing foregoing with following sins . . .[63]

Jude 7: . . . *strange flesh,* i.e. that which is strange, improper, and unfit for such an end. It is the description of the unnatural filthiness of the Sodomites . . .[64]

It should be understood that Henry's and Poole's Bible teachings on homosexuality not only were standard for their day, but also are reflective of the teachings of all true Bible-believing preachers and teachers down through the ages. Tragically, such voices are few and far between today. One does not often hear the equivalent of such teachings ringing forth from most pulpits, let alone from the radio and television preachers, of the present time.

To his credit, the late J. Vernon McGee (1904-1988) minced no words when he dealt with homosexuality on his nationwide "Thru the Bible Radio" commentary series, which has also been made available in written form. Dealing with Leviticus 18:22 and going against the grain of fluffy modern evangelicalism, McGee described homosexual acts as "disgusting" and homosexuals as "sexual perverts."[65] Concerning homosexuality, McGee warned, "My friend, God condemns it!"[66] and went on to say this:

The depravity that is mentioned here is common today. The United States is like Sodom and Gomorrah. It makes me weep to see the way my country is going. I love this country. It's the land of my birth. I hate to see these dirty, filthy, immoral people bringing us into judgment. Believe me, friends, the judgment of God is already upon us today. We can't have peace abroad and we can't have peace at home. Why not? "There is no peace, saith the LORD, unto the wicked" [Isa. 48:22].[67]

In many, if not most, evangelical circles today, it is considered un-Christlike and unloving to portray homosexual activity as dirty, filthy, or beastly. Satan has turned the tables, and now those who speak about homosexuality with appropriately descriptive language and within Biblical parameters are often themselves regarded as sinful.

Allow me to submit just one more example to confirm that amazing reality. Under the banner of responding in love and truth, we are given the following instruction in the July-August 1996 issue of the Christian Coalition magazine *Christian American:* "Examine your own attitude. Being squeamish about homosexuality is one thing but having a reaction of revulsion, hostility or violence is sin."[68]

Considering how evil homosexual acts are and how the Bible repeatedly and in various ways commands God's people to hate evil, how is it that we have come to a place where it can now be considered a sin to feel revulsion and hostility toward filthy, wicked practices which God so soundly condemns in His Word? By today's "Christian ethic," the likes of Poole, Henry, McGee, and any number of other great men of God would be looked upon with more abhorrence than would be those who commit homosexual acts. That is a fact of which some of us are painfully aware. Has homosexuality become a sort of sacred sin to many Christians? Sadly, yes; and for the sake of everyone concerned, that must change.

And others save with fear, pulling them out of the fire;
hating even the garment spotted by the flesh.
Jude 23

CHAPTER THREE

Serving Satan in the Name of God

*Now the Spirit speaketh expressly, that in the latter times
some shall depart from the faith, giving heed to seducing spirits,
and doctrines of devils; speaking lies in hypocrisy;
having their conscience seared with a hot iron.
I Timothy 4:1-2*

November 20, 1997 was a glorious day for the Reverend Troy Perry. On that day, Perry and 120 other religious leaders were honored by President Bill Clinton at a White House ecumenical breakfast. During the event, Perry, the founder of the "gay" Metropolitan Community Church denomination, reportedly sat next to President Clinton. High honors indeed for a defender of sado-masochism who traded his marriage covenant with his wife for perverse sexual relations with other men!

Troy Perry is just one of many clergymen in America who claim the name of Christ and preach doctrines of devils. Virtually every mainline Christian denomination in America has a growing, active pro-homosexual movement within its ranks, as do the Catholic Church and the Jewish faith. I have had the privilege of defending the Word of God against the pro-sodomites in a variety of venues ranging from structured television and radio forums to impromptu sidewalk debates at homosexual events. My adversaries have included fems and butches, a homosexual U.S. congressman and a lesbian state representative, men in dresses and "gay" lawyers in suits, Catholic priests, mainline pastors, public school teachers, leaders of homosexual political groups, and relatives of homosexuals. To me, the most bizarre of all of my opponents have been the perverted pastors and religious leaders. When I say bizarre, I am alluding to their beliefs, not necessarily to their appearance, although the adjective is often appropriately descriptive in that sense also.

Once while witnessing with other Christians at a Milwaukee "gay pride" event, I was confronted by a United Church of Christ pastor dressed in clerical robes including a rainbow stole. This two-fold child of hell was holding a sign which assured homosexuals, "Don't let the Judgmental annoy you. God loves you just as She made you!" This same man was heard to tell a number of the sodomite carnival-goers, "Ralph Ovadal is the most evil man in Wisconsin." Sharing the gospel is evil, but sodomy is good?

On a raw spring evening during a Wisconsin Christians United event in front of a pro-homosexual church in Madison, Wisconsin, I found myself confronted by a lesbian Jewish "rabbi" complete with a yamaluk. The woman, who was built like a bulldog and possessed a similar disposition, let me know that I was hell-bound for preaching hate and that she would like a chance to work me over before I departed for that place of torment.

These two examples of pro-homosexual religious leaders are not all that unusual. I have interacted with many such interesting specimens from the "gay" clergy corps. Yet this is not a group which can be strictly stereotyped by looks or temperament. Pro-homosexual clergymen run the gamut from flaming queer "reverends" to urbane intellectuals, from strident feminists to stodgy, old mainline pastors. The devil truly is an equal opportunity employer. The rank and file of the sodomite nation who crave the "homosexualization" of the Bible to justify their own perverted behavior can now count on a broad array of clerical allies from the Troy Perrys of the world to the likes of Dr. Anthony Campolo, the famous and wildly popular Baptist preacher, author, and lecturer.

Campolo, a charismatic speaker, is still highly regarded and warmly welcomed in many conservative evangelical circles. This is nothing short of astounding considering that Dr. Campolo is not only pro-homosexual, but also, at times, plainly preaches what can only be considered as heresy regarding the central tenants of true Christianity. For instance, during a January 24, 1997 television interview with Charlie Rose, Campolo made this statement: "However, I'm not convinced that Jesus only lives in Christians."[1] In his book, *Following Jesus Without Embarrassing God,* Campolo writes about Earth Day, saying:

> I believe that Christians should be a prominent presence on these occasions, bearing witness to the God who so loved the world that He sent His only begotten Son to deliver it from the ravages of sinful humanity.[2]

Whether Campolo's durability in many Bible-believing evangelical circles is due to ignorance or to apathy is open to conjecture, but the truth is that Dr. Campolo teaches that homosexuals are born that way,[3] that the civil government should bar all discrimination against open homosexuals,[4] that such persons should be welcomed as "brothers and sisters" into Christian churches,[5] and that the body of Christ should make it a goal to "eliminate . . . homophobia."[6]

In *Following Jesus Without Embarrassing God,* Campolo equates those of us who oppose homosexual activity to a group of very unsavory characters which a part of him would like destroyed!

> I pray that Jesus will bring out in me that blessed trait (which some disparage as feminine weakness) that will enable me to find the good in the racist, the homophobe, the fascist, and the militarist. The side of me that the world calls masculine would want them destroyed.[7]

In his book *20 Hot Potatoes Christians Are Afraid to Touch,* Campolo blasts parents and other concerned citizens who resist the idea of impressionable children being taught by homosexuals:

> One of the meanest arguments against public schools comes from alarmists who contend that public school students can be forced to study under homosexuals and might even be subjected to homosexual seduction. This contention makes me furious—not because I believe there are no homosexuals in the public school system, but because of the implication that homosexuals are some kind of special threat to children.[8]

Of course, Campolo labels such concerned parents as "homophobics."[9]

Campolo's wife Peggy has been known to wax eloquent over the privilege and benefits of spending time in the homosexual community and has taken a public stand for the state recognition of "gay marriage."

One of Dr. Campolo's close friends is Reverend Peter J. Gomes, the Plummer Professor of Christian Morals at Harvard College. Gomes, an out-of-the-closet sodomite, is also the minister of Harvard's Memorial Church and the author of *The Good Book: Reading the Bible with Heart and Mind.* In his book, Reverend Gomes rails against Biblical literalism as "dangerous and wrong" and confidently (and incredibly) writes that "no credible case against homosexuality or homosexuals can be made from the Bible unless one chooses to read scripture in a way that simply sustains the existing prejudice against homosexuality and homosexuals."[10]

The bitter poison of homosexuality, one of the fruits of our hedonistic, narcissistic times, has captured the minds and hearts of many American clergymen and now permeates many American institutions labeled as "Christian." Tragically, even many Bible-believing pastors and conservative, pro-family organizations are unwittingly doing their part to advance the cause of the sexual libertines. But more of that in later chapters.

Concurrent with the growth of the "gay Christian" movement has been the promulgation of homosexual-friendly Bible hermeneutics and the institution of blasphemous sacraments and liturgy tailored to fit various occasions and all geared to lending credibility to the farce that homosexual activity is acceptable to God and consistent with the Christian life. Many of these ceremonies, such as the example reprinted below, spring from the presupposition that those Christians who do not accept homosexuality are in sin. The following ritual, "Embracing Our Cause," appeared in the June-July 1996 *More Light Update,* the newsletter of Presbyterians for Lesbian and Gay Concerns. Its purpose is the commission of missionaries to work on behalf of the homosexual cause.

Embracing Our Cause
A Ritual of Commitment to Justice

[This is written for a person or persons (represented by "N.") who wish to publicly commit to working for justice for lesbian, gay, bisexual, and transgendered people, both in the church and in society. The individual(s) responses are italicized.]

Readings: Exodus 3:1-12; Esther 4:6-16

[An Interpretation, Homily, Sermon, or Discussion may be added here, if desired.]

Sometimes God gives us a visible sign such as a burning bush to call us to commitment. But often, the only visible signs that call us are the circumstances of injustice.

We must turn to see the signs of our times. We must turn to listen for God's voice.

N.! Remove the sandals from your feet, for the place on which you are standing is holy ground.

Here I am, Sovereign God. [N. removes shoes.]

I am the God of your fathers and mothers, the God of Abraham and Sarah and the God of Mary and Joseph. I have observed the misery of my Rainbow people: I have heard their cry, I know their sufferings, I have come to deliver them. So come, I will send you to bring my people, my lesbian, gay, bisexual, and transgendered people, out of oppression.

Who am I that I should bring your Rainbow people out of oppression?

I will be with you; and this shall be the sign for you that it is I who sent you: when you have brought the people out of oppression, you all shall worship here together.

You know what happens to those who go uninvited into the courts of power and stand up for the oppressed!

Do not think that in this place of worship you will escape injustice. Who knows? Perhaps you have been created for such a time as this!

Then fast and pray with me, and I will work for justice. If my well-being is threatened, so be it.

Hymn: (See next page) "Walk With Me" Words & Music by John Rice

> [Add this verse between verse 1 and 2:]

> Though Esther had the privileges of royalty
> She was called to risk it all by her loyalty.

Laying On Of Hands:

[N. kneel(s); all gathered lay hands on N. for the commission to justice.]

You will receive power as the Holy Spirit comes upon you, and you will be God's witness(es) here and to the ends of the earth. (Acts 1:8)

See, I make you as God to those who oppress. (Exodus 7:1)
To the oppressed you will bring light and gladness, joy and honor. (Esther 8:16)

Let us pray:

The Prayer that Jesus Taught Us. [Please begin, "God, father and mother of us all..."][11]

Before we go any further, perhaps it would be good to drive home the extent to which the homosexual movement has sunk its roots into America's religious institutions. In the interest of doing just that, allow me to list a number of very active so-called Christian and Catholic homosexual groups along with the denominations in which they "minister." Certainly a few of these groups are acting covertly, but the vast majority are not. My research shows that thus far there has been very little effort by church leaders to confront and oust unrepentant members of these organizations from the denominations to which they belong. Indeed, many church leaders are very supportive of the particular "gay" group which calls its denomination home; many others have struck what is, in essence, a neutral position in the matter. In any event, sexual perversion has been the victor.

Affirmation: United Methodists for Lesbian, Gay and Bisexual Concerns
American Baptists Concerned
Association of Welcoming and Affirming Baptists (American Baptists)
Axios/Eastern and Orthodox Christian Gay Men and Women
Brethren/Mennonite Parents of Gay and Lesbian Children
Conference for Catholic Lesbians, Inc.
Connecting Families (Brethren, Mennonite)
Dignity/USA (Roman Catholic)
Evangelicals Concerned, Inc.
Friends for Lesbian and Gay Concerns (Quaker)
Gay, Lesbian and Affirming Disciples Alliance (Disciples of Christ)
Integrity, Inc. (Episcopal)
Interweave: Unitarian Universalists for Lesbian, Gay, Bisexual and Transgender Concerns
Lazarus Project (Presbyterian USA)
More Light Churches Network (Presbyterian USA)
National Gay Pentecostal Alliance
The Network (Evangelical Lutheran Church of America)
New Ways Ministry (Roman Catholic)
The Oasis (Episcopal)
Office of Bisexual, Gay, Lesbian, and Transgender Concerns (Unitarian Universalist)
Open and Affirming Program/United Church Coalition for Lesbian and Gay Concerns (United Church of Christ)
Parents of Lesbians and Gays (United Church of Christ)
Presbyterian AIDS Network (Presbyterian USA)
Presbyterians for Lesbian and Gay Concerns (Presbyterian USA)
Presbyterian Parents of Gays and Lesbians (Presbyterian USA)
Reconciled in Christ Program/Lutherans Concerned (Evangelical Lutheran Church of America)
Reconciling Congregation Program (United Methodist)

Semper Reformanda (Presbyterian USA)
Seventh-day Adventist Kinship International, Inc.
Shalom Ministries (United Methodist)
Supportive Congregations Network/Brethren/Mennonite Council for
    Lesbian and Gay Concerns
Telos Ministries, Inc. (Baptist)
That All May Freely Serve (Presbyterian USA)
Universal Fellowship of Metropolitan Community Churches
Wingspan (Evangelical Lutheran Church of America)
The Witherspoon Society (Presbyterian USA)

As shocking as it is to come to grips with the number of homosexual groups which are working within the various denominations, it is even more shocking to peruse the vast array of pro-homosexual "Christian" literature which these groups are disseminating, often times to the Biblically illiterate. To scan their resource catalogs, to examine the slick literature they produce in large quantities is to understand that the "gay Christian" movement is an extremely dedicated, well-funded group of people consecrated to destroying the authority of the Holy Scriptures, at least concerning the sin of homosexuality. Of course, their father the devil takes great cheer in such a vision, first, because of his delight in seeing sexual perversion justified in the name of the Lord, and secondly, because once one part of the Bible is no longer seen as the literal, immutable Word of God, what is true for the part eventually becomes true for the whole.

A little later on we will be taking a look at the contorted, demonic hermeneutics of the homosexual church movement. They are doctrines which are alien to truth and which are, to any honest person with a rudimentary knowledge of God's Word, non-sensical on their face. However, to the Biblically illiterate, as many Americans are today, the deceptive arguments of the "gay" theologians no doubt often seem perfectly sensible, not to mention eminently loving. This, of course, is all the more reason Christians need to equip themselves to defend the faith and the Holy Scriptures which so many saints have shed their own blood to defend over the centuries. The arguments of the wicked may be clever, but they are easily put to shame by a Christian armed with a knowledge of the truth. Proverbs 18:17 tells us, "He that is first in his own cause seemeth just; but his neighbor cometh and searcheth him." It is important to understand that silence is often taken as approval by the unknowing. When only one side of an issue is presented, many can be won to the cause being championed. When both sides of a contention are presented, truth becomes apparent to those who still have eyes to see and ears to hear. Christians must first learn how the sodomites use the Bible and then learn the Biblical response which dismantles our enemies' arguments.

Earlier it was mentioned that the homosexual "Christian" movement is producing and disseminating great quantities of literature in order to deceive the unwary into accepting the lie that God condones homosexual acts. Increasingly, books with that identical goal can be found on the shelves of bookstores across America. Much of the literature is expensively done, attractively packaged, and complete with commentaries and endorsements from pastors, professors of theology, and Doctors of Divinity. As to the treatment which individual Scripture passages relating to homosexuality receive in the pro-homosexual books and literature, that we will save for upcoming chapters.

For now, let us take a quick look at just one representative Bible study made available by Lutherans Concerned in cooperation with a number of other "gay Christian" groups. The name of the much heralded and widely distributed study is *Claiming the Promise: An Ecumenical Welcoming Bible Study Resource on Homosexuality.* It is presented in a forty-eight page, glossy-covered, full-color book containing a number of bright pictures and attractive drawings. A similarly packaged leader's booklet is also available. A list of consultants for the *Claiming the Promise* course contains no fewer than thirteen individuals with Ph.D.'s. The project coordinator holds a doctoral degree in religion. The entire study makes ample, though grossly improper, use of many individual Scripture verses to justify homosexual acts and also attempts to convince its students that passages which condemn such acts actually do not do so. We will examine several key statements from the study, statements which give insight into the methodology used by those who would promote evil as good while serving Satan in the name of God.

The introduction begins with a quote from John Newton, author of "Amazing Grace," followed by this comment:

> *Our God has promised good to us. God's word our hope secures.* This old familiar hymn claims the promise that the Bible offers. We are daughters and sons of God, heirs apparent of the Divine One! God calls us to claim that promise! To live it out! To be new creations in Christ. As we do so, we experience "many dangers, toils, and snares."
>
> Today we are called to face with courage a troubling dilemma in the church. This dilemma is a danger and snare that divides and hurts us all. Simply put, this dilemma is: Will the church unconditionally welcome, or refuse to welcome, lesbian women and gay men into the full life and ministry of the church? Will we affirm that people of all sexual orientations can claim kinship as daughters and sons of God, heirs apparent with Christ?[12]

Each chapter of the *Claiming the Promise* study includes four segments titled "Golden Calf," "Pillar of Fire," "Prophetic Voices," and "Promise." According to the introduction, the "Pillar of Fire" segment "is a reflection on broader intents, contexts, and messages related to the 'golden calf' biblical interpretations."[13] (See explanation of "Golden Calf" in the next paragraph.) The function of "Prophetic Voices" is set forth with these words: "These reflections, especially as they come from lesbian women and gay men, are powerful symbols that new life is rising from an oppressed group. They offer possibilities of new life in the Spirit for all of us."[14] The "Promise" segment of each chapter is explained this way:

> The fourth section focuses on the biblical promise that we are God's heirs through God's promise to Abraham. God reaffirmed that promise through the Christ-event. God's claim on Christians requires a response: be "new creations" (2 Corinthians 5:17-20). The butterfly, a symbol for new life, reminds us to explore what it means to claim the promise and be new creations.[15]

In each chapter of the study, Scriptural passages which are "often used as a 'biblical condemnation' of same-sex conduct" are introduced with a picture of a golden calf and then explained away as being misinterpreted by many Christians, and worse, even "worshiped." The reasoning is given thus:

> Like the Hebrews who worshipped a calf, we sometimes idolize static interpretations about same-sex conduct rather than hearing the Bible's story of God's promise to include all people in full kinship with God (Exodus 32).[16]

The "Golden Calf" segment is consistent with a false teaching which warns against the dangers of "Bibliolatry."[17] The thrust of the teaching is a warning against taking the Bible literally! We are told that God speaks in many extra-Biblical ways that sometimes contradict the Holy Scriptures which were written by fallible men eons ago.

The central tenant of the bibliolatry scam is the fallacious claim that the Bible and God do not always agree and that to elevate over God a book written by men when the two supposedly conflict is idolatry or bibliolatry. The whole thrust of this satanic con is to condition people to accept certain behavior which God condemns in His eternal, immutable Word, behavior such as homosexuality. The author of *Claiming the Promise* repeatedly warns against "worshipping" the Scriptures by taking them literally and makes it plain that she favors the "critical approach"[18] to the Bible, stating on page five the basis of such an approach:

> The Bible is the Word of God, but it is not the words of God. Although it witnesses to God's Word and saving actions, it was written by fallible human beings whose evolving understandings—and errors—exist in the words. Our task is to approach the words with historical-critical methods of interpretation to hear the Word that transcends the historical human context.[19]

Concerning II Timothy 3:16-17, which clearly states that "all scripture is given by inspiration of God," the *Promise* author writes:

> Dangers: A literal interpretation of 2 Timothy may lead us to equate the authority of the Bible with the authority of God. We potentially worship the Bible rather than worshipping the living God who speaks through and beyond it.[20]

On page six of the study book, we find this statement regarding II Timothy 3:16, 17:

> . . . the writer of 2 Timothy probably did not mean that every verse of scripture was relevant for all time to come. After all, this letter was a very practical one, addressing very specific concerns of the church around 90-110 C.E. The writer was not addressing us in the twentieth century and had no understanding of many of our twentieth century realities. Biblical writers wrote to their own people in their own day for their own reasons. . . .
>
> We believe that God's Word is not synonymous with all the words of scripture.[21]

It is certainly interesting and more than a little insightful that the "Christian" author of the *Claiming the Promise* Bible study chooses to use C.E., which stands for *Common Era*, as her historical point of reference rather than the long-established A.D., which stands for *anno Domini* or *in the year of our Lord.*

Of course, a book could easily be written disproving the critical approach to the Bible, refuting the heretical nonsense that God can somehow be separated from His Word and that the Bible, faithfully translated, is less than the immutable, infallible Word of God, completely applicable and fully authoritative for all men for all time. Millions have given their lives standing by and defending the absolute, unchanging authority of God's revealed Word. Those "Christians" who would claim that the Holy Scriptures cannot be taken literally regarding homosexuality should be asked, "Why then do you take the Bible literally concerning grace, salvation, mercy, heaven, God's love and providence? If one part of the Bible cannot be trusted as written, then no part of it can be trusted as written, and faith in Christ is in vain."

Happily for the true believer and unhappily for such as those of whom we have been speaking, this is not the case.

Consistent with her stance that the Scriptures should be read critically, the *Claiming the Promise* Bible study author endorses the "sociocultural approach" to God's Word. This defective form of exegesis, as explained on page seven of the study guide:

> . . . acknowledges that much of the Bible and most Biblical interpreters reflect the dominant social, cultural, and political view of their day. As a result, they have usually misrepresented or ignored marginalized and oppressed peoples.[22]

The writer includes among the misrepresented, marginalized, and oppressed peoples "gay men and lesbian women" and goes on to encourage readers of the Bible to ask:

> "How does this passage speak to *my/our* experience? Who's invisible here? What's *not* being said? Who is powerless? Who benefits? What are the economic implications of a law or custom? *Why* is something so important in early Hebrew or Christian communities?"[23]

On page eight we are told, "Gay and lesbian interpreters are just beginning to help us see the underlying structures of heterosexual bias and privilege in Biblical passages."[24] When reading such arrogant claptrap, many verses enter into one's mind, including Jude 8: "Likewise also these filthy dreamers defile the flesh, despise dominion, and speak evil of dignities."

To hold that the Scriptures simply "reflect the dominant social, cultural, and political view of their day" once again denies the divine authorship of the Bible and so far misses the truth as to be almost ludicrous. The Bible was written over a period of approximately 1,600 years by dozens of authors with all types of experiences; under all kinds of conditions; under various covenants from God; in the midst of different cultures, geographic regions, and political situations.

The writer of the first five books of the Old Testament, Moses, was first a Hebrew baby condemned to death, then a prince in Egypt, then an alien in Midian, then a prophet back in Egypt speaking on behalf of an enslaved people, and finally the leader of a free people in the Sinai Desert. Nehemiah was an exile from Judah who became a cupbearer for a Persian king and later a leader and architect of the Jerusalem wall rebuilding project. Daniel, a Judean exile in Babylon who did time in a dungeon and a lions' den, ended up being appointed "ruler over the whole province of Babylon and chief of the governors over all the wise men of Babylon." Daniel was also made a high official in the court of Darius the Mede after God gave Babylon into the hands of the Medes and Persians. The book of Job may have been written by a non-Hebraic author. The book of Psalms was written by two different kings, a priest, a group of singers, several wise men, Moses, and a number of unidentified authors. The prophet Isaiah was apparently from a distinguished Jewish family and married to a prophetess. Jeremiah, who was single, and Isaiah both lived in Judah. Ezekiel, who became a widower during his ministry, lived in Babylon. Hosea lived in Israel and was married to a harlot. Amos was a herdsman and a gatherer of sycamore fruit. Zechariah, Ezra, and Samuel were all priests.

David went from being a lowly shepherd living in the fields to a mighty king living in ornate luxury. In the interim, he was an outlaw wanted by the state and an honored soldier of the same state. At one point in his life, he was an adulterer and a murderer. For most of his life, the Bible says that he was a man after God's own heart.

Before his conversion to Christ, Paul was a "Hebrew of Hebrews," a Pharisee from an apparently prosperous, influential family living within the highest circles of Jewish society. He was a persecutor of Christians who became a Christian himself. After his conversion, Paul was an itinerant preacher and a part-time tent maker who lived in a variety of cultures during his lifetime. He became "all things to all men." During his life, Paul was both rich and poor. He wrote his epistles while in bondage and while free. He wrote surrounded by hostile pagans and while in the midst of loving brothers and sisters in Christ. He wrote while he was relatively young and while he was old.

James and Jude, the sons of a carpenter, became leaders of the early church as did Peter and John, who were fishermen by trade. John became a follower of Christ as a young man living in Galilee. He is said to have written his gospel while living among the Ephesians. He wrote the book of Revelation as an old man living as an exile on the Grecian island of Patmos. Luke was a physician; Matthew was originally a tax collector; Mark was a missionary who had become a disciple of Christ at a young age.

To say that the Old or New Testament is simply a reflection of the dominant social, cultural, and political surroundings of the writers is, first and foremost, a denial of the true Author of the sacred text; but it is also foolish and ridiculous, perhaps especially so regarding the New Testament writers. The dominant culture surrounding the early Christians, worldwide, was the Roman culture, a culture which centered around sensuality, brutality, and statism. It was a culture which exalted the emperor as god, allowed fathers to "legally" murder their own children, viewed some humans as less than human, and demanded unquestioning obedience to the civil government. This is hardly the worldview or culture reflected in the New Testament. In fact, the early church suffered greatly precisely because the gospel they preached, lived, and died for stood in stark opposition to the dominant culture of their day! Far from representing the "dominant social, cultural, and political view of their day," the writers of the New Testament were representatives of a people group which truly was "marginalized and oppressed."

To summarize, the Bible was written over a long period of time, by individuals from various backgrounds, under all kinds of conditions; yet the contents of every book and every page in the Bible is in complete harmony with every other part. The Bible is obviously the revealed, immutable Word of God, rather than simply the studied opinion of man corrupted by cultural surroundings. To say otherwise is to perpetrate a calculated lie. In spite of this, the critical approach to Bible hermeneutics, including relegating the Word of God to a cultural context along with claims of interpretive error, are the pillars upon which rests the homosexual-friendly gospel, the preaching of which causes the speaker to be accursed as explained in Galatians 1:6-9. Later we will delve further into how this approach to Scripture is being used with regard to specific Scriptural passages. For now, let us return to our brief overview of the more general pretenses presented in the Bible study *Claiming the Promise,* a study very typical of pro-"gay" theology.

A number of pages of the study are spent turning the just alluded to admonishment in Galatians 1 on its head. According to the author of *Claiming the Promise,* Paul is warning in that passage against those who would teach that homosexuality violates God's law![25] The study's author freely juxtaposes the Christian liberty spoken of in the Scriptures with the fictional freedom to express oneself as a sexual pervert and says this on page twenty:

> If we move beyond a literalist assumption that views all same-sex conduct as sin and claim instead with Paul that sin is turning away from God, we might read Psalm 139:14 and affirm together:
> *I will praise you God, for I am fearfully and wonderfully made. You have made me as I am; and I am your child.*[26]

Such gross misuse of Scripture is enough to make any true Christian quake with fear, not to mention be vexed with righteous anger. While the study's writer is claiming that God wonderfully knit together certain people to be sodomites, why not also give Him the credit for making other people to be pedophiles, adulterers, whoremongers, prostitutes, and murderers? Did it ever strike the author that committing homosexual acts falls within the category of "turning away from God?" Paul wrote as much in Romans 1, I Corinthians 6:9-11, and I Timothy 1:8-11. Such is the absolute absence of the fear of God and respect for His holy Word exhibited by the false prophets among us.

With relation to the commandments of Scripture, the eminent theological scholars responsible for *Claiming the Promise* propose a *"'discernment-based' ethic* based on *'doing least harm'"* rather than a *"'rules-based ethic.'"* [27] Under such an "ethic," which is actually the standard that most Americans live by today, there are no objective rules of behavior or any acknowledgment of any moral authority higher than the individual. The golden rule of the doing-least-harm sexual paradigm, as stated in the study we are examining, is: "'How do I avoid doing harm to myself and to another?'"[28] Of course, the true answer to that question is to obey God. There are five guidelines listed in Appendix A of the Bible study under "Doing Least Harm: An Ethical Standard and Five Relational Guidelines." Obeying God is not among the five. It is worthwhile to include the list in full, as it truly does reflect the philosophical basis of the so-called gay Christian movement. These then are the five:

Peer Relationships: *Is my choice of intimate partner a peer, i.e. someone whose power is relatively equal to mine? We must limit our sexual interaction to our peers. Some people are off limits for our sexual interests.*

Authentic Consent: *Are both my partner and I authentically consenting to our sexual interaction? Both of us must have information, awareness, equal power, and the option to say "no" without being punished, as well as the option to say "yes."*

Stewardship of Sexuality: *Do I take responsibility for protecting myself and my partner against sexually transmitted diseases and to insure reproductive choice? This is a question of stewardship (the wise care for, and management of, the gift of sexuality) and anticipating the literal consequences of our actions. Taking this responsibility seriously presupposes a relationship: knowing someone over time and sharing a history in which trust can develop.*

Sharing of Pleasure: *Am I committed to sharing sexual pleasure and intimacy in my relationship? My concern should be both for my own needs and those of my partner.*

Faithfulness: *Am I faithful to my promises and commitments? Whatever the nature of a commitment to one's partner and whatever the duration of that commitment, fidelity requires honesty and the keeping of promises. Change in an individual may require a change in the commitment, which hopefully can be achieved through open and honest communication.*[29]

The wickedness of the above "rules" is evident as is their humanistic, even demonic origin. Such doctrine is part and parcel of a man-centered, "enlightened" philosophy that sparked the bloodbath of the French Revolution and laid the foundation in Germany for Hitler's rise to power as well as the groundwork for many other tyrannical convulsions and bloodletting orgies over the centuries.

It is especially interesting to note the contorted reasoning under "Faithfulness." In essence, the "ethic" promoted is that an individual must be faithful to his promises and commitments, unless he changes his mind! Of course, this is a philosophy which has flowered in a homosexual community where the vast majority of individuals are constantly seeking more thrills, more perversion, and therefore, quite naturally, new partners.

Regarding the clearly stated parameters within which God has allowed intimate sexual relations, the marriage covenant, page twenty-six of the *Claiming the Promise* Bible study contains this bit of wicked irrationality:

> The rule that encompasses all the rest has been "no fornication—no sex outside of marriage." This "rules-based" sexual ethic *seemed* to work. In reality, however, it made marriage so sacrosanct that few if any rules stated what was "right" or "wrong" *within* a marriage. Now the assumed superiority of marriage is under question for many legitimate reasons. This is not to say that marriage is no longer viable or sacred. It is only to say that the church is long overdue to rethink its sexual ethic and its process for ethical decision making. For example, suppose we redefined fornication as "sex without a covenant of caring, sex without mutual respect and concern for the welfare of the partner, or sex without justice and love in right relationship." We would put the emphasis on the *quality of relationship* rather than on positions, techniques, or the gender of the people involved. . . .
>
> For Paul, the basic Christian ethic was not a set of rules. It was a way of being and living. We are to claim the promise. We are to be a new creation in Christ. . . .

> *Regardless of sexual orientation, the fruit of the Spirit (love, joy, peace, patience, kindness, generosity, faithfulness, gentleness, and self-control) will be visible in any right relationship and lacking in any wrong or corrupted relationship . . .*[30]

Unbelievable! "Suppose we redefined fornication as . . ." So speak the ones who would be gods.

Perhaps this is a good place to wrap up this brief look at a very representative pro-homosexual Bible study. The study contains a good deal more than we have touched on, including teaching on a number of specific Scripture verses. Let us close this revealing look at a system of beliefs called Christian, which is anything but, with one last quote from the author of *Claiming the Promise: An Ecumenical Welcoming Bible Study Resource on Homosexuality.* Explaining the purpose for the study, the writer says this on the inside back cover of the Machiavellian masterpiece:

> Over the past three decades, Biblical scholars in many faith traditions have questioned the interpretation that the Bible condemns all homosexual persons and same-sex love. . . .
> The idea for *Claiming the Promise* arose out of the need expressed by many Christians to engage the best modern biblical scholarship available on the references or allusions to same-sex conduct in the Bible. . . .[31]

To individuals who are feverishly determined to wrench a license to sin out of the Scriptures, the "best modern biblical scholarship available" is that which justifies their own desires. It makes no difference to such individuals that the scholarship chosen to buttress their evil worldview is dishonest scholarship which is textually twisted, spiritually wicked, and intellectually bankrupt.

To examine material of this kind is to realize that intellect is not equivalent to honesty any more than education is analogous to righteousness. The lettered contributors to the *Claiming the Promise* Bible study, like their comrades responsible for other like-minded, pro-homosexual books and literature, have quite obviously predicated their research and teachings on one non-negotiable flawed presupposition: Homosexuality is not a sin. In so doing, they have substituted their own evil desires and vain imaginations for the eternal, unchanging standard of God's holy ordinances. While such false teachers may be held as heroes in some circles of men as they wax eloquent in their dissertations on behalf of sin today, they will have cause for eternal regret soon enough, for they stand accursed before God due to the false gospel which they preach.

CHAPTER FOUR

High Rollers in a Cosmic Casino

For what shall it profit a man,
if he shall gain the whole world, and lose his own soul?
Or what shall a man give in exchange for his soul?
Mark 8:36-37

The first reaction of many Christians upon coming face to face with the sort of false teachings and false teachers common to the "Christian gay" community is that the people in question are just deceived, as in "poor things, they don't know what they are saying." Is this true? I would submit that it is inherently unbiblical and patently dangerous to credit such extreme rebellion and desperate wickedness to simple confusion or a lack of understanding and discernment. Certainly it is possible to be ignorant of the Scriptures; however, the homosexual religionists eagerly study the Scriptures so as to twist them to their own advantage. Many have theological degrees. All of them quote the Bible; in fact, they boast of their knowledge of the Scriptures. By their own lips, they indict themselves before the Supreme Judge of the universe. The truth is that those who preach the sodomite gospel cannot claim to be ignorant of the fact that they are preaching perversion, because they are not ignorant. They can read, and God's written Word makes it abundantly clear that homosexual acts are an unmistakable violation of His law. The Scriptures are "quick, and powerful, and sharper than any two edged sword, piercing even to the dividing asunder of soul and spirit, and of the joints and marrow, and is a discerner of the thoughts and intents of the heart" (Hebrews 4:12). This written revelation of God thoroughly condemns homosexual activity.

All homosexuals, Bible-reading or not, and their supporters know that homosexuality is a sin against God. They know because God has told them in two other ways in addition to His written Word. Romans 1 makes it clear that those who engage in gross rebellion against God are without excuse, as it says in verse nineteen, "Because that which may be known of God is manifest in them; for God hath shewed it unto them." Not only does God's revealed Word testify against homosexuality, but God's law dictated through His created order also proclaims homosexual acts to be wrong and, in fact, to be "against nature" as Romans 1:26 says. A careful examination of God's created order makes it obvious that God forbids and abhors homosexual acts. God made mankind male and female. From a purely physical perspective, the indications are what is commonly known as a no-brainer. Beyond that, godly marital unions between a male and a female create order, happiness, health, and children. Homosexual unions, which are always ungodly, create disorder, destruction, disease, and death. It is a self-evident truth that homosexual acts violate the laws of God's created order, which "from the creation of the world are clearly seen, being understood by the things that are made, even his eternal power and Godhead; so that they are without excuse" (Romans 1:20).

In addition to God's written and dictated law, the law of God written on people's hearts tells them that homosexual acts are wrong. Romans 2:14-16 is a distinct testimony that God has written His law on the heart of every person in the form of a conscience. Certainly some ignore this law to the point of having a "conscience seared with a hot iron."[1] Nevertheless, the fact remains that even the most reprobate was once warned by his conscience, the same conscience which our merciful Creator gave to each of us.

No, the "Christian" homosexualists in the American church are not deceived by the devil into thinking that God approves of sexual perversion. They are, in fact, taking the ultimate gamble, betting their very souls that the Supreme Judge of the universe will not hold them accountable for their violation of His law. If they have swallowed any satanic lie, it is the belief that they will get away with their rebellion, that the Lord will not judge and condemn them for it.

Perhaps a look at the first sin committed will help to clarify this point. The third chapter of Genesis contains the tragic account of man's fall in the garden of Eden. The serpent tempted Eve; she sinned; she then tempted Adam, and he sinned. When our first parents were confronted by God, as recorded in verse thirteen of the account, Eve's defense was, "The serpent beguiled me, and I did eat." Of course, God did not allow such a defense and pronounced Adam and Eve guilty of rebellion, ejected them from the garden, and announced a curse upon them and all their descendants, a curse brought about by their disobedience. Was God wrong to punish these two confused, deceived individuals? Was He unjust to throw out Eve's (or for that matter Adam's) ignorance defense? Of course not! "God forbid: for then how shall God judge the world?"[2] Then, as now and forever, "true and righteous are Thy judgments."[3]

Yes, Satan is a great deceiver, but we cannot blame him for our sins. As was said earlier, God has made his law manifest to every man. Eve's defense before God in the garden of Eden was that she had been deceived. She was obviously hoping that God would not hold her accountable for her actions. But God did. Why? Because Eve knew the law! God had clearly stated the law to Eve, and she related it to the serpent:

> And the woman said unto the serpent, We may eat of the fruit of the trees of the garden: But of the fruit of the tree which is in the midst of the garden, God hath said, Ye shall not eat of it, neither shall ye touch it, lest ye die (Genesis 3:2-3).

The serpent did not deceive Eve by convincing her that eating from the tree of knowledge of good and evil was not a sin. She knew it was a sin; she knew the law, as did Adam. The deception Satan succeeded in getting Eve to accept was that she could break God's law and He would not punish her. Considering the fact that eating the forbidden fruit was a capital crime, who in their right mind would hold that Adam and Eve decided it was worth the death penalty to eat anyway simply because the fruit was "pleasant to the eyes, and a tree to be desired to make one wise"? Crimes are generally committed either in the heat of passion or because the criminal feels that he can elude punishment. Obviously, Adam and Eve's crime was not a crime of passion. The truth is that Eve wanted the forbidden fruit; she wanted it badly enough to allow Satan to convince her, not that her actions were right, but rather that she could get away with them. Satan first tried to confuse Eve by asking her, "Yea, hath God said, Ye shall not eat of every tree of the garden?" When he realized that Eve knew the law, he then switched tactics and planted in her mind doubt that her loving Creator would actually punish her for rebelling against His clearly stated law. "Ye shall not surely die," he said, and the rest is history.

As it was with Eve and, of course, Adam, so it has been over and over throughout all time. In His love, God makes His will apparent to mankind in three ways: through His creation laws, through His revealed or written law, and through men's consciences. When it comes to rebellion against God, none of us can blame Satan for deceiving us. In relation to those homosexuals and their supporters who claim Biblical justification for their perverted acts, they, like Eve, know in their hearts that such acts violate God's law. If such "Christians" are deceived, their deception is in thinking that they will actually get away with their blasphemy, perversion, and rebellion. Here is where Satan may well have deluded them.

After all, what individual would trade a few moments of fleeting perverted pleasure or the "privilege" of defending such perversion for an eternity in torment, complete with weeping and gnashing of teeth? Which human being, if he were to actually consider the raging fires of hell and the tormented souls in that inferno, would willingly live in such a way as to guarantee his future in such a place? Those who promote homosexuality in the name of God are without excuse. What then can explain why so many today justify and promote homosexuality if the eternal consequence of such rebellion is so horrible? Since we have been assured that God has made their sin known to them and that they are not truly deceived in that fashion, we can only surmise that, in their feverish desire to justify the forbidden, perverted fruit of homosexuality, they have allowed themselves to be deluded into thinking that they will escape God's righteous judgment.

In an updated version of "Ye shall not surely die," Satan is whispering in their willing ears, "Your God is a loving God who surely would not condemn anyone on the basis of whom they love." Because the forbidden fruit, whether it be committing the vile acts themselves or receiving the praise of men for justifying such acts in the name of Christian love, is desirable to them, many homosexualists today have accepted the serpent's deception. They try to rationalize their position by twisting the Scriptures to make it appear as if homosexual acts are not sinful and they proclaim as much. Others admit homosexual acts are perhaps sin but claim that God, in the name of love, has granted a blanket pardon for such perversion because those committing it just cannot help being who they are. Whatever the approach, whatever the justification, those who defend homosexual acts know in their hearts that such acts are strictly condemned by God, but they are banking on Satan's lie—"Ye shall not surely die!"

Over the years, I have spoken personally or via letter or telephone with literally thousands of individuals who have bought this lie. For every one person who has defended homosexuality on the basis that there is no God, I would estimate that at least one hundred have told me that God approves of homosexual acts or, at the very least, is ambivalent toward them. Obviously, these people know better, but they have decided to justify that which they know in their hearts that the Lord condemns. They have created a god in their own image, one who may or may not care about how people behave sexually, but either way, a god who certainly will not judge and punish sexual immorality. Allow me to share just a few very representative quotes from people who have clearly swallowed the satanic lie that man can live as seems "right in his own eyes"[4] and still be welcomed into the kingdom of God:

> Homosexuality is not an evil work of the devil. God created all of us—why is that so difficult to understand? Homosexuals do not need to repent [of] their sins to God (or apologize to you) because they have done no wrong. God intended them to live and enjoy life as he made them, as homosexuals. God loves us unconditionally and accepts us for all that we are....
>
> I sincerely hope that Pastor Ovadal will repent [of] his sins of hate to the Lord and that he will find a place in his heart to accept all children of God because truly, that is what we all are.
>
> —A letter to the editor, *Oconmowoc Focus* [5]

While your organization [Wisconsin Christians United] and its supporters exude hateful attitudes and actions, I and countless other gay and lesbian Christians exemplify Christly love in our lives.... Continued anti-homosexual policy and activity—based in hatred and exclusion rather than on Love of God and inclusion—will continue to undermine the centuries of consecrated work of our predecessors in Christianity....

Teachings that miss the mark and promote hatred toward homosexuals ignore God's all-inclusive nature and wonderful diversity. Your publications tend to add to the murky world of misinformation, prejudice and bigotry toward homosexuals who express pure love but with a different sexual orientation than heterosexuals.... Do you take the Bible literally or do you take it seriously???...

The real work of the Christian Church is to build up, encourage, and embrace society in Love. Christ admonished us to stay abreast of the times.

> —A letter from Bayside, Wisconsin

Please do not leave any more of your homophobic propaganda on our door.... My God's love and compassion is unconditional and I believe that John speaks for Him when he says, "And you shall know the truth and the truth shall set you free."

> —A letter from Milwaukee, Wisconsin

I have just finished reading your "Homosexuality: The Truth" brochure and I feel ashamed to even have wasted my time. I am a Christian and I would rather burn in hell than damn someone for being gay.

Your view is one I pity. You do not know love, or love the diversity of humanity. Everyone is different and GOD LOVES EVERYONE. . . .

The brochure's title and its contents don't belong on the same piece of paper. What is written is the truth according to SOME uneducated, unaccepting, and unethical Christians, not a Christian like me.

—A letter from Ashland, Wisconsin

WCU professes a faith that has as its central core the idea that love is the most powerful force in the cosmos and that all people are worthy of dignity and respect.

In our opinion, WCU has betrayed that faith, betrayed it so badly that its actions threaten to bring the very word "Christian" into disrepute.

—An editorial in the sodomite newspaper the *Wisconsin Light* [6]

The garbage you have written about is very disturbing and I'm wondering if you've ever given any thought to where such trash may put you in the eyes of God. . . . I personally believe God is an all encompassing person who loves all mankind. . . . I feel what you're doing is immoral and against anything God would ever want.

—A letter from Madison, Wisconsin

The sad fact is that we live in a self-centered era, one in which man's pleasure, not God's law, is pre-eminent on most human beings' priority lists. Many people, and especially those in the homosexual community, have determined that they will follow their own desires, God's commands notwithstanding. Since many also realize their own mortality, they still desire the assurance of a Supreme Being who will comfort them here on earth and save them from what, for them, is the unknown in the hereafter. Hence, they simply custom-build their own god, crafting him from Biblical passages taken out of context, and then work such concepts into their theology. In their hearts they know the law, but they have decided that it simply does not apply or will not be applied to them. At this point, it would be profitable to engage in a very brief overview of what the Bible actually does say about homosexuality.

At the very beginning of the Scriptures, God clearly defines the only righteous, acceptable intimate sexual relationship between two human beings. Genesis 1:27 states, "So God created man in his own image, in the image of God created he him; male and female created he them." In Genesis 2:24 we are told, "Therefore shall a man leave his father and his mother, and shall cleave unto his wife: and they shall be one flesh." The Bible condemns all sexual activity outside of marriage; and this model in Genesis, which is reiterated elsewhere in Scripture, is the only one given within which God allows such activity. Hebrews 13:4 warns against defiling the marriage bed and goes on to say that "whoremongers and adulterers God will judge." A male and female who are husband and wife may become "one flesh." Any other sexual relationship is forbidden and is a grievous sin.

The eighteenth and nineteenth chapters of Genesis relate how Sodom and Gomorrah, along with several surrounding towns, were destroyed by God because they were given over to homosexuality, a sin the Lord defines in Genesis 13:13 as "wicked" and exceedingly sinful. Genesis 18:20 proclaims that the sodomite cities' favorite sin was "very grievous."

Judges 19 includes the sordid account of another town given over to homosexuality, Gibeah, which was in the land of the Benjaminites. It was here that a group of "gay" men insisted on having sexual relations with several travelers. When the sodomites were unsuccessful in their attempts, they then turned on a concubine and so abused her that she died. Because such sexual perversion was allowed to exist in their land, the men of Benjamin later suffered a great slaughter.

In Leviticus 20:13, we see that under the Law of Moses, God demanded the death penalty for homosexual acts. Certainly Christians may debate over proper penalties for homosexual acts under God's law as promulgated through the New Covenant which we are under, but to say that God has gone from demanding the death penalty for homosexual acts to no longer considering them as sin is no less than ridiculous and blasphemous. How dare any man portray God as being arbitrary and capricious rather than unchanging and holy! Our Creator has told us, "For I am the LORD, I change not."[7]

The Scriptures commend those Hebrew kings who, even though some of them may have been rebellious in other ways, would not tolerate open homosexuality in the land. I Kings 15:11-12 says, "And Asa did that which was right in the eyes of the LORD, as did David his father. And he took away the sodomites out of the land, and removed all the idols that his fathers had made." I Kings 22 lists some of the righteous accomplishments of King Jehoshaphat, including this in verse forty-six: "And the remnant of the sodomites, which remained in the days of his father Asa, he took out of the land." II Kings 23:3 tells us that good King Josiah and his people made a covenant with the Lord "to walk after the LORD, and to keep his commandments and his testimonies and his statutes with all their heart and all their soul." Verse seven tells us that Josiah, in remaining true to that covenant, broke down the houses of the sodomites. King Rehoboam, on the other hand, did not rule righteously. I Kings 14:22-24 contains an account of what Judah was like under the unrighteous Rehoboam:

> And Judah did evil in the sight of the LORD, and they provoked him to jealousy with their sins which they had committed, above all that their fathers had done. For they also built them high places, and images, and groves, on every high hill, and under every green tree. And there were also sodomites in the land: and they did according to all the abominations of the nations which the LORD cast out before the children of Israel.

Today in America, our civil government has once more tolerated sodomites in the land. Rather than punish such perverted, outrageous behavior, the state now protects and promotes it just as did wicked King Rehoboam. II Chronicles 12:1 says that once Rehoboam "had established the kingdom, and had strengthened himself, he forsook the law of the LORD." Verse fourteen of the same chapter tells us, "And he did evil, because he prepared not his heart to seek the LORD." How like the American saga! As a young, vulnerable nation we did our best to follow God's law. In the twentieth century, we have reached a point where we are strong and well-established. We feel no imminent danger; therefore, we no longer seek the Lord. Consequently, we have become an evil nation governed primarily by wicked men who are more than willing to tolerate not only open homosexuality but also other abominable practices such as adultery and the murder of preborn babies.

Moving to the New Testament, we see that God defines homosexual activity in Romans 1 as "uncleanness," "dishonor," "vile," "against nature," "unseemly," and the product of a "reprobate mind." I Corinthians 6:9-11 includes homosexuals who refuse to repent in a list of rebels who "shall not inherit the kingdom of God," thus precluding the possibility of a Christian sodomite. I Timothy 1:8-10 calls homosexuals "lawless," "disobedient," "ungodly," "unholy," and "profane" persons who "defile themselves" by their perverted acts.

In both the I Corinthians and the I Timothy passages in the King James Bible, the original Greek word *arsenokoites,* which means sodomites or homosexuals, is translated into one settled definition of homosexuality common during the era in which the King James Bible was written, calling such persons "abusers of themselves with mankind" and "them that defile themselves with mankind." Other Bible translations such as the New American Standard Version and the New King James Version more simply translate *arsenokoites* as *homosexuals* or *sodomites.* Either way, the condemnation of homosexual acts as grievous sin is clear in both passages.

Jude 7 tells us that God has continued through the ages to use Sodom and Gomorrah as "an example, suffering the vengeance of eternal fire." The passage further states that the inhabitants of those cities came under this eternal damnation because of their "giving themselves over to fornication" and not heterosexual fornication, but fornication with "strange flesh." Of course, the "strange flesh" relates back to Genesis 2:24 where God defines the only acceptable joining of two persons as one flesh as being male and female within a marriage covenant. When a man and a woman become one flesh outside of marriage, they are committing fornication. The inhabitants of Sodom and Gomorrah not only fornicated, but they engaged in sexual activity which was "strange" or unnatural. Any fornication among same-sex individuals is perversion of the worst stripe, a "going after strange flesh."

II Peter 2:6-10 defines homosexual sin as "unlawful" and "ungodly" and states that because of their sin God turned "Sodom and Gomorrah into ashes condemned them with an overthrow, making them an example unto those that after should live ungodly." The II Peter and the Jude passages give sodomites as an example of a group of people who are "filthy dreamers," "brute beasts," "presumptuous," "self willed," individuals who "despise government" (righteous authority).

Throughout the Scriptures, the infamous sodomite cities are held up as the eternal benchmark of rebellion, depravity, and wickedness. Deuteronomy 32:32-33 metaphorically describes the wickedness of Sodom and Gomorrah as the cruel venom of asps and grapes of gall, bitter clusters which produce poison wine. In Isaiah 1:10, the prophet drives home just how evil the leaders of Judah were at that time by using the extreme pejorative expression "rulers of Sodom." In chapter three, Isaiah again references Sodom to emphasize how wicked the nation of Judah had become. Isaiah 3 points out that they are so vile and apostate as to be proud of their sin, just as was Sodom. This passage is especially relevant to a modern America, where sexual perverts parade through our nation's cities in celebration of Gay Pride Month. Isaiah 3:9 holds an ominous warning for such individuals and the nations which allow such activity: "Woe unto their soul!" Jeremiah 23:14 compares lying, adulterous prophets committing "an horrible thing" as being "unto me as Sodom." The prophet Ezekiel used Sodom as a comparative example of extreme wickedness and rebellion, as did Christ.[8] In Romans 9:29 Paul references the two accursed cities as prime examples of desolation and hopelessness. Other passages of Scripture which put forth the destruction of the sodomite cities as warnings against rebellion to God include Deuteronomy 29:23, Isaiah 13:19, Jeremiah 49:18, Jeremiah 50:40, Amos 4:11, and Zephaniah 2:9.

In summary, the Scriptures relating to homosexual acts are clear, concise, unambiguous, and vigorous in their condemnation of those acts. Those who claim the name of Christ and yet attempt to explain away that condemnation are completely without excuse. Jeremiah speaks of such persons and asks the question with which each who perverts the Word of God will someday be confronted when they stand before the Author of that Word. "The prophets prophesy falsely, and the priests bear rule by their means; and my people love to have it so: and what will ye do in the end thereof?" (Jeremiah 5:31).

CHAPTER FIVE

Anything But Sin

That which we call a rose
By any other name would smell as sweet.
—Shakespeare

The May 27, 1996 issue of *Time* magazine included an editorial by author and critic Wilfrid Sheed. The article, "Gays in the Eyes of God," contained this statement:

[A]s it becomes likelier that homosexuality is a physical predisposition, presumably God-given, the next kind of question has to be, What might God have had in mind, and is it significant that Christ never mentioned the subject? . . . What injustices may have been done to homosexuals under the old understanding, and what can be done to avoid more of them?[1]

Such is the measure of the wickedness in America that arrogant men now routinely place more authority with junk science than in the immutable Word of their own Creator. Such is the depth to which we have fallen, that men will now glibly identify an abominable sin as a God-given character trait. Mr. Sheed's proposal that homosexuals are born that way is one which is being busily disseminated by the "gay

Christian" movement and its sympathizers. The suggestion that homosexual acts must be acceptable since Jesus never mentioned them is another favorite subterfuge of those who would condone homosexual acts in the name of God. This claim will be taken up in a future chapter.

For now, let us deal with the outrageous assertion that God is responsible for all the homosexual activity that has taken place in the history of the world. Let us be perfectly clear; that is exactly what is being claimed by those who say that certain individuals are born or, more accurately, created with an inborn God-given drive to commit sodomy and other homosexual acts. Obviously, those who brazenly promulgate such misrepresentations of God's Word and nature will someday, to their own horror, discover the extent of their error unless they first repent.

> . . . Depart from me, ye cursed, into everlasting fire, prepared for the devil and his angels (Matthew 25:41).

Certainly the sort of doctrines of devils so popular today will one day be refuted once and for all, to say the least. Meanwhile, those who are called to be "the pillar and ground of the truth"[2] have the duty to reprove such "unfruitful works of darkness"[3] and "earnestly contend for the faith which was once delivered unto the saints."[4] To hear it said that our God purposely created men and women to engage in perverted sexual acts of any kind, including homosexuality, should spark a righteous anger in any Christian who truly loves the Lord.

As an example of the lengths to which the homosexualists go in their attempt to Biblically prove that homosexuals are created that way by God, consider this quote by Harry C. Kiely, pastor of St. Paul United Methodist Church. Writing in the *Gay Theological Journal,* Kiely pens this bit of desperate irrationality:

> For those who feel that homosexuality is a sin because it is "unclean," I would ask you to consider what God said to Peter: "Do not call unclean anything that God has made clean." In other words, homosexuality is not a defect to be corrected, but is a God-given trait

to be celebrated. Homosexuals did not choose their sexual orientation any more than I chose mine—God made us as we are. Most people are heterosexual, and a few are homosexual, just as most people are right-handed while a few are left-handed.[5]

It would be relevant to ask Pastor Kiely if his gross misuse of Acts 10 to justify sexual perversion would declare rape, incest, bestiality, and necrophilia "clean" as well. Oh, but how foolish of me! I had forgotten that Pastor Kiely and his pro-perversion associates do not claim that all sexual outlaws are created as such by God, only sodomites are. In the homosexualists' fantasy world, God created mankind not only as male and female and different races, but also as homosexuals and "heterosexuals."

The *Gay Theological Journal,* from which I just quoted, is published and distributed three times a year. This large and wildly pro-"gay" publication, featuring "Homosexual Hermeneutics on Religion & The Scriptures," is a collection of writings from pastors and religious leaders. Contributing writers include the open sodomite Dr. Ralph Blair, founder of Evangelicals Concerned; and Peggy Campolo, wife of the famed evangelical pastor, writer, and speaker Dr. Tony Campolo.

Earlier I referred to the assertion that homosexuals are born that way as being based on junk science, and so it is. There is not one shred of credible evidence which proves that certain people are born programmed, if you will, to commit sodomy and other vile acts. The very few studies that have supposedly proven as much have been discredited by real researchers, many of them extremely liberal but honest scientists. At the same time, there is an abundance of empirical evidence and documentation available which amply proves that homosexuals choose to commit sexual perversion. It is not the purpose of this book to deal with every aspect of the subject of homosexuality, but rather to look at the issue as it relates directly to God's Word. Therefore, we will not get into scientific studies, but rather we will deal with the foundational question of the origin of homosexuality with foundational truth.

Not only is it junk science to claim that homosexuals are born or created that way, but it is also junk theology! If God creates certain persons to be homosexual, then such activity would be in conformity with His dictated or creation laws. Yet, as was pointed out in the last chapter, it is obvious to anyone with eyes to see and ears to hear that homosexual acts are a gross violation of God's creation laws. Those same acts are, of course, also declared a violation in God's revealed law, the Holy Scriptures. Still, the homosexuals continue to push the notion that they were created "gay" by God, that God Himself gave them their "sexual orientation." How the homosexuals and their allies love to wax eloquent on the "gift of homosexuality" and the joy of coming to terms with one's God-given sexuality!

Even sodomite congressmen have gotten into the act. The December 8, 1996 edition of the *Chippewa Herald Telegram* newspaper ran a feature article on "devout Christian" Steve Gunderson (R-Wisconsin) entitled "Reconciling Faith, Homosexuality." The article included this excerpt:

> To pray for a "cure" for his homosexual orientation, Gunderson said, would be the same as repudiating his most precious human relationship.
>
> "That would be like a heterosexual man who is married praying to God to make him gay, and then giving up the woman he loves," Gunderson said. "I hope no one would pray for that. . . ."
>
> In 1982—when he'd been in Congress for almost two years—a "strong, compassionate" voice spoke to him in the solitude of his apartment. In the book [*House and Home*], Gunderson recalled, the voice said:
>
> *Why are you so unaccepting of the person I made you to be? Why, if it's OK with me, isn't it OK with you? . . .*
>
> Ultimately, he said, it was his belief in God's constant presence in his life that helped him come to terms with his homosexuality.
>
> "Nobody," he said, "is going to deny me the love of my God."[6]

The "strong, compassionate voice" which Mr. Gunderson heard was obviously either a figment of his imagination or a seducing spirit. It is sheer lunacy, not to mention blasphemy, to say that God "made" people to perform acts which are vile and an abomination to Him, acts which He has clearly outlawed. The Scriptures repeatedly condemn homosexual acts; hence we can safely draw the conclusion that the Creator would not mandate, by virtue of an immutable congenital characteristic, that certain people engage in activity which He so hates. One does not have to be a Bible scholar to grasp that simple truth!

To maintain that homosexuals are created that way is to pave the way for acceptance of the presupposition that other deviants are also created sexually perverted. The homosexual community has certainly accepted this norm in a big way. Publicly, "gay and lesbian" spokesmen divide the world up into neat categories of homosexual and heterosexual. In their policies and publications, including those directed to youth, they are far more diversified in their words and actions. Here it becomes g/l/b/t, which stands for "gay, lesbian, bisexual, transgendered." Increasingly, a question mark has also been added to represent those individuals who have not yet decided by which perverted lifestyle they want to be identified!

The December 4-17, 1997 issue of the homosexual newspaper the *Wisconsin Light* contained an article about a transgender rights organization named It's Time Wisconsin. The article defined some of the various subgroups in the sodomite community:

> "Trangendered" is an umbrella term often used to refer to a group of people whose gender identities differ from the sexual identities assigned them at birth.
>
> "Transsexuals" are people who have a gender identity that differs from the sexual identity assigned them at birth. To correct the mismatch, some Transsexuals transition to live full-time in their preferred identity.
>
> "Transition" is a period of time when these transsexuals match their physical and social presentation with their preferred gender, taking medical and legal steps to assist them. . . .
>
> Crossdressers are people who are comfortable with the identity assigned them at birth and dress periodically in the clothing of the opposite sex.
>
> Drag queens and drag kings are people who are comfortable with the identity assigned them at birth and occasionally dress in the attire of the other gender and a sometimes exaggerated fashion.[7]

It's Time Wisconsin is just one group which is working to "make a case ... to include gender expression as a protected behavior and Transgenders as a protected class."[8]

As might be expected, many in the liberal media are more than willing to work toward that goal as well. The June 1, 1997 edition of the *Eau Claire Leader Telegram* featured a lengthy, very sympathetic article on an open transgender. The piece told of a forty-year-old man who wears woman's clothing, makeup, and has changed his name to Ann. At the end of the article "Ann," who believes God created him as a woman with a man's body, shared his perception of how God feels about his lifestyle: "'God has a special place in heaven for people like me ... Nobody can tell me that God isn't with me. I'm a good and worthwhile person ...'"[9]

If homosexuals are born that way, is it far-fetched to think that bisexuals, transgenders, drag queens, and crossdressers are likewise created by God to do the things which they do? If homosexual behavior should be protected, rather than censored, by the civil government based on the notion that its practitioners are only acting as they have been divinely programmed to act, what basis is left to deny similar status to all those involved in sexual perversion of any sort? The proposition that homosexual perversion is a hereditary trait opens up a veritable Pandora's box. If certain persons are created by God to commit homosexual acts, would it not be consistent to believe that other individuals are programmed to commit incest, pedophilia, bestiality, and necrophilia? Some individuals report of having very strong urges to the point of feeling driven to commit such shameful, illegal acts. Certainly if asked, few would remember the exact moment they became interested in, much less made a decision to be engaged in, the sexual perversions of the variety named. Is all of this evidence of being born that way? If one sexual deviation can be attributed to simple biology, why not all sexually deviant behavior? Those homosexualists who insist that God created certain persons to be homosexuals should hold a consistent position regarding individuals who feel a strong, inner "God-given" urge to have a sexual relationship with their biological siblings or parents, very young partners, animals, or the dead.

Some Christians say that they do not condone homosexuality but do believe that discrimination on the basis of "sexual orientation" should not be allowed since homosexuals cannot help being born with an intrinsic disorder or a sexual proclivity toward members of the same sex. These Christians ought to be asked if they are willing to be consistent and hire, rent to, be governed by, or have their children taught by open transsexuals, crossdressers, and flaming drag queens. Such are the logical and inevitable conclusions of accepting that sexual perversion of any type is an inherent trait. If any sexual perversion is God-given, then it follows that all sexual perversion must be God-given.

God's written Word testifies that those who engage in same-sex relations actually must make a concerted effort, a decision, to do so. Romans 1:26-27 says:

> For this cause God gave them up unto vile affections: for even their women did change the natural use into that which is against nature: and likewise also the men, leaving the natural use of the woman, burned in their lust one toward another; men with men working that which is unseemly, and receiving in themselves that recompense of their error which was meet.

This passage not only identifies homosexual activity as an error, a wrongful act; but it also clearly tells us that those who engage in such activity do so based on a decision which they have made to "change" into a homosexual. In other words, such persons are not born to commit homosexual acts; they are not oriented toward such acts; they do not have an intrinsic disorder which compels them toward such acts— quite the contrary. In Romans 1:26-27, God tells us that such persons actually have to change from what they were created to be to what they were not created to be. Beyond that, the same passage literally eliminates any notion that certain individuals were naturally born homosexual when it explains that homosexual acts are "against nature." Summed up, Romans 1:26-27 states that homosexuals are what they are because they made a change from what comes naturally to engage in acts which are unnatural.

It has only been in the last several decades that the homosexualists have used the word *orientation,* having previously tried the *preference* approach. The early strategy was at least philosophically honest. What was first being claimed was that individuals should have the choice to engage in any sort of sexual perversion that their hearts desire. Such a claim was wicked, but those espousing it were up front with what they believed. Eventually realizing that they could not gain ground by telling the truth, that the public would not wholeheartedly buy the idea of decriminalizing and even protecting certain perverted sexual practices based solely on the idea that certain persons want to engage in them, the homosexualists shifted their strategy and their terminology to embrace the orientation theory. The last claim is worse than the first and, unfortunately, has been much more effective.

Convincing people that homosexuals are born that way is a win-win situation for the sodomites. For their purposes, the best case scenario under such a methodology is that most people will simply say, "Well, homosexuality can't be wrong if God created homosexuals that way. In fact, it must be wrong to speak ill of such behavior or to discriminate against those practicing it. We had better make sure that the law reflects as much." At the very worst, from the homosexualists' standpoint, people who swallow the orientation lie will see homosexuals in the same light as they do a handicapped person. In other words, they will see homosexuals as persons with a cross to bear through no fault of their own. Of course, the logical conclusion of such an understanding is that homosexuals should not be discriminated against in any way or, much less, have their sexual conduct proscribed by law. After all, what decent person would tolerate discrimination against a handicapped person or, even worse, agree that such a person should be punished by the civil government for being handicapped? Of the two strategies, preference and orientation, the latter is by far the more wicked and diabolically effective in advancing the sodomite cause.

Of course, there is no shortage of "Christian" and religious organizations which have been more than happy to lend credence to the lie that God created a certain class of individuals to engage in perverse sexual activity. To make matters even worse, there are now two schools of born-that-way thought. For those who are squeamish about accepting the proposition that God creates homosexuals and blesses the perverted behavior by which they claim their identity, there is the just-don't-act-on-it branch of sexual orientation theology. According to this twilight zone theory which incorporates pseudo-science and pop psychology into a rough Biblical framework, God creates certain individuals as homosexuals, but He considers it a sin (at least a little one) for them to act upon the constant urges which He has programmed into their very essence. Tragically, some ex-"gay" ministries ascribe to this flawed anti-Biblical notion, a notion which can easily metamorphose into "If God made me this way, surely He will not condemn me for acting on it."

Dr. Tony Campolo's position on the origins of homosexuality typifies this grotesque endeavor to pander to a certain class of sinners by attempting to reconcile Biblical truth with wicked human desire. In his book *20 Hot Potatoes Christians Are Afraid to Touch,* Campolo writes:

> It is *very* important that all of us distinguish between homosexual *orientation* and homosexual *behavior.* Homosexual orientation is an inclination to desire sexual intimacy with members of the same sex. Homosexual behavior is "making love" or seeking sexual gratification through physical interaction with members of the same sex. The first is desire. The second is action. . . .[10]

> I think that many of the despicable attitudes toward homosexuals stem from an ignorance of what science is discovering, as well as a lack of understanding as to what the Bible says. First of all, there is a growing body of evidence that suggests that most homosexuals have the orientation that they do through no choice of their own nor any failure on the part of their parents to socialize them properly. More and more research suggests that in a great number of cases, if not in an overwhelming majority, homosexual orientation is inborn. . . .[11]

> If many of those who have a homosexual orientation are the way they are through no fault of their own, but rather as a result of inborn

conditions or hormonal changes, then it becomes dubious that much can be accomplished simply by asking such persons to repent and choose to be heterosexuals.[12]

Based on his view that homosexuality is an orientation which is only sin if acted upon, Dr. Campolo has endorsed homosexual "covenants" in which two same-sex "oriented" individuals pledge to live together in a life-long, marriage-like covenant but to remain celibate![13] In light of his same-sex celibate marriage covenant scheme, one cannot help but wonder if anyone has ever had the foresight to offer Dr. Campolo a good deal on the Brooklyn Bridge!

As intimated earlier, it is not always just the so-called liberal religious leaders who undergird the devastating deception that homosexuals are born that way. Mixing a sincere respect for the Bible and a love for God with a misplaced desire to be compassionate, many conservative Christian spokesmen and leaders have bought into the lie that homosexuals are born that way, but they must not act upon their orientation. I must quote several such individuals in the following paragraphs, not because I desire to attack them personally, but because their publicly stated views on the particular issue with which we are dealing are typical of a new philosophy that is contrary and damaging to the cause of Christ. The examples given are just several of many which could be cited.

Joe Dallas is a conservative Christian, a former homosexual, a past president of the ex-"gay" ministry Exodus International, and the director of a Biblical counseling practice. While declaring homosexual acts to be sin, in his book *A Strong Delusion,* Mr. Dallas says this regarding those who state that homosexuality is a choice: "It is not. No one *chooses* to be homosexual. People do choose, however, to *act* on their homosexual desires. Make the distinction and keep it clear."[14] By stating that "no one chooses to be homosexual," Dallas is, in essence, claiming that homosexuality is a God-given orientation, even if it is one not to be acted upon!

Mr. Dallas is far from being alone in his claim. For a number of reasons, many Christian leaders increasingly seem to feel the need to somehow soften the Biblical truth concerning homosexuality, thus pandering to the homosexual in ways which would never be considered for an adulterer, a pedophile, or an individual involved in bestiality—at least not yet!

The November 1996 issue of *Christianity Today* contained an article by Donald A.D. Thorsen who is a professor of theology in the Graduate School of Theology at Azusa Pacific University in Azusa, California. In the article "Revelation and Homosexual Experience," Thorsen states very clearly and correctly, "And when we thoroughly consider the various contexts of Scripture, we discover that its teaching remains consistent: Scripture prohibits homosexual activity."[15] Unfortunately, the professor doesn't stop while he is ahead. In the same article he makes these statements:

> We need to test our beliefs and not consider them self-authenticating or beyond question. Reason would have us consider new evidence with open minds, such as the causes of homosexuality. . . .

> Indeed, science has provided a number of helpful insights for reflecting upon homosexuality. The distinction between homosexual activity and homosexual orientation helps us to realize that—like alcoholism—homosexuals may be dealing with a psychological and/or biological orientation that should be viewed as given rather than chosen. . . .[16]

> The distinction may not change our Biblical understanding of the appropriateness of homosexual activity, but it will affect how we view and minister to those who may be experiencing psychological and/or biological factors beyond their control.[17]

Before commenting any further on the allegations contained in the preceding statements, let us also take a look at the current stand of the Roman Catholic Church on this issue of sexual orientation. *The Catechism of the Catholic Church,* as of the writing of this book, includes this about homosexuality:

> The number of men and women who have deep-seated homosexual tendencies is not negligible. They do not choose their

homosexual condition; for most of them it is a trial. They must be accepted with respect, compassion, and sensitivity. Every sign of unjust discrimination in their regard should be avoided. . . .[18]

In all fairness, as of this writing, the Roman Catholic Church is in the process of modifying this portion of its *Catechism.* I have seen the proposed modifications, and quite frankly, they are no great improvement as the new statement will apparently still portray homosexuality as a genetic trait. Even the conservative Joseph Cardinal Ratzinger, Prefect of the Sacred Congregation for the Doctrine of Faith and the overseer of the *Catechism* modification, has explained that he believes homosexual tendencies are "not simply a matter of choice or will."[19] In other words, if homosexuality is not a matter of choice or will, then it must be a matter of heredity. Unfortunately, it would appear that many in the Roman Catholic Church's leadership, at this point in time, have taken a very unbiblical position on homosexuality.

On September 10,1997, the National Conference of Catholic Bishops issued a pastoral statement titled "Always Our Children." This official document expressed the belief that homosexual orientation is "a fundamental dimension of one's personality" and that "homosexual orientation is experienced as a given, not as something freely chosen." The letter also called upon parents and others to "confront their own fears about homosexuality" and urged families to view homosexuality as a "gift" to help families toward "becoming more honest, respectful, and supportive." The bishops' letter alleged that homosexuality is caused by "multiple factors—genetic, hormonal, psychological"—but did not mention sin as a possible cause! The bishops also made these astounding statements:

Sexual identity helps to define the unique persons we are. One component of our sexual identity is sexual orientation. . . .

It is not sufficient only to avoid unjust discrimination. Homosexual persons "must be accepted with respect, compassion and sensitivity" . . .

Nothing in the Bible . . . can be used to justify prejudicial or discriminatory attitudes and behaviors. . . .

> We call on all Christians and citizens of good will to confront their own fears about homosexuality and to curb the humor and discrimination that offends homosexual persons....

The bishops' letter also instructed church leaders to "welcome homosexual persons into the faith community" and repeatedly referred to "our homosexual brothers and sisters."[20]

Certainly it is easy enough for a true Christian to take issue with those who call themselves Christian but nevertheless condone homosexual activities in the name of God. It is yet another story to break ranks with individuals and organizations which claim to operate under a Biblical worldview but, in fact, take a very unbiblical position on homosexuality. Because a number of well-meaning Christians and Catholics may espouse a certain view does not make that position right.

Those who take the stand that homosexuals are born that way but should not act consistent with their "orientation" are not only teaching error, but they are also giving aid and comfort to the enemy. They are, in fact, loosing on earth a great tool for the advancement of a satanic movement in every human arena, including in the legislative arena. For instance, commenting on the bishops' pastoral letter, Kevin Ivers, director of public affairs for the sodomite Republican group, the Log Cabin Club, had this to say:

> "This message from the bishops breaks with some of the rhetoric of the anti-gay movement. It has had an impact on Capitol Hill and could signal a step forward for the Church on legislative issues down the road."[21]

Kevin Ivers and other sodomite leaders celebrated the bishops' pastoral letter, not because it was everything they wanted, but because it was a part of what they wanted. The Roman Catholic bishops' statement, like the stance taken by Christians such as Joe Dallas, advances the notion that homosexuality is genetically determined. The acceptance of such an opinion as fact in turn precludes righteous discrimination against and certainly civil punishment of open homosexuals.

It is foolish to think that a religious organization as large as the Roman Catholic Church has no impact on public policy and private morals. Likewise, Christian pastors and leaders must also understand that great weight is put on the words which they speak. Recognizing that fact, the Scriptures say, "My brethren, be not many masters, knowing that we shall receive the greater condemnation" (James 3:1). Beyond helping to move forward the homosexual political agenda, the born-that-way-but-don't-act-on-it position deceives persons who have fallen into a wicked and dangerous thought life to continue that pattern.

The question must be asked, What defines a homosexual? The answer is the committing of homosexual acts. What then defines this so-called homosexual orientation with which some say certain persons are born but must not act out? We are told that it is identified by homosexual urges. Those who defend the existence of such a status are telling us that certain persons are born with an urge to commit homosexual acts. But where do such urges have their genesis? In the mind, of course. Then the born-that-way-but-don't-act-on-it message to persons who believe that they have a homosexual orientation is first, that they cannot control their thoughts and secondly, that they can control their actions even as they let perversion run riot in their minds.

The truth is that God expects us, with His help, to take authority over our thought lives. This may not always be easy, but those who refuse to take authority over their thoughts usually end up losing control of their actions. This is what we are told by the Word of God. It is a truth which has been borne out by human experience. The simple reality is that it is a sin both to think about or to perform homosexual acts. While it can be a tremendous battle to bring the mind and imagination under control, it is a battle which God has commanded us to fight and, with His help, to win. No one is suggesting that it is possible to achieve perfection in one's thought life; but, by the same token, the Scriptures make it very plain that Christians should not be thinking about or, to put it bluntly, fantasizing about sexual perversion such as adultery, rape, fornication, or homosexuality.

II Corinthians 10:3-5 gives us instructions concerning our minds and imaginations:

> For though we walk in the flesh, we do not war after the flesh: (For the weapons of our warfare are not carnal, but mighty through God to the pulling down of strong holds;) casting down imaginations, and every high thing that exalteth itself against the knowledge of God, and bringing into captivity every thought to the obedience of Christ.

In light of this Scripture, the question must be asked, Are we being obedient to Christ if we allow ourselves to dwell on acts which are forbidden by the Word of God? This passage tells us that we are to bring "into captivity every thought to the obedience of Christ." By virtue of commanding us to do such a thing, God is also telling us that it is possible!

Nowhere in the Scriptures are we told that it is permissible to allow our minds to be "the devil's playground." Nowhere in God's Word is there any indication that certain people are born with a genetic code which causes them to be homosexual in their mind. It is quite the contrary. The Scriptures teach that our minds are not to be conformed to wicked, worldly thoughts. God created us for a better purpose. Romans 12:2 says, "And be not conformed to this world: but be ye transformed by the renewing of your mind, that ye may prove what is that good, and acceptable, and perfect will of God." Our Creator has made it clear in no uncertain terms that we are not to dwell on the wicked things of this world. The Scriptures instruct those who have become new creatures in Christ to renew their minds. Obviously, this eliminates the possibility that it is permissible to continue clinging to the lie that persons are born with a homosexual orientation, unless one holds the unbiblical notion that homosexuals cannot be saved.

How does God look upon a person who justifies fantasizing about homosexual acts or lusting after another person on the pretense that he, the person fantasizing or lusting, was born with a homosexual orientation? In His Sermon on the Mount, Jesus warned that a man lusting after a woman to commit adultery with her is committing adultery in his heart. What then is a person committing who entertains homosexual lusts in his mind? Now, if one does not commit homosexual acts, he is not a homosexual by definition. If one does not even think about committing homosexual acts, that person would not be a homosexual by "orientation."

The Scriptures tell us that it is possible to refrain from fantasizing about wicked things and that it is dangerous not to refrain from doing so. Proverbs 23:7 says, "For as he thinketh in his heart, so is he . . ." James 1:14-15 warns, "But every man is tempted, when he is drawn away of his own lust, and enticed. Then when lust hath conceived, it bringeth forth sin: and sin, when it is finished, bringeth forth death." This passage makes it clear that the progression of rebellion against God is this: first lust is entertained in the heart. The lust facilitates toying with temptation which, in turn, further inflames the lust until finally thought turns into deed and the wages of sin are reaped.

Those who comfort individuals struggling with the temptation of homosexuality by telling them that they were born that way but should just not act out their desires are themselves sinning. Instead of praying for and discipling such individuals properly so that their mind and body might be freed from the grip of Satan, they are providing an excuse for them to cling to a sinful, dangerous thought life. It is a life from which the individual can be set free by the blood of Jesus and by the power of the Holy Spirit. "And such were some of you: but ye are washed, but ye are sanctified, but ye are justified in the name of the Lord Jesus, and by the Spirit of our God" (I Corinthians 6:11).

Since it is possible and, in fact, commanded by God for a homosexual to stop acting like a homosexual and to stop thinking like a homosexual, what is left to identify a person as a homosexual? Nothing! There is then no such thing as inborn homosexual orientation. Those who claim otherwise do violence to the Word of God and a grave disservice to all those enslaved by a wicked perversion.

For whatever reason, homosexuality has apparently become a sort of sacred sin considering how it is treated by many Christians and Catholics. Sadly, we live in a very subjective era in which we are more influenced by the world's standards and "wisdom" than we know. When it comes to homosexual acts, many Christians take great strides to avoid the obvious—homosexuals are sexual outlaws. They are people who are living incredibly wicked lives and engaging in extremely vile acts which allow Satan to have a powerful influence in their lives, thus often making it very hard to break free from the perverted activity. For any number of reasons, many well-meaning, truly Bible-believing Christians treat homosexuals with a special deference and go to great lengths to portray homosexual acts as almost anything other than what they are—gross sin. Shakespeare pointed out that a rose by any other name would smell the same. Homosexual acts are sin and are committed by choice. Wrongfully attributing them to any other cause does not change the fact that they are a stench in God's nostrils.

Homosexuals are not born that way; they do not have an intrinsic disorder, as some well-meaning Christians would insist; and they certainly are not sick people in need of recovery. I have often heard Bible-believing pastors rightly expound on the "anti-homosexuality" passages of Scripture, only to then hear them talk of the need for the body of Christ to help homosexuals recover from their homosexuality. This is not Biblical. Homosexuality is not a sickness; it is a sin. People recover from strep throat; sinners must repent.

In spite of the extensive use of the word in the Bible, *repent* has fallen into disuse within many Christian circles. The prophets of the Old Testament preached repentance. Jesus preached repentance. In fact, the very first quote from Jesus in the gospel of Mark is a call to repentance. John the Baptist's message was repentance-based. Peter at Pentecost confronted the sin of his listeners head-on and in no uncertain terms and, as a result, his listeners were "pricked in their heart, and said unto Peter and to the rest of the apostles, Men and brethren, what shall we do?" Peter's answer? "Repent, and be baptized every one of you in the name of Jesus Christ."[22]

Today, many Christians approach the homosexual as if he were a dilapidated, old couch in need of re-covering. The individual is not urged to repent but rather encouraged to put on a covering of cross-less Christianity via the cheap grace now offered in so much of American Christendom. This is seen as the key to "recovering" from homosexuality. The sin of homosexuality must be portrayed as more than some kind of sad, self-destructive sickness if we are to see homosexuals truly become new creatures in Christ.

It is interesting that homosexuals are treated so much differently than others who are involved in gross rebellion against God. Those of us who have attempted to take a Biblical stand against homosexuality are often told that we should be more gentle in our preaching. After all, it is so difficult to stop committing homosexual acts. Surely this may be true with certain individuals, but if this is a basis for soft-soaping the sin of homosexuality, then we should be consistent. Does anyone in their right mind think that it is easy for a promiscuous "heterosexual" young man in this sensual, sex-soaked society to totally renounce his old ways, including the use of pornography? Perhaps we should down-play the wickedness of male-female adultery and fornication, considering how hard it can be for some individuals to relinquish those activities and relationships. What about the abortionist who, as one told me, feels "a spiritual need to kill babies"? Perhaps it would be best not to use words like *murder* or *innocent bloodshed* or *repent* in connection with those activities. Before he was executed, serial rapist and murderer Ted Bundy shared how he had developed a consuming need to commit his barbarous acts. Does this mean that we should take a soft, gentle approach to rape and murder?

It is vital for a number of reasons that Christians approach the sin of homosexuality in the way that the Scriptures approach it. Homosexuals are not ill; they are sexual outlaws engaged in perverted, vile sin. Unless they understand the depth of the depravity in which they are involved, they may never understand the need for brokenness and repentance before God. When we use words such as *recover* relating to the homosexual, we are providing an excuse for backsliding and even for maintaining a secret life of sin. After all, a person should not be blamed for being sick, and sometimes recovery from sickness takes a long time. Sometimes a person is chronically ill all his life. By not portraying the Word of God as written to homosexuals, we may well play a part in false conversions which bring a certain amount of comfort to the individual but not salvation and liberty.

Sadly, it has become increasingly popular for many who profess to accept the authority of Scriptures to nevertheless speak of homosexual activities with such words as *disorder* and *recover.* This approach may emanate, at least in part, from a latent tendency to be affected by the born-that-way deception and as a result of so often hearing homosexuals insist that they never made a decision to become a homosexual. "I didn't just wake up one morning and decide it would be neat to be gay" is the way they put it. This all seems very confusing to Christians and to others with an essentially Biblical worldview. Not wanting to blame someone for something which seems to be out of the individual's control, the logical conclusion is to embrace either the orientation, disorder, or sickness myth, or perhaps a combination of all of these.

Homosexuality is a chosen condition. Some homosexuals remember making the decision to commit perverted sexual acts; others do not. This is no different from many other lust-driven sins. Many people who live "heterosexually" immoral lives do not remember the first time they thought of becoming a fornicator or adulterer. Individuals choose to commit homosexual acts and, with God's help, they certainly can choose to cease from committing such acts.

A bit earlier, we touched on the National Conference of Catholic Bishops' statement on homosexuality. Personally, if I were asked to write a brief statement on the same question, it would be something like this: While some individuals may not remember the exact moment that they began to think about engaging in homosexual acts and the actual decision to do so may have, in fact, been formulated over a period of time and influenced by various environmental factors, all persons who engage in homosexual activity are in open rebellion to God's law, the law which is not only revealed in His Scriptures but also dictated through His creation and written on every human being's heart. According to the Bible, homosexuals are to be considered as sexual outlaws whom the civil government should prosecute, the church should discipline and expel, and the family should shun. This is to be done not out of hate for the individual, but in obedience to God's Word and in the hope that the homosexual will experience the godly sorrow which leads to repentance and rebirth as a new creature in Christ. At every opportunity, the gospel of Jesus Christ should be shared with individual homosexuals in hope that they will see their need to be washed, sanctified, and justified in the name of the Lord Jesus and in the Spirit of our God.

It's All Just a Big Mistake

Men do things which their fathers would have deprecated,
and then draw about themselves a flimsy cordon of sophistry,
and talk about the advance of humanity and liberal thought,
when it is nothing after all but a preference for individual license.
—John Hall, Nineteenth Century Presbyterian Pastor

The Scriptures contain many exhortations for God's people to stand for His eternal truth. These are admonitions that Christians are bound to obey. In this day and age of political correctness, subjective truth, and man-centered religion, standing for God's immutable, eternal absolutes can garner one no end of hostility and demonization. As pointed out in a previous chapter, there is a form of fascism afoot in our land which requires the neutralization and isolation of those who refuse to buy into the pagan worldview which dominates our culture. The strategy is simple, tried, and true—link an honestly held moral position to an immoral, illogical position in hopes that the reputation and credibility of the targeted person will be destroyed. Christians who, in obedience to and love for the Lord, take a public, Biblical stand against homosexuality are often cast by the media and the homosexualists as Nazi-types who not only hate all homosexuals but Jews and blacks as well. For the educational benefit of those Christians who have not experienced this phenomenon first-hand, I include these two excerpts from the sort of letters routinely received at Wisconsin Christians United:

- [Y]our rhetorical tactic of casting homosexuals as "depraved" . . . in order to quickly drum up extreme hatred and perhaps violence against them is highly reminiscent of Hitler's attempt to portray Jews as sub-human vermin and rats. . . . your Biblical quotations reveal that you are not inspired by God or acting on behalf of God, but are rather filled with boiling hate and find some diabolical need to engage in a Salem-style witch hunt. . . . you misleadingly call yourselves "Wisconsin Christians United"; you are not "united" with most Christians in your blatant Hitler-style hate mongering tactics. You are rather a fringe group attempting to get the pot of hate boiling, which may well lead to violence against persons whom, for all your rhetoric, are still part of the bounteous creation of your precious God.
NAME AND ADDRESS WITHHELD DUE TO CONCERNS
FOR SAFETY
cc: Wisconsin Department of Justice-Human Rights

- Where does your hate come from? Who taught you such intolerance? Were you picked on by a bully in 2nd grade that you feel you must now pick on someone else? Groups such as yourself who disseminate these shallow attitudes and judgmental stances are the true Neo-Nazis of our time. Who is next? Jews? Catholics? Blacks? Hispanics? . . . P.S. Stay the hell off Charles Lane in Madison. We have no time for you. P.S.S. Mt. 7:1-7

The homosexualists place great value on the strategy of portraying true Christians as Nazis and are busily trying to work that image into the public's conscience. The Campaign to End Homophobia distributes a brochure titled "Homophobia and Anti-Semitism: Making the Links." The brochure contains this statement:

Jewish people and lesbians, gay males, bisexuals, and transgender people are natural allies; they share a history of oppression.

However, a dominant Christian and heterosexual culture has prevented such alliances from forming. This pamphlet offers some information about the connections between homophobia and anti-Semitism and some guidance on building alliances.[1]

As painful as it may be, Christians must not be intimidated into silence by fascist-like attempts to lump us with Nazis and racists. It has been my experience that such tactics have begun to wear thin with the general public, especially in those instances when the targeted Christian refuses to be intimidated and continues to lift up a truly Biblical standard in the face of character assassination. God truly does vindicate His people when they are willing to stand firm for His kingdom and His righteousness.

For a fascinating, detailed look at the history and philosophy of fascism, I highly recommend the excellent book, *Modern Fascism: Liquidating the Judeo-Christian Worldview* by Gene Edward Veith, Jr.

In addition to being stereotyped as Nazis, those of us who resist the "gay" agenda are often portrayed as just plain stupid. After all, to be against an activity which has received the stamp of approval by the modern enlightenment philosophes must surely be a clear sign of ignorance and mental deficiency!

Once after Wisconsin Christians United did a literature drop in Oconomowoc, Wisconsin, a weekly columnist in the local paper wrote an incredibly vitriolic editorial which ended with this amazingly intolerant, elitist statement: "The protesters need to gather up their leaflets and go back to their caves."[2] Go back to our caves? Yet it is no surprise that distributing a gospel tract containing the Biblical truth about homosexuality would earn such a scathing, demeaning remark.

Again, there is a form of fascism afoot in America which insists that those who do not get with the post-Christian, pagan program must be hounded from the public scene. It simply will not do to have people who believe in the eternal, transcendent law of God accorded respect or even civility. After all, unless such persons are discredited as Nazis, idiots, or both, their views may be heard, considered, and may even prevail. Such a situation could certainly impede America's relentless march into a brave new world where the unspeakable sin is judging others and the only moral code is to do the least harm in pursuit of personal gratification.

Then there are those who attempt to justify homosexual acts with the very eternal standard which condemns such acts. These are the ones who have truly honed the ridicule, demonize, and isolate paradigm to a fine edge. Woe to that Bible-believer who would even mispronounce a word when defending the Scriptures against the homosexualists! During my years of ministry, I have had the blessing of defending the Scriptural truth about homosexuality on radio, on television, on the telephone, and on the street. More than once, I have felt blessed by God and anointed by the Holy Spirit to rise above my own natural limitations as I shared truth, publicly or privately, with one of Sodom's apologists. Yet every so often, after having demolished all the strongholds set up against the truth of God, my flesh will fail as it does for all of us from time to time, and I will commit some grammatical or pronunciation error. It is precisely upon that human error that my antagonist will pounce to once more "prove" the stupidity of us "fundamental" Christians. Let me give you an example.

One fine day after some ministry in Madison, Wisconsin, passing out a tract which I wrote titled "Homosexuality: The Truth," I was interacting on the telephone with one of many irate individuals who does "believe in the First Amendment but not for this sort of hate speech." My opponent obviously had come to the debate equipped primarily with an arrogant, elitist attitude and a hotter-than-average temper. Concerning the Scripture, the Constitution, and even common sense, the man was armed only with an impressive array of skewered history, mindless slogans, and out-of-context Scripture verses on love. When I challenged him to substantiate his repeated and loud proclamations that the brochure which I had written was all lies and distortions, he was helpless, falling back to the God-haters' Siegfried line and turning those big guns of tolerance, freedom, and non-judgmentalism against my Christian "bigotry, hatred, and ignorance." But then came the break every defender of the indefensible hopes for—I made a grammatical error! Summing up our conversation I said, "The truth is, you cannot refute a thing I have said and you cannot refute a thing in the brochure you are attacking. There isn't nothing in the brochure you can refute!"

Aha! I had slipped and used a double negative, clearly a blunder which destroyed my credibility and rendered all of my arguments moot. With an air of great superiority, my antagonist announced, "You people can't even talk right," and hung up the phone. And so it goes. Well, at least he did not call me a "clown" and "a semi-literate farmboy" as did one editorial in the "gay" *Wisconsin Light* newspaper.[3]

In 1997, a friend of mine wrote a letter to several pastors who had signed the pro-homosexual manifesto "On Homosexuality and Christian Faith: A Madison Affirmation" which proclaimed homosexuality not to be a sin and called upon those who say it is a sin to repent. In her letter, this dear lady simply defended the Holy Scriptures as best as she could using verses from the Bible. As I read several of the replies to her letter which she received from the homosexualist "men of God," I could not help but think of the "mockers in the last time" spoken of in Jude 18. For instance, a letter signed by two United Church of Christ pastors from Madison, Wisconsin, contained this loving little caveat:

> Yes, my dear, Romans is *still* in the Bible. (We checked, too, just to make sure). The last time we looked, (which was just today), it read *"Therefore you have no excuse, whoever you are, when you judge others; for in passing judgment on another you condemn yourself . . ."* (Romans 2:1a).
>
> We might also point out that our Bible also has the book of Genesis where we can read about the destruction of Sodom and Gomorrah (not *Gomorra,* as in your letter, unless Gomorra is some other place we're not aware of.)

These clergymen may not view it a sin to commit sodomy, but apparently a typo warrants merciless scorn. The letter closed with this caustic remark: "Your sarcasm and clearly holier-than-thou-attitude, so over-ride whatever reasonable arguments you may wish to put forth that we sense only your hostility. Perhaps the fault is entirely ours."

Another Christian brother wrote to a different pastor who had also signed the same manifesto the pastors just quoted had signed. That man of the cloth, a United Church of Christ pastor from Plymouth, Wisconsin, responded in a fashion similar to his brother "wolves," saying in part:

> Thank you for your handwritten "biblical rebuke in love."
>
> First of all, it dispels the belief that persons holding your judgment of other brothers and sisters in Christ can't read or write (although you did misspell my name).
>
> Secondly, I'm sure that we never met, for I'm not welcome in your circles. I don't keep company with modern day Pharisees, nor they with me. You remember the Pharisees, don't you? Those self-righteous, pious, holier-than-thou, judges . . .
>
> I hope that your prayer for my "eyes to be open" and the speck to be removed, includes a prayer for your own eyes, where a log has situated itself. . . .
>
> Your letter prompted me to prayer. A prayer for the strength to love you in Christ...a prayer for the light to come to you in the midst of your present darkness. A prayer that you might not be judged by God as severely as you have judged others.

This book could be filled with similar first-person examples such as those mentioned. Believe me, I know. Such is the wilting rhetoric turned on any who dare to question the wisdom of those who preach doctrines of devils in the name of love during the closing years of the twentieth century. The question may rightly be asked, Who are the true elitists; who are the consummate snobs? Why, the very people who rail against faithful Christians as narrow-minded and bigoted!

Those who stand on Biblical absolutes defend an inerrant, transcendent body of morality, truth, and law. We make no apology for that fact, nor should we. Our opponents likewise defend a distinct system of beliefs. The difference is that we are not like our opponents, defending an evolving, philosophical set of subjective "ethics" conditioned by human passion, pride, and opinion. We can substantiate our position with the Word of God, as written and delivered by Him. Our opponents, on the other hand, must somehow justify assertions which clearly fly in the face of not only God's dictated or creation law, but also His revealed law, the Holy Scriptures. When faced with a Christian wielding the "armour of righteousness on the right hand and on the left,"[4] they must first demonize the messenger in an attempt to discredit the message; and secondly, they must construct a theoretical basis which will support their false presuppositions under the color of truth and fact.

In recent years, the "gay Christian" movement has assembled an array of wolfish theologians who, in turn, are busily assembling systematic demonic doctrines which can be referenced as "proof" that the Bible condones sodomy and other acts central to the perverted activity known to us as homosexuality. When it comes to homosexual acts, the Scriptures are so clear that it would seem impossible, and certainly audacious, for any mortal to attempt to prove that the Bible which calls homosexual acts vile and an abomination actually contains no prohibition against those same acts! Yet that is exactly what is happening today. Before we examine individual verses, it would seem profitable to look at some of the general arguments used to portray God's holy Word as pro-homosexual.

There are two major claims used to achieve this wicked goal. The first relies heavily on intellectual intimidation. Why are we not surprised? This particular strategy is designed to shame the vast majority of Christians into silence by convincing the masses that only those who can read the Bible in its original languages can understand what the Scriptures truly say. According to those wielding this elitist weapon, many mistakes were made in the translation of the Scriptures into English. They then go on to make numerous claims regarding what the early Hebrew and Greek texts supposedly really say about homosexuality. It is always gratifying to watch such liars self-destruct when confronted by godly men who can read the Bible in its original languages. But what of those Christians who are not Greek or Hebrew scholars? How do we defend against this mistranslation deception when confronted with it?

I have had this easy-to-refute, original-language challenge thrown at me many times. I always answer something like this: *Are you advocating a return to pre-Reformation times? Are you insisting that we revert to a past when the Scriptures were only available to an elite priesthood? Are you saying that the very Book upon which Western Civilization's laws, customs, and culture was built is filled with interpretational mistakes? Are you insinuating that you have discovered something that Biblical scholars, preachers, teachers, translators, and evangelists throughout the centuries have missed? Are you suggesting that the Bible, for which so many have laid down their lives and upon which millions more have based their temporal actions and eternal future, is no longer to be trusted?*

While I believe that there are several very accurately translated versions of the Bible available today, the Bible which much of Christendom has defended for over three hundred years is the 1611 King James Bible. All English translations prior to the King James Bible, including the Geneva Bible, consistently agree with each other and the King James on the rendering of the "anti-homosexual" passages of Scripture.

To suggest that the 1611 King James Bible is unreliable due to being mistranslated is simply an outrageous lie. If the passages of that Bible or, for that matter, the Geneva Bible which was the Bible of the Puritans cannot be trusted and taken at face value as written regarding homosexuality, then neither can the Biblical passages on any other subject be trusted. This would mean that millions have shed their blood and multitudes have staked their lives and eternity on lies. It would mean that the Book upon which, along with the Geneva Bible, much of our western culture, our church governments, and our civil laws have been built is a fraud. What unmitigated arrogance to claim such a thing! "Let him be accursed"[5] who, for the sake of justifying a favored perversion, would attempt to strip the Holy Scriptures of divine authority and portray the Bible as less than the immutable, authoritative Word of God.

Certainly we live in a time of paraphrased, amplified, gender neutral, dynamic equivalent, and so-called living bibles. I, for one, strongly counsel against using such books as Bibles. Even so, as of the writing of this book, I have yet to see a version which does not still plainly condemn homosexual acts as sin. Perhaps someday soon a "bible" will come out which contains the many extreme textual changes which would be necessary to erase the obvious in order to represent homosexual acts as being acceptable in God's eyes. Of course, that would be a "bible" which is not true to the Scripture's divine origins and is mistranslated. As such, it could not rightly be considered as Holy Scripture. Suffice it to say, the claim that one cannot understand what the Bible says concerning homosexuality, or any other sin for that matter, unless one is a Hebrew and a Greek scholar is obviously a pathetic, evil attempt to justify the unjustifiable.

Another related ploy used by the purveyors of perversion is their contention that there is no Greek or Hebrew word for *homosexual.* Such an assertion is disingenuous at best. Here are some examples of this tactic:

[A]s Calvin Theological Seminary Old Testament scholar Marten H. Woudstra says: "There is nothing in the Old Testament that corresponds to homosexuality as we understand it today" and as SMU New Testament scholar Victor Paul Furnish says: "There is no text on homosexual orientation in the Bible." . . .

The Bible is an empty closet. It has nothing specific to say about homosexuality as such.[6]

—Evangelicals Concerned, "The Bible Is an Empty Closet"

The Scriptures are very important because they teach us God's love for all, gay or straight. But the Scriptures are old, thousands of years old, written even before the word "homosexual" existed.[7]

—Rev. Dr. George R. Edwards, "Is Homosexuality a Sin?"

As for the Bible, *the word "homosexual" never appears there,* and the passages which some regard as condemning homosexuality are few and subject to varying interpretations.[8]

—Pastor Harry C. Kiely, "A Plea for Compassion"

The distinction that one now routinely makes between heterosexuality and homosexuality was not made, and could not have been made, in the ancient world. . . . The word *homosexual* was not coined until 1869 . . . Since the biblical languages (ancient Hebrew and Greek) had no words for *sexuality, heterosexuality,* or *homosexuality,* it is anachronistic and misleading when, as occasionally happens, the term *homosexual(s)* is used to translate some biblical expression.[9]

—New Testament scholar Victor Paul Furnish,
"What Does the Bible Say About Homosexuality?"

The Bible does not have a great deal to say about homosexuality, and in the original languages the term itself is never used.[10]

—Letha Scanzoni and Virginia Ramey Mollenkott,
Is the Homosexual My Neighbor? Another Christian View

Our Bible was originally written in Hebrew and Greek. All modern translations purport to be based upon the oldest copies available in those languages. However, in spite of the fact that there was NO word for "homosexual" in either ancient Hebrew or ancient Greek, some of the modern English Bibles contain the word.[11]

—National Gay Pentecostal Alliance, "Homosexuality and the Bible"

Those who claim that the Scriptures have been mistranslated and really do not condemn homosexuality because there is supposedly no word for *homosexual* in the original languages in which the Scriptures were written are simply engaging in bait and switch linguistics. They are talking about *transliteration,* not *translation.* To *transliterate* is to write or spell words in the characters of another alphabet that represent the same sound or sounds. *Transliterating* a Greek word into English makes it possible to spell and pronounce the word using English characters, but for anyone but a Greek scholar, the word is still meaningless. With regard to language, to *translate* is to change words from one language into words of another language which have corresponding meanings. *Translating* a Hebrew or Greek word into English makes it possible for an English speaking person to read and understand it. Of course, the process works the same in reverse.

The word *blood* starts out $\alpha\tilde{\iota}\mu\alpha$ in Greek. This means absolutely nothing to those who cannot read Greek, which is most of us. $\text{A}\tilde{\iota}\mu\alpha$ *transliterates* as *haima* in English letters, which still means absolutely nothing to most of us. However, a Greek scholar knows the meaning of the Greek word, what it is representing. He knows that αἷμα or *haima* means the red fluid which circulates through the heart, arteries, and veins of humans and animals. He knows which English word has the corresponding meaning. Not only is he able to *transliterate* the Greek letters of the word into English letters, but he is also able to *translate* the word into a corresponding English word. In this case, the English word is *blood.* Of course there is no word in the Greek which *transliterates* into the word *blood,* but there is a word which *translates* into the word *blood.*

When the pro-homosexual theologians say that there is no word in the Greek or Hebrew for *homosexual,* they are relying once again on subterfuge to make their case. Certainly there is no word in either language describing what we understand to be a homosexual which transliterates from Hebrew or Greek into *homosexual.* But both languages do contain words which describe a person who engages in same-sex sexual acts, just as the words *homosexual* or *sodomite* do in English. These words are accurately translated in our English Bibles as *homosexual* or *sodomite;* and in several instances, they are translated into a phrase which captures the meaning of the word as expressed at the time of the translation.

For instance, the Greek word ἀρσενοκοίτης, which is transliterated into *arsenokoites* (ar-sen-ok-oy'-tace), describes persons who commit homosexual acts. While the New American Standard version translates *arsenokoites,* which appears in I Corinthians 6:9, as *homosexuals,* the translators of the King James Bible chose to translate the same word into the phrase *abusers of themselves with mankind.* That phrase was in settled use at that time in England to describe the persons we commonly call homosexuals today. The King James also uses the very descriptive word *sodomites* to describe the people most Americans today call homosexuals. The important thing in all of this is that both the Old and New Testament contain words which properly translate into English the Greek and Hebrew words which describe homosexuals as persons who commit specific perverted sexual acts.

Another ploy of the bait and switch mistranslation crowd is to claim that the writers of the Old and New Testaments were not condemning same-sex acts in general, but rather "abusive" same-sex acts such as cultic male prostitution and pederasty (men having sexual relations with boys). In essence, this socio-cultural claim is that the translators of all the English Bibles ever put into general use misunderstood the cultural and societal context of the verses relating to homosexual activity. It may be considered an understatement to say that those modern scholars who claim to have discovered this massive and systematic mistranslation and misunderstanding in the Biblical texts condemning homosexual activity have assumed quite an impressive mantle for themselves. Imagine that after all those years, they alone have discovered what all the great Bible scholars, teachers, and expositors over the centuries have missed! Stop the presses; it's all just a big mistake! Such is the arrogance of fools claiming to be wise.

The Bible, both the Old Testament and the New Testament, clearly condemns homosexual activity as a violation of God's law, not only by identification, but in some cases by description. Leviticus 18:22 and Leviticus 20:13 both give graphic descriptions of same-sex activity and condemn it. There is no talk of cult prostitutes or pederasty or anything else in those passages. The passages clearly prohibit men having sexual relations with men—period. No other meaning can be attached to the verses except via fertile imagination and vain thinking. Romans 1:26-27 likewise graphically describes same-sex sexual relations, including a condemnation of what today is commonly called lesbianism. The book of Jude sets forth the cities of Sodom and Gomorrah as examples of divine wrath which came about because those cities' inhabitants insisted on giving themselves over to homosexual fornication, fornication with strange flesh.

In light of all of this, how can "gay" theologians attack the Biblical sanctions against homosexuality as simple misinterpretation and misunderstanding? One immediate reason is whom they are serving. They are clearly two-fold children of hell serving their father the devil who "was a murderer from the beginning, and abode not in the truth, because there is no truth in him."[12] The fantastic contention that the Bible has been misinterpreted to condemn homosexual acts is merely one of many convenient ruses used to seduce the unwary into believing that God's blessing rests upon some of the most disgusting, filthy acts that human beings can commit.

In reality, the homosexualists do not really care what the Bible says, notwithstanding all their pious concerns over the "real meaning" of the Greek and Hebrew texts. They really do not care what the Bible says in the Greek or Hebrew texts anymore than they care what it says in the English text, as they often give away in their own publications. "Gay" author, lecturer, and theologian Chris Glaser certainly reveals that much in his messages which are aimed at his peers. Writing in the *More Light Update,* a publication of Presbyterians for Lesbian and Gay Concerns, Glaser shares this revealing look into his exegetical methodology:

> We who believe in Jesus will never be put to shame. Paul affirmed this [in Romans 10:11] and then proceeded in the next verse to say, "For there is no distinction between straight and gay..." At least, that's how I read it in my Bible. Those who trust God will not panic at such an understanding.[13]

So we see that it does not really matter what the Word of God says, but rather what the homosexualists want it to say. Glaser does not bother with the misinterpretation fantasy in this instance when writing to kindred souls; he simply explains that the words of the Bible metamorphose right before his eyes to validate his "gay Christianity."

There is no great mystery as to why certain clergymen, authors, or theologians make the pretense that the Bible has been mistranslated and misunderstood and really does not proscribe homosexual acts. They are simply promulgating a lie.

Christians must not be intimidated by the sophistry and theological smoke and mirrors of the pro-homosexual apologists. President Andrew Jackson once remarked about the Bible, "That book, Sir, is the Rock upon which our republic rests!"[14] The sexual libertines and moral relativists have managed to push our American Republic off the rock upon which it once rested. We must not allow them to do the same with our Christian faith. The body of Christ must take a bold, uncompromised stand for God's holy ordinances as delivered to us and preserved by Him down through the ages. It is the strategy of the devil to shake our confidence in our ability to defend the unchanging Word which showed us the way of salvation and instructs us how to live in a way which pleases God and advances His kingdom and His righteousness. The Holy Scriptures contain God's law which is applicable and binding to the whole world, every individual, every nation, every believer, and every unbeliever. Disbelief in God and His law does not invalidate God or His law.

It was by the will of God that we, the English-speaking peoples and eventually people of other languages, have been gifted with the translation of the Bible into our own tongue. The Bible is more than a church document or a position paper subject to rewriting and reinterpretation as the desires and lusts of men dictate; it is the written revelation of God delivered to us and preserved for us by the Holy Spirit and at great human cost. May we be faithful to the sacred obligation which we bear to defend the veracity and immutability of the Holy Scriptures against all who seek to erode its authority! We must confront those who would so arrogantly claim that the average man and woman cannot read the Scriptures and gain an understanding of God's will. For the love of the Lord and His Word, for the sake of the lost and vulnerable, we must also vigorously defend the Scriptures against those who so flippantly speak of the need for dynamic, evolutionary, critical, or socio-cultural readings and versions of the Bible. These are the ones who seek to reject the Scriptures as written and turn centuries of Christianity on its head with claims of misinterpretation and misunderstanding. This is our calling; this is our duty to our Lord and to those who follow behind us.

For all flesh is as grass,
and all the glory of man as the flower of grass.
The grass withereth, and the flower thereof falleth away:
but the word of the Lord endureth for ever.
And this is the word which by the gospel is preached unto you.
I Peter 1:24-25

CHAPTER SEVEN

God vs. God?

He saith unto them, But whom say ye that I am?
Matthew 16:15

I t is no secret that false doctrines are being systematically preached and taught in many churches and peddled to the public by the pro-homosexual movement. Why is this happening? For the Christian, the answer is obvious: human rebellion coupled with satanic inspiration. America has now entered into what is obviously a post-Christian era. Although our laws, civil institutions, religious organizations, and culture once were grounded on a Christian, Biblical worldview, this is no longer so. Far from it. In the past, most American citizens recognized the existence of an eternal, unchanging standard of right and wrong, a standard which transcends the temporal ordinances and turbulent passions of mortal men. Today, most people decide what is right or wrong based on feelings and on what the present governing authorities say is right or wrong at this particular moment in history.

For graphic proof of this reality, one has only to spend time on a sidewalk in front of our nation's modern-day death camps speaking to abortion-bound mothers. Upon having truth and help offered to her by Christians stationed near an abortion clinic entrance, it is not the least bit unusual to hear a mother flippantly respond, "I know it's a baby, but it's my right to decide whether or not to have it. Besides, abortion is legal." Over the years, I have heard many mothers coldly say, "So what if it's a baby? If I want to kill it, I can. Abortion is legal." We have clearly reached a dangerous point in our nation's history, an era when good is evil, evil is good, and God's binding, unchanging objective standard for human behavior has been rejected by most of our citizens.

There are historical parallels to America's current crisis, parallels from which we can learn. In his excellent book *Modern Fascism: Liquidating the Judeo-Christian Worldview,* Gene Edward Veith, Jr. explores a much overlooked aspect of fascism—the desperate need the fascists in Germany and Italy had to strip the Bible of its authority and the church of her fidelity to her Head. True Christianity is the natural enemy of fascism. The former is dependent upon God's unchanging, immutable truth as revealed through His Holy Scriptures. The latter in its full manifestation is a pagan religion rooted and grounded in utilitarian philosophy and spiritual existentialism.

In his book, Veith documents the strategy which fascist philosophers and theologians employed in their largely successful attempt to destroy the German Protestant church's witness for God's eternal truth. In order to consolidate their power over the German people, it was vital for the fascists, eventually embodied by Hitler's Nazis, to erode and destroy the power of their archenemy, the church of Jesus Christ. After all, no man can serve two such diametrically opposed masters as a fascist state and Christ. A population informed by God's unchanging law and animated by His Holy Spirit is a population which will resist the actualization of fascism. To remove the threat of a people pledged to "obey God rather than men,"[1] the fascists in Germany knew that they must wear away and ultimately destroy the confidence which many German people had in the Bible as the literal Word of God. The groundwork for such an endeavor was laid by a growing theological movement espousing "higher criticism" of the Bible, a movement which found common ground with a resurgent nature-worshipping, Darwinian, pagan culture which especially began to blossom in post World War I Germany.

Gene Edward Veith and other historians have succinctly documented the methodology of those who were determined to undermine the authority of God's Word and clear the way for an "enlightened" fascist regime in Germany. Steps included the disconnecting of the Old Testament from the New Testament. The Old Testament, along with its graphic account of creation, its documentation of God's various covenants with man, its many Messianic prophesies about Jesus Christ, its attestation of God's holiness, and its historical accounts of His judgment against those who spurned His eternal standards, simply had to go. Consequently, it was portrayed as an irrelevant collection of out-of-date, even mythical, Jewish writings. The enlightenment thinkers of Germany, along with the fascists, pushed a "positive" Christianity which focused almost exclusively on various compassionate acts done by Jesus as recorded in the New Testament while at the same time doing everything possible to distance God the Son from God the Father. In short, the approach that the fascists took to undermine the credibility and authority of the Scriptures was to set the Old Testament against the New Testament, the law of God against the love of God, and the Son of God against God the Father.

For more background on the connection between fascism and the critical interpretation of the Bible, I strongly suggest reading *Modern Fascism.* For more insight into fascism and homosexuality, read *The Pink Swastika* by Scott Lively and Kevin Abrams. A thorough study of fascism would be beneficial for every Christian who has determined to answer God's call to "contend for the faith."[2] Such a study will quickly prove once more that there truly is "no new thing under the sun."[3] Those who would attempt to justify homosexual acts today use the fascists' tactics from yesteryear which proved to be so effective.

It is not the purpose of this book to delve into the many historical parallels to the heresies being peddled by the modern "Christian" homosexual movement, but rather to alert the reader to the lies which are currently being promulgated by that group and how those deceptions compare to what God has stated in His Holy Scriptures. It does not take a great thinker to see the fascist heart of not only the homosexualists' tactics but also their theology. It is also beyond the mission of this book to document case after case of a particular pro-homosexual argument or doctrine. Make no mistake about it; the examples used are representative of a rapidly growing body of pseudo-Christian doctrine which is being expounded from church pulpits; in church newsletters, books, magazines, and pamphlets; and on "Christian" radio and television as well. Sooner or later, every Christian who takes a public stand against homosexuality will be faced with the distorted arguments and twisted theology with which we are dealing. My goal is to make the reader aware of the various claims of the promoters of perversion and to provide at least some simple, rudimentary arguments against those claims.

In previous chapters, we have taken a look at some of the more general deceptions being circulated by pro-homosexual religionists. In this chapter and in succeeding chapters, we will look at some of their specific subterfuges. It seems appropriate to begin with one of the most outrageous and blasphemous of all claims—that being that Jesus never said anything about homosexual acts, thus signifying His approval of those acts. This grossly disingenuous assertion is rapidly becoming a favorite among sodomites and their allies. The hoped-for result is confusion, pure and simple. The homosexualists hawk this disgraceful lie in hopes of convincing the average person (and perhaps themselves) that homosexual acts are not sinful. Other less radical homosexual apologists apparently promulgate this myth in an attempt to downplay or neutralize the many severe Biblical condemnations of homosexual activity.

Dr. Tony Campolo evidently falls into the second category as exhibited by some of his comments such as this statement from his book *20 Hot Potatoes Christians Are Afraid to Touch:*

Actually, Jesus never alludes to homosexuality in His teachings. The fact that homosexuality has become such an overriding concern for many contemporary preachers may be more a reflection of the homophobia of the church than it is the result of the emphasis of Scripture.[4]

Dr. Campolo is obviously highlighting Jesus' "silence" on homosexuality as a mechanism to encourage, or perhaps intimidate, Christians who have taken a Biblical stand against homosexuality to be as silent on the issue as Jesus supposedly was. Campolo is troubled that "many contemporary preachers" have made homosexuality "an overriding concern." He does not seem to grasp that it is the calling of a pastor to preach against sin, especially those sins which most stir God's wrath and which most predominate a given age. Today in America, abortion and sexual immorality of all kinds, best exemplified by homosexuality, are the pre-eminent modes of rebellion against the Lord. Certainly preachers must make it a priority to speak out against such devastatingly vile acts!

I suppose that the Tony Campolos of Moses' day felt that Phinehas exhibited quite a bad case of "fornophobia" when he stayed the plague which God had brought upon the Israelites because of their determination to commit whoredom with the daughters of Moab. Phinehas certainly displayed his "overriding concern" for the popular sin of his day by plunging a javelin through the body of an Israelite man and a Midianite woman. Numbers 25:11-12 tells us how God felt about what Phinehas had done:

> Phinehas, the son of Eleazar, the son of Aaron the priest, hath turned my wrath away from the children of Israel, while he was zealous for my sake among them, that I consumed not the children of Israel in my jealousy. Wherefore say, Behold, I give unto him my covenant of peace.

I am certainly not suggesting the spearing of homosexuals. As a priest under the Mosaic Law, Phinehas had the authority to administer the death penalty. On the other hand, if the response of Phinehas to the pre-eminent sin of his day is a measure of zeal for God's righteous precepts, much of the American church is certainly the opposite in its response to the gross rebellion of our day.

While Tony Campolo uses Jesus' supposed silence on homosexuality to tone down criticism against that behavior, an increasing number of "Christian" homosexualists claim that same silence means Christ approves of homosexual activity; therefore it is not sin. Let me give you a few very random examples.

Telos Ministries, Inc. is a "gay" Baptist group. Telos's November 1994 newsletter contained an article from the August 1994 edition of the *Washington Blade.* The article, entitled "Alarmed by What's Done in the Name of Jesus," is a treatise on why the Bible supposedly does not condemn homosexual acts. The writer, Nicole Gibeaut, begins with this statement: "Because of my beliefs as a born-again, spirit-filled Christian, I oppose discrimination on the basis of sexual orientation." Gibeaut ends with this:

> Fortunately, most Christians see their mission as modeling Jesus' teachings of love, forgiveness, and brotherhood. But if you are a Christian who uses Christ's name to condemn and judge homosexuality, I plead with you to stop. I do not ask you to change either your beliefs or your prejudices. I do, however, ask that you keep quiet and not add to the hatred and bigotry.
>
> Since Jesus did not discuss homosexuality, I ask that you refrain from doing so, too.[5]

Mark Olson is an editor of the *Other Side* magazine. The publication's purpose is touted as being to "advance a healing Christian vision for our times."[6] Founded in 1965, the editors frame the objective of the magazine this way: ". . . as a witness to the Biblical call to justice for all people, *The Other Side* has consistently sought to follow Christ."[7] In a 1994 special edition of the *Other Side,* Olson shared these nuggets of "wisdom" concerning Jesus and homosexuality:

> And as we look to the New Testament for advice on homosexual behavior, the first thing we're struck with is the complete silence of Jesus on the subject. Jesus addressed many issues. He pointed through our human follies. He poked holes in our false gods. He got devastatingly specific in calling God's people to lives of love not hate. But he never, in the Gospel record, addressed the question of homosexual behavior.
>
> So when we look to Jesus on this question, we get many important general principles about righteous living. But we get no spe-

cific answers. Either homosexual behavior was not an issue for Jesus—or he (and the Gospel writers) deliberately chose not to address it. And that's something we must not lose sight of as we examine other New Testament passages.[8]

The article ended with this summation from Olson:

> . . . I have seen God blessing and using homosexual Christians who have united with each other in loving sexual relationships. In faithful, committed relationships, gay and lesbian Christians find God at work. We must not be so attached to a few verses of Scripture—or our own interpretations of them—that we miss this witness of God's Spirit.[9]

In my home state of Wisconsin, we have many pro-homosexual clergymen who have been outspoken in defense of the sexual perversion which we have been discussing. United Methodist Pastor Dianne Reistroffer is one of the most outspoken of all. On Sunday, February 25, 1996, in response to Wisconsin Christians United's ministry activities in Madison, Reistroffer delivered a message entitled, "Why We Stand with the GLBT Community." The sermon was a classic, garden-variety, pro-homosexual propaganda piece filled with out-of-context conclusions and exegetical acrobatics. Midway through her message, Reistroffer posited this concerning the New Testament, Jesus, and homosexuality:

> The New Testament is not clear on the matter at all. Paul, from my reading, speaks against male prostitution. We are not at all sure what the Greek words actually mean, despite the definiteness of the English translations. There is no other mention of homosexuality in the New Testament. Jesus spoke no direct word on homosexuality that was recorded in the Bible.[10]

As was said earlier, dubbing Jesus as pro-homosexual because He is not quoted as saying anything about that particular abomination has become an increasingly popular ruse among the pro-homosexual clergy. As always, wicked leaders produce wicked followers.

At Wisconsin Christians United, it is a common occurrence to receive letters from angry "Christians" who point out to us poor idiots that there cannot be anything wrong with homosexuality since Jesus never said anything about such activity. Whenever homosexual behavior becomes the subject of public debate, editorial columns and letters to the editor parroting this same trite nonsense invariably show up in the local newspapers.

In 1994, a newspaper in my area did a large article on the local Parents and Friends of Lesbians and Gays (PFLAG). The paper highlighted this quote from one of PFLAG's state leaders:

> The truth is it doesn't say anything about homosexuality in the Bible. The word wasn't even invented then. The Bible is a product of time and culture. Jesus didn't say a word about the subject.[11]

In PFLAG's booklet *Is Homosexuality a Sin?*, Unitarian Universalist Rev. Dr. William F. Schulz presents this supposedly compelling proof that Jesus had no problem with homosexuality:

> Turning to the New Testament, we discover that Jesus has nothing whatsoever to say regarding homosexuality. Inasmuch as he frequently condemned others of whose behavior he disapproved (e.g., the money-changers in the temple), it is significant that he makes no reference to homosexuals or their practice.[12]

In 1997, several major Wisconsin newspapers carried a guest editorial by Adam Chase Korbitz, the organizer of the Wisconsin chapter of the Interfaith Alliance and state chairman of Republicans for Choice. Korbitz's article was titled "Jesus' Answers to Religious Right Found in Gospels." The purpose of his column was to prove that Jesus was (and presumably is) pro-homosexual. So what was the set piece of his position? In Korbitz's own words, "The Bible contains only four or five references to homosexuality, and Jesus never talked about homosexuality. Not once."[13]

To present Jesus Christ as being pro-homosexual for any reason is an abomination in at least three ways:

1. It accuses Christ of condoning behavior which the Bible condemns.
2. It denies the deity of Christ by separating the Son of God from God the Father and places the two at enmity with each other over the issue of homosexuality.
3. It makes the claim that Christ approves of any activity which He did not specifically condemn during His time on earth.

In the interest of equipping ourselves to deal with the allegation that homosexual acts are not a sin because Jesus supposedly never said anything about such acts, let us briefly look at each of the points just raised beginning with the last. To say that homosexual acts are not sin because Jesus is never recorded as having directly addressed such acts is a ridiculous, if not a desperate, position which is easy to dismiss. It should be understood that the Bible does not contain every word which Jesus spoke while He walked this earth. This is not to say that He spoke anything which would conflict with the Scriptures, because He most surely did not. However, since homosexual acts are so consistently and severely condemned in the Scriptures, it is certainly possible and perhaps even likely that Jesus did verbally condemn such activity while on earth, but that His words on that particular issue are not recorded in Scripture. The Bible does not record any words from Jesus about sexual perversions such as bestiality, pedophilia, rape, incest, or necrophilia. Are we to believe then that these acts are not sin and that Jesus, in fact, condones them? Such would be a logical conclusion of a consistent application of the Jesus-never-said-anything-about-homosexuality argument.

So much for this scurrilous attempt to cast our Lord of lords as a promoter of sexual perversion, which brings us to point number one. To accuse Jesus of condoning homosexual acts is to accuse Him of promoting activity which God's Word describes with such words as *vile, an abomination, lawless, disobedient, ungodly, profane, unrighteous, unnatural, worthy of death,* and *unseemly.* To imply that Jesus Christ, God the Son, approves of behavior which the revealed Word of God so clearly and vigorously condemns is sheer wickedness, to say the least, not to mention senseless to the extreme. Those who claim that Jesus approves of homosexuality are accusing Him "who did no sin"[14] to be a promoter of lawlessness!

Of course, to substantiate their allegation, the homosexualists must attempt to achieve point number two, at least in the minds of those whom they are striving to win to their way of thinking. They must empty Christ of His deity by covertly or overtly casting Him as being of a different nature, even as holding different standards than does God the Father. This misrepresentation of Christ is blasphemy of the worst stripe.

Jesus clearly and repeatedly reminds us that He and the Father are "one."[15] He said, "For I came down from heaven, not to do mine own will, but the will of him that sent me" (John 6:38). Hebrews 1:3 says, "Who [Christ] being the brightness of his [God's] glory, and the express image of his person, upholding all things by the word of his power, when he had by himself purged our sins, sat down on the right hand of the Majesty on high." The Son of God is the express image of God the Father! Colossians 2:9 testifies, "For in him dwelleth all the fullness of the Godhead bodily." How utterly foolish and demonically evil to claim any sort of doctrinal dichotomy between the Father and the Son!

Those who make such allegations would be well-advised to remember the reason that the Sanhedrin wanted Jesus dead. It was because Jesus had testified that He is God. In John 8:58, He tells the Jews, "...Verily, verily, I say unto you, Before Abraham was, I am." With that statement, Jesus flatly identified Himself as God (see Exodus 3:14). Because such a claim is blasphemy if not true and because the Pharisees did not believe that Jesus was God, they tried to stone Him.

The Lord Whom we know now as Jesus Christ is not only God in the Person of God the Son, but He pre-existed as God before His earthly incarnation as well. About Jesus Christ, John 1:1 plainly states, "In the beginning was the Word, and the Word was with God, and the Word was God."

John 1:3 tells us regarding Christ, "All things were made by him; and without him was not any thing made that was made." All things were made through Christ—all things, including God's creation law and

His revealed law, the Holy Scriptures, both of which clearly condemn homosexual activity. To accuse Jesus Christ of condoning homosexual acts because of His supposed silence on the issue while He walked this earth denies the fact that He has spoken quite loudly and clearly on it. We must also realize that the Bible, both Old and New Testaments, was written through men by the Holy Spirit. The passages in Genesis, Leviticus, Romans, I Corinthians, I Timothy, II Peter, and Jude which condemn homosexual acts were all written by God; and so they were also written by Christ.

The very essence of God is holy perfection and perfect righteousness. To claim that God the Father and God the Son or, for that matter, the Holy Spirit would have different "opinions" or "beliefs" regarding the rightness or wrongness of any given act, including homosexuality, is to accuse One of Them of being in error. The argument that our Lord condones homosexual acts by His supposed silence is a theologically bankrupt argument which is put forth by people who are desperate to justify the unjustifiable and condone the condemned. Those who make this argument should be ashamed to do so in light of its evil nature and ridiculous conclusions.

Some are even bolder and suggest that Jesus Himself may have been a sodomite! One voice uttering such unthinkable blasphemy is the Metropolitan Community Church. MCC is a rapidly growing "gay" church which claims to be Bible-believing and Christian, but which, in reality, is busily proselytizing America with doctrines of devils in the name of Christ. MCC's brochure "Homosexuality: Not a Sin, Not a Sickness" makes this declaration concerning the Holy Scriptures: "Most Christian churches, including Metropolitan Community Church, believe the Bible was inspired by God and provides a key source of authority for the Christian faith."[16] After that opening statement, the brochure proceeds to systematically deny the authority of the Bible, just as do other MCC materials and statements.

One segment of the MCC brochure "Homosexuality: Our Story Too" is titled "Jesus Lived an Alternate Lifestyle" and includes this vile utterance:

John's gospel refers no less than eight times to the "one whom Jesus loved," also called the "beloved disciple." Scholars rarely explore that fact that Jesus obviously had a particularly close friendship with one man. Whether or not Jesus was gay, homophobia has silenced exploration of this relationship.[17]

MCC's evil missive also maintains that many of the righteous characters in the Bible were actually homosexual. The possibility is raised that Mary and Martha may have only called each other sister but were in reality lesbians. Concerning the book of Ruth, this is written:

> The book of Ruth is a romantic novel but not about romance between Ruth and Boaz. Naomi is actually the central character and Ruth is the "redeemer/hero." Boaz' relationship with Ruth, far from being romantic, is a matter of family duty and property.[18]

As a supposedly convincing evidence of Ruth and Naomi's lesbianism, "Homosexuality: Our Story Too" quotes Ruth's moving pledge of love and loyalty to her mother-in-law recorded in Ruth 1:16.

David is cast as a "gay" due to his close relationship to Jonathan. MCC's so-called proof in this instance is II Samuel 1:26, which is referred to in the brochure as "one of the most direct expressions of same-sex love in the Bible."[19] Too bad for David that he valued the brotherly love of Jonathan even over the romantic love of a woman. Such a sentiment voiced today wins the label of "gay" for the one expressing it. Thus are the demented workings of minds deformed by perversion.

> Unto the pure all things are pure: but unto them that are defiled and unbelieving is nothing pure; but even their mind and conscience is defiled. They profess that they know God; but in works they deny him, being abominable, and disobedient, and unto every good work reprobate" (Titus 1:15-16).

To identify David, Ruth, and even Christ as being sexually perverted is clearly the machinations of a homosexual movement intent on sweeping away the most formidable roadblocks standing between them and total success in their drive to homosexualize America. Of course, MCC and other pro-homosexual "Christian" groups do not limit themselves to labeling only the aforementioned individuals as "gay." It is in their best interest to similarly slander many of God's righteous servants whom we read of in the Bible.

To summarize this topic, those who make the claim that our Lord approves of homosexual acts based on His supposed silence on the issue are accusing the Supreme Judge of all mankind of breaking His own immutable precepts. They are also denying the Trinity by pitting God the Son against God the Father and against God the Spirit. Lastly, they are denying that Jesus Christ is God. This outrageous accusation that Jesus Christ is pro-homosexual on the basis that the New Testament does not record Him dealing directly with that perversion should be zealously confronted and vigorously refuted by those who love the Lord, especially by pastors and other Christian leaders.

Jesus once asked his disciples, "But whom say ye that I am?" The time has come when the body of Christ in America must provide the answer to those who are wondering who Christ really is. Today men are creating a false christ in their minds, a messiah who will conform to their own vile lusts and vain imaginations. Consider this excerpt from the article "A Thousand Trains to Heaven" which appeared in the *Other Side:*

> My own experience of Christ is diverse. I have known Christ as straight, as gay, as man, as woman, as stranger, as friend. . . .
>
> As a gay man, I have found the encounter with Christ as lover to be fundamental to my religious experience. Jesus is my most intimate companion, skin-close and spirit-close as only a lover can be. In certain crises, only his arms wrapped around me keep me from falling apart. I talk to him, yell at him, berate him, thank him, listen to him, feel his spirit breathing upon me, wrap myself in his embrace.
>
> In my dreams, I have also met Christ as a woman. She has danced before me and beckoned me toward the earth and its abundance. I have followed her, fascinated, hoping to discover the secrets she holds in her hand. And through her kisses, I have received a wisdom I cannot verbalize.[20]

Today men say that Jesus is any number of things from a "gay" lover to a pro-homosexual earth goddess. If the true church of Jesus Christ will not define the true Jesus to the world, the followers of Satan will define Him their way.

By the way, Dr. Tony Campolo has endorsed the *Other Side* with these words: *"The Other Side* provides the kind of commentaries and critiques of societal realities that people committed to peace and justice must have. *The Other Side* is Christianity at the cutting edge."[21]

Earlier, I related an account of Dr. Campolo musing over why some preachers have an "overriding concern" with the rise of a sodomite nation in our land. The man obviously does not realize the responsibility which ministers of God bear to speak out against the wicked movements and popular sins of the day, beginning with the most destructive and rebellious activities first. Of course, there have always been critics who would attempt to silence the prophetic voices which God raises up to confront the devil's advocates.

Prior to America's War for Independence, some criticized those pastors who preached against the tyrannical actions of the British. One pastor, the Reverend William Gordon, later answered that criticism with words which strike a chord in many of us today:

> [I]t is certainly a duty of the clergy to accommodate their discourses to the times; to preach against such sins as are most prevalent, and to recommend such virtues as are most wanted. . . . You have frequently remarked that though the partizans [sic] of arbitrary power will freely censure that preacher, who speaks boldly for the liberties of the people, they will admire as an excellent divine, the parson whose discourse is wholly in the opposite, and teaches, that magistrates have a divine right for doing wrong, and are to be implicitly obeyed . . .[22]

Pastor Gordon preached against tyrannical acts and against the idea that men should obey the laws of civil government even when to do so would mean to be disobedient to the Supreme Lawgiver. He naturally came under fire for his Biblical boldness even while other pastors who taught an unbiblical doctrine regarding civil authority were often rewarded with praise from certain quarters. Perhaps Gordon and his associates who championed Biblical law and liberty were classified by some as Britaphobes for vigorously preaching against a predominate evil of their day.

Today, those who are striving to portray homosexual acts as moral and Biblically sound use many tactics to silence the voices which confront such a vile assault upon the integrity of God's Word and the divine order of His creation. Once it is seen that the cry against homosexuality cannot be silenced by ridicule or intimidation, the would-be-silencers often turn to another tactic—shame. As incredible as it is, those who have the most of which to be ashamed often attempt to shame good, decent people who take a stand against homosexual behavior based on their deeply held moral convictions and faith. The shame strategy is multi-faceted. It would be useful to review several aspects of this strategy, and so we will in the next chapter.

CHAPTER EIGHT

Shame on Who?

S hame can be a very powerful emotion. The fear of bringing shame on one's self or loved ones can be, and should be, an inducement to refrain from wrongdoing. Concerning rebellious members of the body of Christ, Paul instructs the Thessalonians:

And if any man obey not our word by this epistle, note that man, and have no company with him, that he may be ashamed. Yet count him not as an enemy, but admonish him as a brother (II Thessalonians 3:14-15).

In this passage, we are charged, along with the Thessalonians, to shun members of the body of Christ who are in obvious rebellion to clear commands of Scripture. The point of such action is multipurpose, as is revealed by reading this instruction in context with other Scriptures relating to the same situation. Shunning a rebel is done to uphold respect for the law of God; to preserve the purity, reputation, and testimony of the body of Christ; to cultivate a fear of doing wrong; and to protect the vulnerable from the adverse effects of bad company. Another purpose for shunning a rebellious Christian is to make him ashamed of his disobedience in hopes that he may repent of his wicked and destructive ways.

Speaking to the worldly and somewhat out-of-control Corinthian church, Paul exhorts, "Awake to righteousness, and sin not; for some have not the knowledge of God: I speak this to your shame" (I Corinthians 15:34). Here Paul was rebuking the Corinthians because some of their number were counted as Christians, yet they did not have a true knowledge of the Lord. He is saying that the Corinthians, as well as any church, should be ashamed to have members who either are not truly saved or are saved but have never moved beyond their initial conversion to a true knowledge of the fullness of Christ, the holiness of God, and the reality that a Christian is constrained to live by the law of the Lord as revealed in the Scriptures.

The book of Titus contains instructions regarding the behavior, responsibility, and interrelations of Christians and their leaders. Titus, who had the job of setting in order the church at Crete, was counseled by Paul in Titus 2:7-8:

> In all things shewing thyself a pattern of good works: in doctrine shewing uncorruptness, gravity, sincerity, sound speech, that cannot be condemned; that he that is of the contrary part may be ashamed, having no evil thing to say of you.

Simply put, what Titus and God's shepherds are being told here is that they are to speak and live in such a way that troublemakers within the church are put to shame when they unjustly attack them.

I Peter 3:15-16 tells Christians:

> But sanctify the Lord God in your hearts: and be ready always to give an answer to every man that asketh you a reason of the hope that is in you with meekness and fear: having a good conscience; that, whereas they speak evil of you, as of evildoers, they may be ashamed that falsely accuse your good conversation in Christ.

In this passage, the Holy Spirit is instructing us to speak and act in such a way that in any culture or nation where justice still prevails, those who falsely attack God's people will be put to shame. Here shame is used as an inducement for unbelievers to refrain from evil. Of course, in times when evil is called good, good is called evil, and consciences are seared, the wicked readily attack Christians since they are no longer deterred from such treacherous activity by simple decency or fear of cultural stigmatization. I Peter 3:17 deals with such a contingency: "For it is better, if the will of God be so, that ye suffer for well doing, than for evil doing."

Shame properly used is a check on ungodly behavior. Once a people loses the capacity to be ashamed of even the vilest of sins, that culture stands on the brink of destruction. The prophet Jeremiah berated a people who refused to be restrained by God's law and who were no longer the least bit ashamed to live in open violation of it.

> Were they ashamed when they had committed abomination? nay, they were not at all ashamed, neither could they blush: therefore they shall fall among them that fall: at the time that I visit them they shall be cast down, saith the LORD (Jeremiah 6:15).

Philippians 3:17-18 speaks of people beyond shame whose only guiding principle is their own carnal appetite:

> For many walk, of whom I have told you often, and now tell you even weeping, that they are the enemies of the cross of Christ: whose end is destruction, whose God is their belly, and whose glory is in their shame, who mind earthly things.

Quite clearly, those who practice and/or promote homosexual acts in the name of Christ do so to satisfy their own appetites. Just as clearly, destruction will be their end, short of true repentance.

Jude 12-13 presents a stark metaphor of those who would preach heresy for their own gain:

These are spots in your feasts of charity, when they feast with you, feeding themselves without fear: clouds they are without water, carried about of winds; trees whose fruit withereth, without fruit, twice dead, plucked up by the roots; raging waves of the sea, foaming out their own shame; wandering stars, to whom is reserved the blackness of darkness for ever.

Tragically, we have reached a point in America today when many of our citizens routinely and shamelessly follow their own foul appetites, urged on by religious leaders, some of them calling themselves Christian. Instead of being ashamed of their actions and their doctrines, these rebels do all in their power to make moral people, especially true Christians, feel ashamed for speaking out against immorality! More than once I have been greeted by chants of "Shame! Shame!" from homosexuals who have surrounded a facility where I have spoken or from individuals at "gay pride" events where Wisconsin Christians United has witnessed and picketed.

After my group literature drops neighborhoods with brochures containing the Biblical truth about homosexuality, we invariably receive letters which literally scream, "Shame on you!" Here is a typical excerpt from one such letter:

SHAME ON YOU!!!!!! I arrived home from work today to find a filthy, hate-filled, factually wildly inaccurate brochure from your group in my mailbox. I am astounded that individuals who claim to be "Christians" could in good conscience spread the intolerant, loveless, WRONG information portrayed in this pamphlet. It is because of people like you that so many are fleeing the Christian churches and turning against any political candidates who identify themselves with groups such as yours. . . .

Your hatred and beliefs are so dangerous that although my husband and I (both professionals with higher degrees) strongly agree with the contents of this letter, we are choosing to remain anonymous because "Christians" of your ilk have hounded families, harassed children, and even killed. We are unwilling to submit to your "Christian" kindness. If you were not so toxic to society I would feel sorry for you for your provincialism and ignorance. May your God forgive you.

Filthy, hate-filled, inaccurate, intolerant, loveless, wrong, dangerous, toxic, ignorant? Hounder of families, harasser of children, killer, the immediate cause of souls turning away from Christ? Such is the wild, vitriolic rhetoric which is heaped upon the heads of those who take a Biblical stand for truth against perversion—all for the purpose of shaming the Christian into silence. Those who promote homosexuality reveal their own intolerant, elitist hearts, even as they attempt to shame true followers of Christ for our supposed persecution of homosexuals.

Here is another typical response to a WCU literature distribution campaign:

> Normally I don't respond to such trash as your publication, but your paper makes me sick. First, let me identify myself as a serious Christian, a student of the Bible, a wife, a mother, a very successful, well educated business woman. My children include two lawyers and two holders of MBA's. . . .
>
> I try to treat all of God's creatures with the respect I think Christ envisioned, and that includes the homosexuals you are crucifying with your heinous rhetoric. SHAME ON YOU, AND MAY GOD FORGIVE YOU for spreading such hatred for His children . . . you should fall on your knees and ask Him how you can learn to love "the least of these, MY CHILDREN."

There is a reason why the homosexualists use shaming tactics against Christians and other moral people who oppose the sodomite agenda. Such tactics work! This reverse shaming tactic has been used to great effect by the homosexual movement. Most Christians shy away from being miscast as cruel, unfeeling, or ignorant. Thus many Christians, including pastors and other leaders, trip over themselves in an effort to avoid being mischaracterized in such ways. Since Biblical words such as *lawless, vile,* and *abomination* play so poorly with the God-haters, many Christians will not even use Biblical terminology when vying with the homosexualists for the soul of America. In failing to do so, they reveal themselves as being ashamed of the Word of God. Meanwhile, the homosexualists feel no hesitation whatsoever to use whatever rhetoric which will best advance their corrupt cause. Indeed, they seldom go into battle without wheeling out the biggest rhetorical guns in their arsenal.

In the spring of 1997, the Wisconsin State Assembly was debating AB104, legislation to enact a ban on state recognition of "same-sex marriage." Commenting on that situation and on a public hearing attended by many Christians who testified for passage of the bill, the sodomite newspaper the *Wisconsin Light* wrote a typically acidic editorial containing these remarks:

> The bill, currently being considered seeking to ban recognition of same-sex marriages in Wisconsin does not have its roots in reason and clear thinking. We are forced to believe that its roots lie elsewhere; in the dark, irrationalities of bigotry and ignorance.
>
> We are forced to believe as well that the hearing held Monday, March 10th, in Wausau, had as its sole purpose the airing of ignorance, flung against a minority who it is acceptable for some to hate.
>
> *We decry the hateful, ignorant words that were spewed out in Wausau by the Religious Right. We were taught that before you open your mouth, you should know what you're talking about. Given the presumed fact that the Religious Right people aren't Lesbian or Gay, we find it outrageous they should speak about a subject they know nothing about.*[1]

The May 13, 1997 Assembly debate on AB104 opened with a prayer by Pastor Dianne Reistroffer, who intoned, ". . . each of us must find our own truth . . . who know God by many names. . . . In your holy name, God of the rainbow."

During the course of the day-long debate, opponents of AB104 made generous use of shaming. Representative David Travis had just returned from a trip to Washington, D.C., where he had visited the Holocaust Museum. Comparing supporters of AB104 to the German Nazis, Travis exclaimed, "They didn't start with gas chambers. They ended with gas chambers. They started with stigmatizing people." Representative Marlin Schneider called AB104 "poison." Representative Frank Boyle insisted that it was a denial of constitutional rights to disallow state-sanction of homosexual "marriage." In an ominous tone, Boyle warned, "There's a simmering hatred out there for gays and lesbians," adding that AB104 sent the message, "Go kill a queer for Christ." Representative Barbara Notestein was adamant that AB104 was being "driven by hatred" and was "an abomination . . . being rammed through the legislature to push an agenda of hatred." Representative Rosemary Potter chided AB104 supporters for "putting legal barriers in front of those who want to do what is right." Openly homosexual Representative Tammy Baldwin made the wild-eyed claim that AB104 was "placing me at risk" of personal assault, even murder, along with "thousands of decent citizens." Representative Antonio Riley, who claimed to be a Christian, quoted the Bible and then sanctimoniously lectured anti-homosexuality forces: "Your moral indignation and self-righteousness is wrong. . . . We are all sinners in God's eyes." Representative Spencer Black fumed that disallowing sodomite marriages "sets a very dangerous precedent against religious liberty."

Such are the verbal salvos leveled against anyone who dares to stand in the way of America's "queer nation." We are to be ashamed of our irrationalities, bigotry, ignorance, and hate. We are unloving and unchristian. We constitute a grave threat to life, liberty, the pursuit of happiness, the U.S. Constitution, and, presumably, mom, dad, and apple pie as well. Thus it is that much of the American church has been shamed into ineffectual resistance, and in many cases, silent acquiescence to the twentieth century sodomite revolution. This must cease! An army ashamed to fight obviously has no chance of winning a war.

We have dealt with the shaming tactic in a general sense; now let us look at some of the specific methods which the homosexualists employ to shame their opponents into recoiling from taking the only sort of stand against homosexuality which God will bless—a Scriptural stance based upon eternal absolutes animated by Biblical terminology.

One of the most outrageous shame tactics which the pro-sodomites use is to blame Bible-preaching Christians for the suicides of "gay" youth. Homosexual groups have been busily convincing America, first of all, that homosexual youth kill themselves at a rate which far exceeds their "straight" peers, and secondly, that this is occurring as a direct result of "intolerance." The Stonewall Alliance for Youth puts out information which contains this assertion: "Gay and lesbian youth are two to three times more likely to attempt suicide than other young people."[2] Gays, Lesbians and Allies for Diversity in Education (GLADE) claims that "gay, lesbian and bisexual youth are two to six times more likely to attempt suicide than straight teens and comprise 30% of all completed suicides."[3] Parents and Friends of Lesbians and Gays disseminates the same figures.[4] The pro-homosexual Center for Population Options promulgates the view that "suicide is the leading cause of death among gay male, lesbian, bisexual and transsexual youth."[5] The National Gay and Lesbian Task Force reports that "41 percent of male adolescents seeking services at agencies for gay youths had attempted suicide, compared to 22 percent of the heterosexuals in the same age group at a shelter for runaways."[6]

The National Youth Advocacy Coalition (NYAC) states in their material, "Gay and lesbian youth are three times more likely to attempt suicide than their non-gay peers."[7] NYAC is sponsored by the Hetrick-Martin Institute, a non-profit homosexual advocacy group. Its activities include disseminating a comic book series titled *Tales of the Closet.* *Tales* champions the "gay" lifestyle by promoting the usual myths and portraying true Christians as ignorant, violent individuals who beat up and abuse their own children.

As of this writing, the Lazarus Project is busily promoting the emotionally-charged *Scared to Death: Gay Youth Suicide,* a twenty-nine minute video. A promotional flyer put out by the group says that thirty to forty percent of all youth suicides are "gays and lesbians." Viewers are urged to "Look, Listen, and Learn to help others find the love and acceptance to stay alive and not *Scared to Death.*"[8]

Several years ago, I attended an event in a Unitarian church (complete with a rainbow flag draped over the pulpit) which featured speaker Kevin Jennings. Jennings is the founder of Gay, Lesbian and Straight Teachers' Network (GLSTN). The group has since changed its name to Gay, Lesbian and Straight Education Network (GLSEN). During his presentation, Jennings stated the "fact" that one out of three homosexual students will attempt suicide. According to Jennings, Christians who teach their children that homosexuality is wrong are teaching their children to "hate" and by doing so are committing "child abuse" and are not only perpetrating violence against homosexuals but are also causing homosexual youth to commit suicide.

The suicide shaming tactic is a two-pronged approach. The first step is to convince America that large, disproportionate numbers of homosexual youth are taking their own lives. The second step is to put the blame squarely on those who have taken a prophetic, Biblical (or any other) stand against homosexuality.

The Reverend Mel White is one who relies heavily on shaming tactics. Reverend Mel White was once the colleague of such Christian leaders as Jerry Falwell, James Dobson, and Pat Robertson. White is now an out-of-the-closet sodomite. During a speaking tour in Madison, Wisconsin in 1997, Rev. White pushed the cliché that God made homosexuals just as they are and loves them just as they are. The *Wisconsin State Journal* reported that White:

> . . . spoke movingly of teenagers who commit suicide because they cannot handle the realization they are gay.
>
> "People are literally dying out there because we haven't found a way to reach them with the good news that God loves them," White said.[9]

Mel White is just one of many homosexualists who have turned the shaming of Christians into a fine art. Let us look at several more examples of this technique:

> Much of the human pain and loss represented by these statistics [the rate of "gay" youth suicide] can be avoided if more of us can work through the fog of misinformation, prejudice and fear that surrounds homosexuality.
>
> Gay, lesbian and questioning adolescents often have nowhere to turn. Too often, they lose themselves to suicide . . .[10]

The form of the discrimination may not be so overt as saying that a child is bad or sinful . . . Such discrimination also generates brutal violence against gay youth and leads to suicide and other self-destructive behaviors.[11]

   —*Plain Talk,* a publication of We Are A Family

A pattern of hopelessness and despair is often seen among teens who take their own lives. . . .

A young person's sexual identity does not *itself* cause him or her to attempt suicide. Rather, the experience of growing up "different" in a society that expects, even demands, that everyone be exclusively heterosexual can be devastating for young people who are not.

When youth realize they are lesbian, gay, or bisexual, they already know that society condemns them. . . .[12]

Most religious groups condemn homosexuals and homosexual behavior and further label homosexuals as outsiders, as unfit, as sinners. . . .[13]

   —*Issue Papers One and Two* of the Respect All Youth Project,
   Parents and Friends of Lesbians and Gays

In a 1986 report on suicide among gay and lesbian youth, Paul Gibson found that "the majority of suicide attempts by gay and lesbian persons occurs during their youth, and gay youth are two to three times as likely to attempt suicide as are others. They may comprise 30 percent of youth suicide annually" . . . Very clear about what he sees as the reason for this, Gibson writes, "The root of the problem . . . is a society that discriminates against and stigmatizes homosexuals . . ."[14]

   —"Living Surrounded by Silence," *Christian Social Action,*
   February, 1991

"We have to have an environment to produce self-esteem. If we don't, the young people will be persecuted and this has led to an overdose of suicide among gay and lesbian youths. We don't want that to happen," Joann stressed.[15]

   —April 22, 1994 *Janesville Gazette* interview with
   Joann Elder, a member of PFLAG and a parent of a gay son

"Bobby's death was the direct result of his parents ignorance and fear of the word gay," Mrs. Griffith wrote after much soul-searching and Bible study, guided by the pastor of a church accepting gays and lesbians. . . .

Mrs. Griffith wrote in a letter to her son after his death, "You were the apple of God's eye just as you were. If we had only known."[16]

—"Prayers for Bobby: A Mother's Change of Heart About Her Gay Son's Suicide," *Wisconsin State Journal,* September 23, 1995

The use of a purported Christian bigotry-driven epidemic of suicide among homosexual youth is a classic and reprehensible example of current attempts to shame good people into silence. After all, who would want to think that his words had caused even one young person to kill himself? Some Christian leaders and researchers have disputed the accuracy of the homosexualists' "gay" teen suicide statistics. For instance, many have pointed out the inaccuracies of the Paul Gibson study, "Gay Male and Lesbian Youth Suicide," which was incorporated in a 1989 report by the U.S. Department of Health and Human Services. The report cites sources which claim that three thousand "gay" youths kill themselves every year.[17] This is a bit unlikely, to say the least, since, as of 1996, a total of about two thousand teenagers a year were committing suicide![18] Researchers such as Dr. Paul Cameron of the Family Research Institute and Peter LaBarbera, editor of the *Lambda Report,* have provided compelling evidence that "gay" teen suicide rates have been highly inflated by those intent on shaming America into acceptance of the sodomite agenda.[19]

While it is very worthwhile and important to expose the duplicity being used by the homosexuals to shame moral Americans into silently enduring gross immorality, the question must still be asked: What if someday homosexual youth did commit suicide in disproportionate numbers to their peers? Or what if it turns out that the numbers currently presented are true? Does this mean that we Christians should soften our Biblical stance and our prophetic preaching regarding homosexuality? Tragically, many Christian leaders have already done just that!

To avoid falling victim to the enemy's shaming strategy, it is important that we approach the issue of homosexual suicide in the same way in which we should approach any other issue—with Biblical truth and godly discernment. Do homosexuals, young or old, commit more suicide proportionately than normal people? Probably so, and that should surprise no one. Let us understand—homosexuality is a filthy, vile, unnatural, extremely perverted sort of behavior which violates man's God-given conscience. People usually experience extreme guilt and shame when involved in such depraved acts, especially when they first begin to commit them. Such feelings are ultimately dealt with by one of three ways: rejection, repentance, or suicide. In other words, the sinner either rejects the conviction, stops what he is doing and repents, or stills the voice of conscience by snuffing it out with the taking of his own life. Given the extreme depravity in which they are involved, the extent to which homosexual acts can aggravate the conscience, and the unstable company which homosexuals keep, it is not impossible and, in fact, it is very probable that young homosexuals take their own lives more often than do well-adjusted, moral teens. By the same token, young people involved in other loathsome, self-destructive activities, such as immoral heterosexual activity or drug or alcohol use, no doubt also have a higher rate of suicide than moral teens from stable families. This is simply common sense.

When a Christian taking a stand against homosexuality has the accomplice-to-suicide charge hurled in his face, perhaps the best way to answer is something like this: It may or may not be true that homosexual teens have higher rates of suicide. If they do, it is not that surprising considering the self-destructive life which they are leading. However, this is no excuse to condone homosexual activity. Youth who use drugs also have a higher rate of suicide. Are you saying that we should tell those young people that they were born with a drug orientation and that they should learn to be proud of being a druggie? What about teenagers involved in promiscuous sex? With all the physical risks and emotional pain involved in such a life, should we tell such kids that they were born with a promiscuous orientation and that they should just accept the fact that they were created by God to be a whore or a whoremonger?

Christians have a holy duty to present the gospel as it is written. We simply have no right to soften the Word of God or to suppress the reality of His judgments and wrath against evildoers any more than we have a right to downplay His love and mercy.

In 1997, Wisconsin's first statewide "gay prom" was held in Milwaukee. Wisconsin Christians United was present on the public sidewalk to witness against homosexuality and to the "gay" teens going into the hotel in which the prom was held. During the course of the evening, I was approached by an editor with the homosexual newspaper the *Wisconsin Light*. The middle-aged sodomite was livid with rage as he screamed in my face: "You are killing kids with your bigotry!"

My answer to the man was simple and Biblical: "No, you are killing kids! Their young conscience tells them it is wrong to commit homosexual acts. They search for help to stop doing what they know in their hearts is wrong. They search for truth, and what do they get from people like you? You tell them, 'Sorry, kid; you were born that way,' and so they despair of ever changing and they kill themselves. Christians offer homosexual kids hope and new life through Christ. All people like you offer them is despair and a lifetime of enslavement to perversion!"

Christians must not allow the wicked to seduce us into committing treason against the Word of God by shaming us into presenting only half of the Biblical truth about homosexuality or into even being silent all together. With concern for the souls of all, we must preach the whole counsel of the Word of God and pray that young people struggling with any sort of sin will come to the conviction that they are in rebellion to their Holy Creator and that Christ is the only One Who can truly set them free from the grip of Satan, sin, and death. An individual must understand the depth of his own sin and his need for Christ before he will repent and be born again. Soft-soaping sin does not draw people to Christ. Soothing troubled consciences may help "self-esteem" in the short run; but in the long run, such a strategy multiplies suffering, sin, death, and damnation. To preach a lopsided gospel big on "unconditional love" but stripped of conviction is to place emphasis upon short-term physical comfort at the price of eternal damnation.

Concerning the strong words of rebuke which he had shared with the wayward Corinthians, Paul says this:

> Now I rejoice, not that ye were made sorry, but that ye sorrowed to repentance: for ye were made sorry after a godly manner, that ye might receive damage by us in nothing. For godly sorrow worketh repentance to salvation not to be repented of: but the sorrow of the world worketh death (II Corinthians 7:9-10).

It is vital that Christians confront the homosexual community with the sharp sword of God's Word. Certainly we will cause some sorrow when we do so, but for many that sorrow may well lead to repentance and salvation. If homosexuals kill themselves after being overwhelmed by sorrow, it is due to the worldly sorrow that accompanies a life of rebellion against God, not the godly sorrow which results from having the Word of God presented to them as written. If the body of Christ in this nation would preach the gospel as it was meant to be preached, the result would be that fewer kids would be seduced into committing sexual perversion; more homosexual youth would come to Christ; and, in the long run, fewer, not more, young people would take their own lives.

When confronted by Biblical truth, the homosexuals and their supporters often respond by alluding to or actually chanting, "Judge not, that ye be not judged!" and "He that is without sin among you, let him first cast a stone. . ." If I had a dollar for every time I have had those verses quoted—sometimes screamed—to me out of context, I would be in far sounder financial shape than I am in now. The purpose of using those verses in such a way is obvious—to portray Christians as pharisaical hypocrites who break the commands of Christ by judging others. Who would want to be accused of acting so shamefully? Often the Scripture quotation is followed up with the questions: "Have you ever sinned? How can you judge others when you're a sinner yourself?" Of course, once again the wicked twist the Scriptures to their own destruction.

Here are a few samples of written comments which I have received from the homosexuals and their champions which were supposed to make me ashamed of having taken a public stand against homosexuality:

- I do not allow hate in my life. Be it thought, word, deed, OR literature. . . . My God is a loving, forgiving God. Judgment is also his. Not yours.

- Jesus also says, "Do not judge, and you will not be judged." . . . It seems that we Christians are so busy judging others and placing ourselves in God's shoes, that we have very little time to meditate on our own errors . . . How is it that we think we can see God's view? How is it that we think we know without doubt all that he wants us to know?

- As a practicing Christian, I strongly object to your manipulative use of the Bible, your slanderous use of the word TRUTH, and your judgmental accusations that you label "Christian."

- Why does your ad on the radio sound so full of hatred? Christ does not hate! . . . He did not judge! What gives you the right to?

- Be careful about casting the first stone, Mr. Ovadal. Are you without sin? Are you so sure that you are right that you defy your own God and His Son? . . . I can't help but wonder what Jesus thinks of this whole mess.

- You cannot judge a person because of who they love. That is immoral and I hope you go to hell for it.

- I am a lesbian and proud of it. I am at peace with God, my creator, who made me exactly the way I am. I will be judged by God alone.

Of course, many of the people in the public and in the pews have been well-trained to embrace various evils in the name of non-judgmental love. Consider these several quotes from pro-homosexual clergymen responding to the distribution of Wisconsin Christians United literature:

- "I'm not the judge. God is the judge . . . My church is open to all people who seek worship and God."[20]

- Isn't it time for all Christians to stop assuming the bad or evil in others and start complimenting the good?
  It would be good for all of us to remember the words of our Lord and Master: "Do not judge, so that you may not be judged . . ."

- [W]ho died and made you God? You see, I too have read the Biblical record of God's job description, especially the part about God being the sole judge of humankind, and I would like to say, the position of God has been filled and we're not it.[21]

As pointed out in chapter two of this book, a reading of Matthew 7:1-5 makes it clear that Jesus is talking about wrongful judging within the body of Christ. The Lord is warning Christians not to judge each other in a harsh or unrighteous manner and not to nit pick at other Christians' minor weaknesses but to instead tend to one's own sanctification. Interestingly, verse five instructs us that once we have dealt with and eliminated the "big" sins (beam) in our own life (eye), we can then help others to overcome the smaller sins (mote) in their lives.

Christians are commanded to exercise righteous judgment regarding the unrighteous conduct of individuals, church leaders, and civil rulers. How else can we fulfill our Scriptural mandates to hate evil, reprove the ruthless, warn the wicked man, establish judgment, and be the pillar and the ground of the truth? How can we speak out against any sin, up to and including murder? Using a stern tone in Luke 12:57, Christ asks, "Yea, and why even of yourselves judge ye not what is right?" In John 7:24 Christ commands, "Judge not according to the appearance, but judge righteous judgment." The Scriptures contain many other exhortations for Christians to judge rightly.

Everyone makes judgments concerning human activity. Would any homosexual not rightly judge it to be wrong to murder people because they are homosexual? Pagans judge Christians when they accuse them of being judgmental. Everyone makes judgments. The question is not whether or not it is permissible to judge the actions of others. The question is when, how, and why to judge.

The important thing for Christians to realize is that we are constrained to judge what is right and what is wrong according to God's Word. The Holy Scriptures are the unerring yardstick that we must lay alongside any act or issue, including our own behavior, to judge its rightness or wrongness. If the body of Christ will not inform the world in this fashion and defend this standard, no one else will! When the church abdicates its duty to announce God's law to the world, the result is moral anarchy, perversion, violence, and death. Yes, we must be very careful about judging the content of a man's heart, judging in arrogance or with wrong motives, or substituting our own judgment for God's. However, Christians are not only permitted, but they are also commanded to judge the rightness of words and actions. To do otherwise is to fail our commission to be the light of the world. The body of Christ is the sole possessor of immutable truth. When we do not make God's judgments known to the world, we are modeling total indifference regarding the eternal destiny of those who are in rebellion to God.

We do not make God's law known because we have never sinned or because we fulfill it perfectly at all times. First of all, we make His law known to the world because His law leads others to Christ. "The law of the Lord is perfect, converting the soul" (Psalm 19:7). Secondly, we make God's law known to the world because we have an obligation to defend that law against those who would denigrate it. After all, if the Lord's people will not stand fast for His Word, who will? Finally, we make God's law known to the world because there is no security for life, liberty, or the weak unless the passions of men are restrained by that law. The civil law, the purpose of which is to punish evil and reward good, must judge the actions of men by God's true law; otherwise, the civil magistrate is powerless to fulfill his sacred duty as a "minister of God."[22]

To attempt to shame Christians away from condemning homosexual activity by quoting Matthew 7:1 is a wicked, wrongful, and an out-of-context use of the Scriptures just as is the misuse of John 8:7 for the same reason. Those of us who have taken a public, Biblical stand against homosexual acts constantly have John 8:7 thrown into our faces by the sexual libertines. This verse is included in the well-known passage about the woman caught in adultery. Without going into an extensive dissertation on the passage, it should be sufficient to point out that Jesus was simply confronting a group of scribes and Pharisees who were attempting to misuse a judicial process in order to tempt Jesus into breaking the law. Since they were acting as if they were greater than the law, as if they were a law unto themselves, Jesus pointed out to them that all who sin are under the law. When He said, "He that is without sin among you, let him first cast a stone at her," Jesus was asserting that unless they were sinless, which no one is, the scribes and Pharisees were subordinate to the law. Human life can only be taken in accordance with God's ordinances for a specific violation. The taking of a human life for any other reason, including vengeance, is the prerogative of God alone, the holy Creator and perfect Judge. In essence, Christ was asking the Pharisees if they thought that they were God and that therefore they were able to exercise complete sovereignty over human life—in this case to even expend a woman's life to accomplish a political goal. Convicted by their own consciences, the would-be judges drifted away. Jesus then very pointedly warned the woman, ". . . Go, and sin no more" (John 8:11).

This passage can in no way mean that men are never to exercise judgment. Such a situation would result in total lawlessness in one's personal life, in the family, in the church, and in society. This passage, taken in context with the rest of the Scriptures, is another warning against unrighteous judgments and the misuse of God's law.

We must always remember: God's Word does not contradict itself. It must always be read in context, both with relation to the immediate text and to the entire Bible. When we do this, we quickly realize that Christians have the right and duty to judge the actions of men, but only for the right reason and in the right manner.

No doubt some homosexualists will point to I Corinthians 5:12-13, which features Paul saying:

> For what have I to do to judge them also that are without? do not ye
> judge them that are within? But them that are without God judgeth.
> Therefore put away from among yourselves that wicked person.

To reiterate what was said in a previous chapter, these two verses are the conclusion of a passage in which Paul commanded the church at Corinth to discipline the unrepentant, sexually immoral among them by throwing such people out of the church and having nothing to do with them unless and until they repent. Paul is talking about a judicial process, complete with a finding of guilt and an execution of sentence, the sentence being the most extreme which God has given the church authority to execute—disfellowship. This is the sum total and type of judging which Paul is talking about. Obviously, Christians have no power to judge and punish non-church members in this regard. It is the responsibility of the civil authorities to "judge them also that are without" when individuals commit crimes which fall within the jurisdiction of civil government—crimes such as adultery, incest, or homosexuality. When such acts are committed by Christians, the case must be adjudicated by both the church and the state.

It would be beneficial to deal briefly with two other ploys which the purveyors of perversion use to shame their theological and ideological opponents into silence. The first approach entails pointing out that many homosexuals are friendly, successful, and hard-working. Some are even famous. The homosexualists are currently making very dubious, reprehensible claims about the sexual "orientation" of a number of great men and women who have long since passed from the scene. They apparently find it useful, as well as safe, to accuse certain respected individuals of homosexual activity based on fabricated evidence, considering that the accused are not here to defend themselves.

The "good citizen" technique is increasingly and effectively being used by Sodom's apologists. And it is no wonder. In a hedonistic society which jealously guards the individual's prerogative to follow the dictates of his own desires and lusts, it becomes expedient for the whole to guard the "right" of certain subgroups to engage in almost any sort of behavior. Plainly put, most Americans do not want to condemn the immorality or even the perversity of any of their fellow citizens for the simple reason that they want to be free of censure when they choose to engage in their own pet sins. In other words, fornicators, adulterers, voyeurs, child abusers, liars, drunkards, drug users, and thieves would just as soon the status quo was such that a person was judged on his personality and job performance rather than on his true character and adherence to a set standard of morality.

Considering the great number of Americans who fit into the just mentioned categories, the sword which hangs over many people's heads is the fear that what is good for the goose is sauce for the gander. After all, if homosexual behavior is condemned as wrong by society and punished by the civil government, what is next? Adultery and fornication could be recriminalized! The local porn shop could be shut down! A standard of absolute sobriety could be set for driving! Perjurers could actually receive their just reward! And so it is that the homosexuals play upon guilt and fear with the tactic of "He's such a nice, accomplished person; so what can be wrong with homosexuality?"

Unfortunately, the homosexualists are often aided in this strategy by evangelical Christians who many times begin by professing that homosexuality is sin and then go downhill from there. Let us look at just one example of this.

Thomas E. Schmidt formerly taught New Testament and Greek at Westmont College in Santa Barbara, California. He is an author of several books. In his book *Straight & Narrow?*, Mr. Schmidt states:

> Without exception in my experience, gay men and lesbians have been among the most intelligent, talented and thoughtful people I have known. Their sexual desires and practices differ from mine, but they do not particularly repulse or threaten me. I simply disapprove, as I do of some heterosexual desires and practices.[23]

This statement is typical of Mr. Schmidt's book. With it he not only downplays the abhorrent nature of same-sex acts, but he also knowingly or unknowingly parrots the sodomite party line that g/l/b/t/? people are not only as intelligent, talented, and thoughtful as "straight" people but, in most cases, more so! Certainly it would be appropriate to inquire of Mr. Schmidt how thoughtful can a person be who engages in the sort of sexual acts which the Bible labels as "vile"? How intelligent is it to build a life around perverted activity which devastates the health of the practitioner and even physically injures the human body? What bearing does a person's talents have on his capability to do wickedness?

Let us quickly dispatch this notion that somehow homosexual practices are acceptable or at least not all that bad due to the talents, job skills, civic consciences, intellectual capabilities, or even the compassionate hearts sometimes modeled by the practitioners. How many cells in America's prisons are occupied by individuals who were competent, dedicated workers at their jobs and well-liked by their neighbors at home? How many times have we seen interviews with the shocked neighbors of the likes of the Son of Sam serial killer from New York City? What do we hear from these people? They are stunned that a man or woman who seemed so kind, gentle, and trustworthy could have been secretly involved in such violent, wicked, and cruel activity.

The truth is that depravity begets depravity. At its heart, the homosexual community is a perverted and often violent culture, regardless of its superficial appearance. Just because an individual is able to perform competently at a job, has a heart for certain acts of compassion, or displays brilliant talent or stunning intellectual capacity, does it mean that every other aspect of that person's life is justifiable? Should the polite bank robber be excused; the artistic child molester be exonerated; the brilliant drug dealer be acquitted; and the philanthropical, homicidal drunk driver be pardoned? The world is full of evildoers, and it is natural for such individuals to downplay the darkness in their lives by turning the spotlight onto their positive attributes. "For every one that doeth evil hateth the light, neither cometh to the light, lest his deeds should be reproved" (John 3:20).

Christians should not be so shallow as to tolerate the minimization or even the justification of rank perversion and gross violations of God's law simply because the offender possesses certain attractive attributes. When we do this, we denigrate God's Word and assist in a demonic campaign which certainly places a stumbling block in the path of the weak, ignorant, and young.

Another increasingly popular shaming tactic that the homosexual promoters employ is pointing out how hard it is to be an out-of-the-closet "gay" and then asking the question, "Given the nature of gay life, who would willingly choose to be homosexual?" I have received scores of letters which have raised that very question as "proof" that homosexuals are born that way. The writers invariably tick off all the awful possibilities which supposedly await the sodomite upon exiting from his closet: the mocking, the ostracization, the discrimination, and the possibility of physical assault. "It is obvious that gay people are born gay; who would ever choose to subject themselves to such abuse?" is the argument offered. It is an argument which has often been used against efforts by Wisconsin Christians United to share truth with the public regarding homosexuality. Here are just two cases in point.

An article which appeared in the *Oconomowoc Press* following WCU activity in that town included this:

> "Why would anyone choose to be gay in this culture?" [Pastor Stephen] Welch questioned, noting that homosexuals are often the object of abuse. He noted that the WCU is treating homosexuals as though they chose their lifestyle. However, he added, that might not be the case. He said he's aware that research is proving homosexuality could be genetic.[24]

After a Wisconsin Christians United Truth Blitz in Stevens Point, Wisconsin, the inevitable appeared in the local paper:

> If you still do not believe that your sexual orientation is out of your control, consider this. Why would anyone choose to be shunned by the entire world? People do not choose to be homosexual.[25]

The goal of the Why-would-anyone-choose-to-be-homosexual? maneuver is to shame those who oppose homosexuality into silence for fear of being lumped in with foul-mouthed skinheads who hate people on the basis of God-given immutable characteristics. In his book *Cease Fire,* Tom Sine makes use of the tactic with what he claims to be a literal example. Sine is a writer, educator, consultant, and an adjunct professor at Fuller Theological Seminary. At one point in his book, Mr. Sine bemoans the fact that "most heterosexuals have little appreciation of the sort of harassment that homosexuals commonly experience."[26] He then proceeds to relate a situation in which he was accosted by several skinheads who thought that he was "gay," saying, "It was a brief taste of the sorts of situations that gays and lesbians have to contend with all the time."[27]

The assertion that no one would choose to be a homosexual based on the various reactions which such a choice precipitates is shallow and disingenuous at its best. Fallen men and women engage in all kinds of immoral and socially despised activities to satisfy their own sinful lusts. Child molesters and rapists are rightfully some of the most detested members of our society. Such individuals place their very lives in jeopardy and are often referred to as "monsters" and "perverts"; yet many choose to commit rape. Increasingly, drunk drivers are looked down upon as the selfish, reckless individuals that they are; yet on Friday and Saturday nights, the streets and roads of America are filled with suicidal, homicidal, intoxicated drivers. Those who sell drugs to young people are not exactly admired in America. Drug dealers are sometimes identified by such terms as "scum" or "slime." Not only are they vulnerable to the long-term loss of their freedom and health, but they also live in a culture of simmering instability and violence in which the loss of their lives is also a very real possibility. Given the facts, who would ever choose to be a child molester, a rapist, a drunk driver, or a drug dealer? Still, multitudes do. Yet there is no serious, well-funded crusade to legitimize such activity—at least not yet.

Christians should never allow this or any other shaming tactic to deter them from taking a bold, uncompromised Biblical stand against the destructive, abominable sin of homosexuality. We are called to be willing to bear shame for our Lord and His righteous standard. Acts 5 contains a narrative of Peter and the other apostles being beaten on account of their public fidelity to the Word of God. Acts 5:41-42 tells us how our spiritual forefathers reacted to such degrading treatment:

> And they departed from the presence of the council, rejoicing that they were counted worthy to suffer shame for his name. And daily in the temple, and in every house, they ceased not to teach and preach Jesus Christ.

The Scriptures teach us that the godly use of shame, done as instructed by the Scriptures, can have a soul-saving effect in a sinner's life. On the other hand, shame can also be used by wicked people in an attempt to paralyze good people and keep them from acting on behalf of righteousness. Christians must not permit themselves to be shamed into betraying or compromising God's eternal truths. To this end, we have an example in Christ:

> Looking unto Jesus the author and finisher of our faith; who for the joy that was set before him endured the cross, despising the shame, and is set down at the right hand of the throne of God (Hebrews 12:2).

Christ did not let the horrible shame which accompanied death on a cross deter Him from being faithful to His commission to become the perfect sacrifice for our sins. How wrong it is for us to allow the enemies of the cross of Christ to shame us into betraying the very Word of our Lord! That is the ultimate shameful act!

CHAPTER NINE

Deadly Deceptions

*Likewise also these filthy dreamers defile the flesh, despise dominion,
and speak evil of dignities. . . . But these speak evil of those
things which they know not: but what they know naturally,
as brute beasts, in those things they corrupt themselves.*
Jude 8, 10

There are generally two reasons why wicked men pervert God's holy Word to condone homosexual acts. Some twist the Scriptures because in their hearts they are at least somewhat concerned about their eternal destination. Such individuals may believe in God, but they do not fear Him. Plainly speaking, they want to have their cake and eat it too. They want to have eternal assurance, or perhaps we should say insurance; and they want to be able to satisfy their own carnal lusts here and now. In order to do both, they simply reinvent God using a rough Biblical outline which has been gutted of those precepts which are not harmonious with their laundry list of traits which a "good God" should possess. They then convince themselves and others that the Creator has indeed given His approval and blessing to the "gay lifestyle." These persons are those whom the Bible describes as "traitors, heady, high-minded, lovers of pleasures more than lovers of God; having a form of godliness, but denying the power thereof: from such turn away" (II Timothy 3:4-5).

On the other hand, there are the avowed atheists who go to great lengths attempting to totally debunk God's eternal truths and prove their own faulty presuppositions as fact. Both groups possess foolish hearts darkened by rebellion; rely on "vain imaginations"; and while claiming to be wise, are the epitome of what it means to be a fool. Members of both circles routinely distort history; scientific fact; and, most grievously, the Holy Scriptures. It does not matter what other label they may claim for themselves—those who use the Bible in an attempt to justify homosexual acts are liars. Regardless of what their motivation is, they are simply liars in the purest sense of the word. In this chapter, we will take a look at some of the deceptions employed by the "Biblical" homosexualists to convince themselves and others that God not only approves of sexual perversion, but also that homosexuals can be a part of the church of Jesus Christ!

One of the most popular verses which the homosexualists distort to convince others that "gays" and "lesbians" can be Christians is Galatians 3:28: "There is neither Jew nor Greek, there is neither bond nor free, there is neither male nor female: for ye are all one in Christ Jesus." As one example of how the pro-sodomite theologians pervert this passage in an attempt to justify their agenda, consider this excerpt from the *Claiming the Promise* Bible study:

> The real point of Paul's message in Galatians is that God made us *all* heirs. Paul says there are now no distinctions: "There is no longer Jew or Greek, there is no longer slave or free, there is no longer male and female; for all of you are one in Christ Jesus" (Galatians 3:28). Gentiles are beloved without becoming Jewish; females, without becoming males; and—dare we say it?—lesbian women and gay men are beloved without trying to become heterosexual or to live "straight" lifestyles. If we believe (belong to Christ), we are all "heirs according to the promise" (Galatians 3:29).[1]

It is somewhat ironic that the homosexualists twist Galatians 3:28 in an effort to reconcile homosexuality and Christianity when one considers that Galatians 1:9 contains Paul's explicit warning against preaching a false gospel. Those who use Galatians 3:28 to homosexualize the body of Christ are truly an accursed breed. They are engaging in an egregious misuse of the Scriptures. Bad hermeneutics would be a gross understatement in this case. Galatians 3:28 has nothing to do with homosexual activity or any other sexual activity for that matter.

In Galatians 3:28, we are plainly told that admission into the family of God is not dependent upon nationality, gender, or position in life. With numerous examples of godly women in the Scriptures, it should not be necessary to convince the reader that women as well as men are eligible for adoption into the family of God.

Galatians 3:28 also assures us that societal position is no barrier to salvation. The lowest person in the eyes of men who repents and gives his life to Christ becomes a highly esteemed child of our heavenly Father. The lake of fire will be populated by many kings, emperors, and presidents while the lowliest slave who picks up his cross and follows Jesus will someday occupy a place at the wedding feast of the Lamb.

Contrary to what some are once more claiming today, race or ethnic background is likewise no barrier to entrance into the kingdom of heaven. Revelation 5:9 pictures the twenty-four elders before the throne of God speaking of Christ:

> And they sung a new song, saying, Thou art worthy to take the book, and to open the seals thereof: for thou wast slain, and hast redeemed us to God by thy blood out of every kindred, and tongue, and people, and nation.

This verse, along with numerous other Scriptures, makes it an indisputable fact that no one is barred membership in the body of Christ on account of race or nationality. At the time of the writing of Galatians 3:28, people were considered either a Jew or a Greek. Galatians 3:28 reminds the Christians of Paul's time and ever since that God's offer of salvation extends to all who will truly repent and accept Christ as Savior and Lord.

Galatians 3:28 has nothing to do with certain acts which identify a person as a lawbreaker. To use the passage to claim that God does not exclude homosexuals from the true body of Christ is equivalent to claiming that God does not exclude thieves, murderers, or, for that matter, rapists or pedophiles from the kingdom of heaven. Assuredly, God's kingdom includes those who had once engaged in all manner of vile activities but have repented and turned to Christ (I Corinthians 6:9-11). Yet thieves who used to steal, rapists who used to rape, or, for that matter, homosexuals who used to engage in that perverse activity but who have repented and been washed by the blood of Jesus are no longer thieves, rapists, or homosexuals; they are rather "a new creature: old things are passed away; behold, all things are become new."[2] Galatians 3:28 is an assurance that no person is excluded from salvation on the basis of conditions over which they have no control—station in life, place of birth, or immutable God-given characteristics. To claim that this passage justifies sin of the most grievous and perverted sort is to truly preach a doctrine of devils. Still, some continue to believe the lie that homosexuals can truly be "one in Christ Jesus." Unfortunately, as we will see in the next chapter, it is not only "flaming queers" and liberal churchmen who are making such an ungodly claim.

It is perhaps fitting that the next "gay Christian" deception we look at is their handling of Sodom and Gomorrah's destruction. While there are many nuances to the homosexualists' revised tale, the most popular lie currently being peddled to explain God's judgment of the sodomite cities is a perverted use of one passage of Scripture. The homosexual apologists' tactic is to set aside the overwhelmingly clear Biblical evidence that God destroyed those cities because the inhabitants were committing homosexual fornication and to instead zero in on one passage which is at least a little easier to take out of context. Ezekiel 16:48-50 says this:

> As I live, saith the LORD God, Sodom thy sister hath not done, she nor her daughters, as thou hast done, thou and thy daughters. Behold, this was the iniquity of thy sister Sodom, pride, fullness of bread, and abundance of idleness was in her and in her daughters, neither did she strengthen the hand of the poor and needy. And they

were haughty, and committed abomination before me: therefore I took them away as I saw good.

This is the passage on which the homosexualists have gleefully pounced. "The stupid fundamentalists have it all wrong," they say. "God's destruction of Sodom had nothing to do with homosexuality. He obviously destroyed Sodom because its inhabitants were materialistic, selfish, and cold-hearted toward the poor." Thus the filthy dreamers haughtily brush aside all the many other Scripture passages which clearly identify the sin for which God destroyed Sodom as sodomy. They have found a passage which they can contort to justify the acts they champion. Based on Ezekiel 16:48-50, the homosexualists deny that Sodom was destroyed on account of being given over to homosexual activity. Some even strive to redefine the age-old word for the signature act which epitomizes such activity.

In their brochure, "The Bible is an Empty Closet," the group Evangelicals Concerned makes this brazen claim:

> According to evangelical Bible scholar William Brownlee: "'sodomy' (so-called) in Genesis is basically oppression of the weak and helpless; and the oppression of the stranger is the basic element of Genesis 19:1-9."[3]

Does it seem at all strange to Evangelicals Concerned, William Brownlee, and others who promulgate the myth that Sodom was destroyed based on its mistreatment of the poor that over all the centuries the word *sodomy* has been used to describe a very specific, perverted sexual act? Even to this day, *sodomy* has a well-defined, exact meaning in our legal statutes and terminology. The word is derived from the name of the city that was made famous by the debauched sexual activity of its "gay" inhabitants. Various terms have been used throughout the ages to define mistreatment of the poor, weak, and helpless; but *sodomy* has never been one of them. *Sodomy* has an exclusive, very definite meaning. That word, the act it defines, and the town Sodom have always been inextricably linked together.

Yet based on an opportunistic, skewered reading of one passage in Ezekiel, the homosexuals and their friends strive mightily to convince the world that homosexual activity had nothing to do with the destruction of Sodom, Gomorrah, and a number of neighboring cities. The Universal Fellowship of Metropolitan Community Churches, a denomination "calling people to new life through the liberating Gospel of Jesus Christ,"[4] is just one of a number of pseudo-Christian church organizations busily spreading this deadly doctrine. The Reverend Elder Donald Eastman is Second Vice Moderator of the UFMCC Board of Elders. An article written by Eastman which appeared in the *Gay Theological Journal* contains these remarks:

> What was the Sin of Sodom? Ezekiel 16:48-50 states it clearly: people of Sodom, like many people today, had abundance of material good. But they failed to meet the needs of the poor, and they worshiped idols.[5]

This claim that Sodom and her sister cities were destroyed for mistreatment of the poor is a misreading of Ezekiel 16:48-50 and nothing less than wicked nonsense. It is so because all the rest of the Bible opposes such a notion and declares that Sodom and her sisters were ultimately destroyed because they had become homosexual cultures. Beyond that, the passage itself does not teach that the destruction came because of materialism and greed, as sinful as those may be.

Ezekiel 16:48-50 is part of a rebuke from the Lord which the prophet Ezekiel is delivering to the inhabitants of Judah. The chapter opens with a recitation of the tender care and great love which God had bestowed upon His chosen people from the very birth of Israel. Verse forty-eight lambastes God's people for being worse than the inhabitants of Sodom. For such a people to commit abominable acts of perversion and idolatry was even worse than what was done by the inhabitants of Sodom in that the acts were being done by a people who had been set apart as a chosen people and singularly blessed by the Lord above all other people. Even Sodom did not combine such a level of treachery with her lewdness and wickedness.

Ezekiel 16:48-50 chronicles the fall of Sodom. Genesis 13:10 tells us that the area where Sodom was built "was well watered every where." The very reason Lot had moved to Sodom in the first place was because it was located in a lush area where a man could prosper. The story of Sodom, as related in Ezekiel 16, is a scenario which has been repeated many times over in the course of history. Verse forty-nine relates how the prosperous inhabitants had become proud, lazy, and selfish. In verse fifty we see that they next became haughty as men often do when living in the lap of luxury. How tempting it is to praise the work of our own hands rather than the God who gave us the hands to do the work in the first place! How easy it is for those who praise themselves for their material blessings to also turn to themselves for the definition of right and wrong!

Prosperity also brings with it the possibility of leisure time which in turn can birth laziness and self-indulgence. Lazy, selfish, arrogant people spend their time striving to fill their days with excitement and satisfy their own ever-increasing desires. The sin nature of man tends toward evil pastimes in such a situation, and the devil is certainly more than willing to provide wicked diversions. It was a natural progression for the affluent, arrogant, selfish, lazy inhabitants of Sodom to slide ever downward in their quest to find fulfillment in life. Eventually, as we are told in verse fifty, they "committed abomination" before the Lord. No doubt the abominable behavior began with various forms of "heterosexual" sin. The Bible tells us how it ended—with wholesale sexual anarchy which featured sodomy as the set piece around which life in Sodom revolved and as the abomination for which God destroyed that city and her sisters. Sodom was a town filled with g/l/b/t people, and that is exactly why God judged it. "[T]herefore I took them away as I saw good" (Ezekiel 16:50).

The story of Sodom's fall is being repeated in America today. We are a nation which first became prosperous, then prideful, then materialistic, then lazy, and then a people always seeking more diversions and recreation. In the last few decades, we have seen the natural progression from the acceptance of opposite-sex fornication, pornography, and adultery to the acceptance of homosexuality and all the vile perversions which accompany it. We now see semi-nude homosexuals literally marching and committing perverted acts in our nation's streets à la Sodom during "gay pride" events. We have truly gone the route of Sodom and we will share her fate in one form or another if we do not put a stop to the madness very soon.

Ezekiel 16:48-50 chronicles the ruin of a civilization. All the sins mentioned in that passage provoke God's wrath, but it was when Sodom's inhabitants began to commit abomination before Him in the form of homosexual acts that God's wrath reached critical mass and "therefore I took them away as I saw good." Rather than make a case for the sodomites, Ezekiel 16:48-50 actually does just the opposite.

Let us look briefly at several more fables that the homosexualists are busily spreading concerning the fall of Sodom and Gomorrah. One school of dreamers would have us believe that the sin of Sodom was "inhospitality to strangers" based on Genesis 19:5: "And they called unto Lot, and said unto him, Where are the men which came in to thee this night? bring them out unto us, that we may know them." The renegade theologians claim that Genesis 19:5 is the key to understanding why Sodom was destroyed. Their contention is that the residents of Sodom simply wanted to know, to get acquainted with, Lot's guests and became angry when they were denied the fellowship. Apparently we are to believe that the sodomites were so hospitable that they became inhospitable when they were not allowed to exercise their hospitality!

In an attempt to make that very point, the homosexual group Lutherans Concerned has circulated the editorial "Does the Bible Condemn Homosexual Acts?" written by Joseph C. Weber, former Associate Professor of Biblical Theology at Wesley Theological Seminary. In his article, Weber insists that the annihilation of Sodom had nothing to do with homosexual activity:

> The passage most quoted in tradition against homosexuality is Genesis 19:4-11. It is questionable whether the sin in this story is "sodomy" at all. . . . The incident can rather be understood as a breach of hospitality. Lot's offer to turn over his daughters is a desperate effort to maintain the sacred trust of hospitality by diverting

the men of Sodom away from their attempt to assert their rights. They are the ones who have the right to decide whether hospitality should be accorded to the strangers, not Lot who is just a sojourner in the city. . . .

There is no evidence that Sodom's sin was homosexuality . . .[6]

The author of the *Claiming the Promise* Bible study likewise insists that God incinerated Sodom and her sister cities at least in part because the inhabitants were inhospitable and asks the reader to subjectively "think about how gay men feel when they hear the story of Sodom interpreted as God's judgment on male homosexuality."[7] Such are the sort of guidelines utilized by many these days to discern God's will! The study's segment on Genesis 19 ends with this lament:

It is ironic and sad that a biblical story about hospitality and God's justice came to be used as biblical support for the church's inhospitality toward, and injustice against, gay men and lesbian women. It is tragic that those who today physically assault gay men and lesbian women (and those who commit crimes of rape and domestic violence against women) are the ones who truly commit Sodom's sins. Sodom's sins are not only general inhospitality. Sodom's sins include violent abuse and extreme disregard for others' well-being.[8]

Daniel A. Helminiak, Ph.D., is a Roman Catholic priest who has written the book *What the Bible Really Says About Homosexuality*, which is forwarded by the wildly pro-"gay" Episcopalian priest John S. Spong. Chapter three of Helminiak's book deals with the sin of Sodom and contains this "insight":

It may simply be that the men of Sodom wanted to find out who these strangers were and what they were doing in their town. After all, Lot was not a native of Sodom. He, too, was an outsider. The townsfolk were not happy with his inviting strangers in. . . .[9]

So what was the sin of Sodom? Abuse and offense against strangers. Insult to the traveler. Inhospitality to the needy. That is the point of the story understood in its own historical context.[10]

Under the subheading "The Sin of Sodom Today," Helminiak ends chapter three by nonchalantly drafting Jesus into the pro-sodomy camp and reinventing the word *sodomite* in a most astounding fashion:

> Even Jesus understood the sin of Sodom as the sin of inhospitality. Other passages in the Bible come right out and say the same thing. Yet people continue to cite the story of Sodom to condemn gay and lesbian people. . . .
>
> Such oppression is the very sin of which the people of Sodom were guilty. Such behavior is what the Bible truly condemns over and over again. So those who oppress homosexuals because of the supposed "sin of Sodom" may themselves be the real "sodomites," as the Bible understands it.[11]

Writing in the *Other Side,* Mark Olson expresses his amazement that so many Christians actually believe that homosexual activity brought about Sodom's destruction:

> An amazing number of Christians, particularly those who haven't looked into the question, assume that the sin of Sodom (for which it was later destroyed) was homosexuality. This interpretation is based on the assumption that the word *know* in this passage is a euphemism for sexual intercourse.
>
> . . . if the word here means something more general, then it's possible that the sin of Sodom was the sin of inhospitality. Maybe the men of Sodom, fearing aliens, wanted to abuse and attack these foreigners. Maybe they wanted to subject them to hostile and suspicious questions. Maybe they intended to kick them out of their city, denying them any gracious hospitality. If you think such a view is far-fetched, don't forget that it was while discussing with his disciples the problem of inhospitable cities that Jesus refers to the destruction of Sodom (Matt. 10:14-15).[12]

In an article distributed by Wingspan, a Lutheran homosexual "ministry," the Reverend Paul A. Tidemann also takes the position that the words of Jesus verify that Sodom was destroyed because its citizens were inhospitable:

I find these comments of Bishop Herbert W. Chilstrom to be helpful in understanding this passage. ("A Pastoral Letter: The Church & the Homosexual Person"). "... if we consider Sodom from the standpoint of subsequent references, we find no suggestion that homosexual acts were the essence of their sin. Instead, it is clear that the lack of hospitality is seen as the basic issue. Neither Ezekiel nor Jesus (Ezekiel 16:48-50; Matthew 10:14-15; Luke 10:10-12) mention homosexuality in referring to Sodom and Gomorrah. Both cite inhospitality—a cardinal sin in that culture—as the primary allegation."[13]

In the two previous quotations, the writers recklessly attempt to commandeer Christ's approval for their own flawed exegesis of Genesis 19 by referencing His words to His twelve disciples as He sent them forth to preach to the lost sheep of Israel. After giving them their commission, Christ tells them how to act in response to those who reject the gospel:

And whosoever shall not receive you, nor hear your words, when ye depart out of that house or city, shake off the dust of your feet. Verily I say unto you, It shall be more tolerable for the land of Sodom and Gomorrah in the day of judgment, than for that city (Matthew 10:14-15).

That the pro-sodomite theologians would take these words of Christ and twist them in a vain endeavor to "prove" that the sin of Sodom was inhospitality shows wicked desperation on their part. Christ was not talking about simple inhospitality in the passages cited; He was telling his disciples what to do when people rejected His gospel even when it was preached by them, His commissioned disciples, and confirmed by great signs from heaven. To reject the gospel is to reject the Lord, and to reject the Lord is a matter of extreme wickedness with serious eternal results. In the passage, the Lord was stressing the deadly consequences of such a reaction to the gospel by citing two cities which are a bench mark of rebellion and wickedness. The book of Jude testifies that Sodom and Gomorrah are literally "set forth for an example, suffering the vengeance of eternal fire." Christ went on to state that those households and cities which rejected the gospel brought to them by His disciples could look forward to being in even more trouble than the sodomite cities on judgment day. Jesus' words as recorded in Matthew 10:14-15 and Mark 6:10-11 should be anything but an encouragement for "gay Christians" considering that they have rejected the true gospel and are also committing the sin of Sodom.

It is a source of unceasing amazement to me to see the length to which the purveyors of perversion will strive to justify the unjustifiable. One would think that a simple aversion to making a fool of oneself would preclude some of the theological fairy tales which are pouring out of the pro-sodomite churches and seminaries; yet desperation is often the mother of invention; and in our American culture, enthusiastically promoted lies which remain unanswered do frighteningly well.

By the way, the assertion that Lot was simply a temporary visitor in Sodom is not an accurate one. Genesis 19:9 does record the sodomites saying about Lot, "This one fellow came in to sojourn." However, this does not mean Lot was a sojourner at the time of the Genesis 19 incident but rather that he was not a native of Sodom. A reading of the chapters preceding Genesis 19 shows that Lot had already lived very near and even in Sodom for a number of years. II Peter 2 reveals that Lot was literally dwelling among the sodomites and that he was vexed by their behavior from day to day. It is also instructive to note that in Genesis 19 Lot had his own home in Sodom at the time of the visitation of the angels. Portraying Lot as a suspicious, haughty stranger just passing through does nothing to get the sodomites off the hook.

The homosexualists' arguments that Sodom was destroyed on account of inhospitality are futile and foolish. Such claims are, quite frankly, laughable. Jude 7 plainly states that the inhabitants of those cities suffered God's vengeance because they gave "themselves over to fornication, and going after strange flesh." This is a clear reference to homosexual fornication. Believe it or not, there are some sodomite-friendly "scholars" who are now insisting that the strange flesh with which the sodomites were fornicating were angels! They are saying that God destroyed the "cities of the plain" because the people were committing sexual acts with angels!

This claim can be, and should be, easily dismissed. With respect to humans, God created them male and female for several express purposes. First, God created the female as a help meet for the male (Genesis 2:18). Secondly, He made the opposite sexes for the purpose of creating a family unit (Genesis 2:24). Thirdly, God made them male and female to "be fruitful, and multiply" (Genesis 1:28). God created mankind in the form of two sexes to fulfill His purposes.

Angels were not created as two sexes and have not been given any of the functions just mentioned. In Matthew 22:29-30, Jesus tells the Sadducees, "Ye do err, not knowing the scriptures, nor the power of God. For in the resurrection they neither marry, nor are given in marriage, but are as the angels of God in heaven." The truth shared here is that marriage and, consequently, sexual relations are earthly institutions which will have no purpose in heaven and will not exist there. Rather, we will be "as the angels of God in heaven."

This is a clear testimony that angels are not sexual beings. There is no place in the Scriptures which even remotely suggests that angels are sexual beings—quite the contrary—much less that angels could have sexual relations with humans even if they wanted to. Adherents to this ridiculous fairy tale point to Genesis 6:2, a passage which speaks of "the sons of God" taking wives. By taking this passage in context with what we know about God's creation from the rest of Scripture, the verse is obviously speaking of men, not angels. All evidence confirms that the fornication with strange flesh spoken of in Jude is homosexual fornication. There is no credible evidence for any other explanation.

But back to the inhospitable sodomites. The "Christian" homosexualists place much emphasis on the verb *to know* which appears in Genesis 19:5. They hold that the sodomites only wanted *to know* who Lot's guests were, to get *to know* them personally; and when they could not, they acted in an exceptionally inhospitable manner by throwing the most famous tantrum in history. This is pure drivel! If the sodomites outside Lot's home merely wanted to get acquainted with his guests, Lot must have been the most unsociable man who ever walked the face of the earth! In Genesis 19:7, we see that he answered the sodomites' requests "to know" his guests by pleading with them,

"I pray you, brethren, do not so wickedly." It is hard to conceive that Lot would label a simple desire for fellowship as being wicked! Of course, this is not the case. Lot was clearly dealing with a crowd of lust-crazed sodomites.

The verb *to know* in the King James Bible is rendered from the Hebrew verb *yada,* which in turn is used in several ways in the Old Testament, including to describe intimate sexual relations or "knowledge." Genesis 4:1 tells us that ". . . Adam knew Eve his wife; and she conceived . . ." Genesis 4:17 says, "And Cain knew his wife; and she conceived . . ." These are just two examples where *yada* is used in the Old Testament to describe intimate sexual relations.

Yada is used in this same fashion in the Genesis account of Sodom. This is obvious from the context. That is why most modern Bible versions translate Genesis 19:5 even more explicitly than does the King James Bible. The New King James Version reads, ". . . Bring them out to us that we may know them carnally." The New American Standard Version states, ". . . Bring them out to us that we may have relations with them." The New International Version renders it: ". . . Bring them out so that we can have sex with them."

Lot had insisted that his guests should not spend the night in the streets. Why? Was he afraid that the sodomites would run over them with the welcome wagon, suffocate them with gifts, or perhaps ruin their sleep by keeping them up talking all night in an attempt to get to know them better? No, Lot obviously feared for his guests' personal safety, and the succeeding events justified his fears. If the mob outside his door simply wanted to get acquainted with Lot's guests, to know them, why did he wickedly try to protect his visitors by offering the sodomites a chance to know his daughters instead? Were they not already acquainted with the girls? In the passage, Lot submits his daughters to the sodomites while testifying that they have never "known" a man. Does this mean the girls had never been socially acquainted with men? In his misguided efforts to protect his guests, Lot was apparently hoping the sodomites would be content with sexually abusing his daughters, but they were not. The men of Sodom had long ago left "the natural use of the woman" and "burned in their lust one toward another." Anyone who has studied the homosexual lifestyle soon learns that eventually most gay men are repulsed by the thought of intimate relations with a woman, as obviously were the sexual deviants of Sodom.

Another thing that students of the homosexual life quickly learn is that the vast majority of sodomites are driven by a consuming lust for perverted sensual excitement. That is why most "gays" and "lesbians" have numerous sexual partners in the course of their lifetimes, even while they sometimes maintain a long-term relationship with one particular person. The men of Sodom were no different. They wanted Lot's guests and they wanted them so badly that they kept trying to get at them even after being struck blind! "And they smote the men that were at the door of the house with blindness, both small and great: so that they wearied themselves to find the door" (Genesis 19:11).

The account of Sodom is the story of the homosexual culture. In spite of the health risks, violence, shame, and filth which accompany the homosexual life; in spite of the obvious truth that homosexual activity violates the laws of God, most sodomites are committed to pursuing perverted sensual pleasure at all costs, just as were the inhabitants of Sodom. Consequently, relatively few truly repent and turn to Christ. There is no doubt that more would repent if Christians would boldly resist the homosexual agenda with the sharp sword of God's Word while praying for and sharing the gospel with the homosexuals themselves.

Those pro-homosexual theologians who do admit that the mob outside Lot's door had a lot more in mind than simply becoming acquainted with his visitors often contend that the sin of Sodom was that the inhabitants had attempted to gang rape Lot's guests. We are told that God's actions against Sodom must not be viewed as proof that God condemns "loving, committed same-sex relationships," but rather that His actions were a punishment for gang rape. What they neglect to admit is that God had decided to destroy Sodom before the angels even arrived in Sodom. The only reason the angels went there was to rescue Lot and his family so that they would not be swept away with the wicked when God poured out His judgment. God also destroyed Gomorrah and a number of other sodomite cities at the same time even though the angels were obviously never attacked by perverts in those cities. Again, we must remember that Jude 7 identifies the sin of Sodom and Gomorrah as fornication with strange flesh, not as gang rape.

God destroyed Sodom, Gomorrah, and the cities about them because a homosexual culture had taken over those cities and the surrounding area. Depravity begets depravity. It is the simple truth that any culture which is literally ruled by homosexuals will be a culture rife with pedophilia, sado-masochism, and violence, including gang rape. The root sin which spawns and undergirds it all is same-sex acts. Variations of debauchery are simply the nature of homosexual depravity. Such was the cultural norm of Sodom and Gomorrah. Such will be a homosexualized America's future if the growing sodomite culture here is allowed to come to full fruition.

Let us move on to several other examples of how the "gay Christians" and their allies pervert the Scriptures. One of the most common comebacks the homosexualists use when confronted with Scripture verses which condemn homosexual behavior is to zero in on the Levitical prohibitions and sneer, "So if you use these verses to say that homosexual behavior is wrong, do you also think that it's wrong to wear a shirt with two types of cloth or to eat shellfish, etc., etc.?" As evidence of this smug approach, allow me to offer excerpts from a response to a guest column I wrote which appeared in the *Wisconsin State Journal*. My antagonist identified himself as Kirk Ormand, assistant professor of classical studies, Loyola University, Chicago.

> I am naturally suspicious of anyone who claims to know what "the truth" is. But let me suggest another "truth" in response to guest columnist Ralph Ovadal: That fully devout Christians of all stripes disobey the words of God on a daily basis.
>
> A quick glance through my Hebrew Bible discovered the following injunctions: The eating of pork and of shellfish is clearly forbidden (Leviticus 11:7,9; Deuteronomy 14:8,10). . . . Persons of either gender may not "wear a garment of divers sorts, as of woolen and

linen together" (Deuteronomy 22:11). . . . Does Ovadal own any permanent press shirts? . . .

Ovadal can credibly argue from the Bible that homosexuality is a mortal sin. It may be comforting, in a world when changes are radical and rapid, to cling to a notion of such unchanging laws. But unless he is willing to obey all the laws of the Hebrew Bible (and condemn those who do not), it seems that his condemning of homosexuality rests on little more than his subjective choice to do so.[14]

The homosexualists often use the ban on homosexual acts in Leviticus, just as Professor Ormand does, as an implement to ridicule and discredit Christians who take a Biblical stand against homosexuality. During her sermon "Why We Stand with the GLBT Community," the United Methodist Reverend Dianne Reistroffer did just that. After declaring the "hermeneutical bottom line" that the Levitical ban on homosexual activity stemmed from the need for the Hebrews "to populate a sparsely settled land," Reistroffer went on to incorrectly state that in the Old Testament "homosexuality gets no more space than the ban on shellfish, and far less than the ban on eating pork." Reistroffer concluded her teaching on the Levitical verses by suggesting, with dripping sarcasm, that Christians who hold the Bible to be literally true "should spend more time protesting county pork queens than drag queens" and went on to exult:

> We do not live in the age of Leviticus; we live instead in a much more diverse, confused and difficult time. Even so, these are exciting days, ones in which we are finally free to affirm our sexuality as a good gift from God and to know what it means to be responsible, faithful sexual persons.[15]

The homosexual Episcopalian group Integrity also uses a misrepresentation of Leviticus 18:22 and Leviticus 20:13 to mock "fundamentalists" who hold that the Bible condemns homosexual acts. On behalf of Integrity and concerning the Levitical prohibitions, Dr. Wilfrid R. Koponen writes:

> This [is] part of the "Holiness Code" of the Old Testament, which also condemns the practice of eating rare meat or wearing a fabric from more than one material—anyone eating a rare steak while wearing a cotton/polyester is doubly violating this holiness code! (Funny: these things don't seem to bother Fundamentalists.)[16]

The aforementioned article by Rev. Paul A. Tidemann which appeared in the Wingspan ministry publication contains this excuse as to why the Levitical condemnations of homosexual acts are supposedly invalid:

> These verses are part of the Levitical holiness code. In the previously quoted Pastoral Letter, Bishop Herbert Chilstrom said, "We who champion evangelicalism in its historic sense will hardly want to retreat to the Levitical code for our understanding of the Gospel." We need to note that if we were to apply all verses of the Bible literally, the church would have to call for capital punishment of homosexuals. Are we prepared to suggest that? By the same Levitical code we would not be allowed to eat pork or shellfish.[17]

The "Christian" homosexualists resort to a misrepresentation of the Levitical ban on homosexual acts because their superficial arguments make sense to the Biblically illiterate while appearing to be a difficult one for true Christians to quickly refute with a short sound bite. However, the answer to this challenge is really quite simple. To declare Biblical license for homosexual acts based upon the misreading of the Levitical passages is corrupt on its face.

First, homosexuality is soundly condemned in both the Old Testament and the New Testament. It is condemned prior to the Mosaic Covenant, in the Mosaic Covenant, and under the New Covenant. Any portion of the Bible that the "gay Christian" might possibly accept includes a condemnation and a prohibition of homosexual acts.

Secondly, God mandated the death penalty for homosexual acts under the Law of Moses. This gives us a crystal clear picture of how He views homosexual acts. "For I am the Lord, I change not . . ." (Malachi 3:6). It is nothing short of ridiculous to think that God has changed His mind regarding homosexual acts, swung 180 degrees around, and now condones such behavior.

Thirdly, God still promulgates His law through the New Covenant.[18] Individuals who use the Levitical passages in the manner of those quoted above display monumental ignorance of the Scriptures and God's covenants with man. It is either that, or they are simply lying. Under the New Covenant which Christ sealed with His blood, God's people are no longer required to observe a number of regulations included in the Law of Moses which God chose not to include in the New Covenant. This is not to say that God's people are no longer under any law; they and the whole world are still under the law of God, but the law of God as promulgated through the New Covenant. All of the Old Testament, which God has not nullified, including the entire Adamaic and Noahic Covenants, is part of that law. A study of the Scriptures shows that the Mosaic dietary, ceremonial, and sacrificial regulations are not a part of the New Covenant.

The important thing in all of this relative to homosexuality is that all Christians should be prepared to explain why homosexual acts are sinful and why they should be punished by the civil government, while at the same time being able to explain why the Levitical regulations in question are no longer in force. As evidenced by numerous New Testament passages, the particular dietary and dress regulations which the homosexualists attempt to exploit to their advantage are not a part of the New Covenant. At the same time, there can be no doubt that God certainly has not and will not change His law prohibiting homosexual activity. As said earlier, this has been made abundantly evident throughout the New Testament.

Another twist that the homosexualists use in an attempt to empty the Levitical passages, and sometimes Romans 1, of any blanket condemnation of homosexuality is to claim that the verses relate only to homosexual acts done within the context of cultic worship. In Rev. Elder Donald Eastman's previously quoted article, "Homosexuality: Not a Sin, Not a Sickness," he attempts to purge the Leviticus chapters of all vestiges of "homophobia" with pseudo-intellectual reasoning of this sort:

Given the strong association of toevah [abomination] with idolatry and the Canaanite religious practice of cult prostitution, the use of toevah regarding male same-sex acts in Leviticus calls into question any conclusion that such condemnation also applies to loving, responsible homosexual relationships.[19]

Concerning Romans 1, Eastman states:

The homosexual practices cited in Romans 1:24-27 were believed to result from idolatry and are associated with some very serious offenses, as noted in Romans 1. Taken in this larger context, it should be obvious that such acts are significantly different from loving, responsible lesbian and gay relationships seen today.[20]

Daniel A. Helminiak writes in *What the Bible Really Says About Homosexuality* that because the Canaanites practiced homosexual acts, "Leviticus condemned homogenital sex as a religious crime of idolatry, not as a sexual offense, and that religious treason was thought serious enough to merit death."[21]

In their brochure "The Bible is an Empty Closet," Evangelicals Concerned also attempts to cast Paul's "anti-gay" remarks in Romans 1 as strictly relating to homosexual cult practices:

In Romans 1, Paul is ridiculing pagan religious rebellion, saying that the pagans knew God but worshipped idols instead of God. To build his case—which he'll turn against judgmental Jews in chapter 2—he refers to typical practices of the fertility cults involving sex among priestesses and between men and eunuch prostitutes such as served Aphrodite at Corinth, from where he was writing this letter to the Romans.[22]

The sources mentioned are just three of many which claim that a number of Biblical condemnations of homosexuality are, in reality, aimed only at same-sex cultic practices. Others also argue that the New Testament prohibitions are only dealing with man-boy sexual relations. To undergird their outrageous claims, the deceivers weave a complicated web of warped history, implied associations, flawed presuppositions, devious juxtapositions, textual misinterpretations, and pseudo-exegesis. There are many different twists, turns, and versions of their sordid fantasy, but the one constant is a heavy reliance upon erroneous but confident assertions concerning various cultures and customs, Biblical history, and the Greek and Hebrew languages. The obvious intention of the counterfeit Christian teachers is to intimidate and confuse everyone who has not achieved a Doctor of Divinity degree into thinking that certainly most Christians cannot ever hope to understand what the Bible really does say about homosexuality, and thus many are embarrassed into silence.

Certainly homosexual cultic practices and pederasty existed during the writing of the Scriptures, just as such practices exist today. This does not justify in any way a reading of the aforementioned Scripture passages in such a context. It is evil and dangerous to read things into the Bible which simply are not there. Revelation 22:18 warns:

> For I testify unto every man that heareth the words of the prophecy of this book, If any man shall add unto these things, God shall add unto him the plagues that are written in this book.

Of course, the immediate context here relates to the book of Revelation, but I personally would counsel prudence with the rest of God's Word as well. It seems obvious that He would not feel any differently about Leviticus or Romans than He does about Revelation, and we know that He does not in light of the many Scripture verses which testify to that truth.[23]

A careful reading of Leviticus 18:22 and Leviticus 20:13 makes it abundantly clear that those passages are condemning homosexual acts as wicked and prohibited in themselves. There is not even a hint that either verse is dealing with cultic homosexual practices. Both verses appear as part of a long list of prohibited sexual activity which includes incest, adultery, and bestiality. There is only one mention of cultic practice in each chapter. If we are to assume that Leviticus 18:22 and 20:13 only prohibit homosexual cultic practice but do not condemn "loving, committed" homosexual activity, may we then assume the same for the other sexual crimes outlawed in the surrounding passages? Certainly various pagan religions have always condoned and practiced sexual anarchy, including incest, adultery, and bestiality, as part of their rituals. Are the prohibitions which God has set forth in Leviticus against those acts relegated to cultic practices only? Does God approve of "loving, committed" sex between fathers and daughters, mothers and sons, men and other men's wives, people and animals? Of course not! Such acts in themselves are wicked, condemned and proscribed by God's law in every circumstance, in any context, all of the time. So it is with homosexual acts. The very acts themselves are what is prohibited and condemned in the Levitical passages. It obviously follows that cultic homosexuality would also be unacceptable.

In a desperate attempt to escape this truth, the purveyors of perversion point to Leviticus 18:21 and several verses in Leviticus 20 which condemn the sacrifice of infants to Molech. This is said to be proof that the surrounding verses prohibiting homosexual acts deal only with Canaanite cultic practices. But again, this is a truly illogical conclusion for all the reasons previously mentioned. Beyond that, the Levitical ban on homosexual acts is echoed throughout Scripture; and everywhere, including in Romans 1, that prohibition is based upon the wickedness of the act itself, not the context in which it occurs. Leviticus 18:22 and Leviticus 20:13 are part of the law of God which was delivered through Moses to the Israelites. Nevertheless, the sexual practices delineated in that law which God prohibited then are still prohibited now. They are practices which God condemned then and condemns now as unlawful no matter what the context or location or time in which they take place.

The portion of Scripture that the homosexualists perhaps hate, fear, and wrestle with most is Romans 1:18-32. And it is no wonder. Here we have a portion of Scripture which, in verses eighteen through twenty-three, describes "vain . . . fools" who have turned away from God's creation and revealed law in the name of wisdom and states that such persons are without excuse and under God's wrath. There is no mention of cultic practices or pederasty here, let alone "orientation" or "intrinsic disorders," only the judgment that individuals who have turned their backs on God and are living a lie are *without excuse!* In verse twenty-eight we are informed by the Lord that such persons are so deep in sin that God gives them over to a "reprobate mind."

Verses twenty-nine through thirty-one paint a picture of the various sins of the heart and body in which members of this rebellious community engage. The verses are in fact a composite of sins which are all too common in a people given over to rank depravity and gross immorality. Verse thirty-two says that the individuals spoken of know that the law of God outlaws their activities, yet they continue on in their rebellion and do so with pleasure. Verses twenty-six and twenty-seven identify the community or people group which the passage deals with as homosexuals. The homosexuals hate this passage because it clearly speaks of them. There is no wiggle room for them here. Certainly Romans 1:18-32 can be related to all those who have turned their back on God, not just homosexuals; but they are the specific group identified in the passage as the epitome of rebellion against God. This identification comes in a New Testament passage and not with a single word but with a vivid description of an act which in turn pinpoints the people being identified:

> For this cause God gave them up unto vile affections: for even their women did change the natural use into that which is against nature: and likewise also the men, leaving the natural use of the woman, burned in their lust one toward another; men with men working that which is unseemly, and receiving in themselves that recompense of their error which was meet (Romans 1:26-27).

These verses graphically describe homosexual acts and state that those who commit them receive what they deserve. So how in the world do the homosexualists attempt to explain away this one, other than with the cultic or pederasty excuses which we dealt with previously? As with all the other Biblical prohibitions against homosexual acts, they first isolate the passage from the rest of the Scriptures which condemn homosexuality.

The next step in the deconstruction of this passage in Romans is one which the reader may have trouble believing; it is that incredibly brash and wicked. It is a maneuver which highlights the willingness of the homosexuals to legitimize their activities regardless of God's truth, His law, and even simple logic. Faced with the obvious in Romans 1:18-32, many homosexualist scholars fall back on a desperate game of "let's just say." But allow me to explain. When I was a child, my playmates and I used that phrase often, as I am sure many children did and still do. Many times of make-believe would begin with phrases such as "Let's just say that you're a cowboy and I'm an Indian." The homosexualists are essentially doing the same thing concerning those verses in Romans which so trouble them. "Let's just say that Paul was talking about something totally different than what he obviously was and what almost two thousand years of Bible teachers, historians, commentators, scholars, and preachers have all agreed that he was talking about. Let's just say that up until recently everyone misunderstood what Paul meant when he used the words 'natural' and 'against nature' in Romans 1:26."

Daniel Helminiak plays the let's-just-say game in his book *What the Bible Really Says About Homosexuality*. Here is an explanation of Romans 1:26-27 according to Helminiak:

> But given Paul's own usage of these terms [*natural, against nature*], the sense is not "in opposition to the laws of nature" but rather "unexpectedly" or "in an unusual way," what we might mean if we said: "Contrary to her nature, Jean got up and danced last night."
>
> So what does it mean when Romans says that the "women exchanged natural relations for unnatural and the men likewise gave up natural relations with women and were consumed with passion for one another"? It means that these women and men were engaging in sexual practices that were not the ones people usually perform. The practices were beyond the regular, outside the ordinary, more than the usual, not the expected.
>
> There is no sense whatever in those words that the practices were wrong or against God or contrary to the divine order of creation or in conflict with the universal nature of things. According to Paul's usage, the words only say that the practices were different from what one would generally expect.[24]

Rather than comment on the preceding quotation, I would like to give several more examples of the desperate alibis put forth by "gay" theologians and their friends regarding Romans 1:18-32. We can then examine both their claims and the truth all at once. Metropolitan Community Church's brochure "Homosexuality and the Bible: Bad News or Good News?" contains this fantastical depiction of Romans 1:26-27:

> John McNeill, a Roman Catholic scholar, says there is ample evidence that Biblical authors probably had in mind what we would also call perversion, namely, the indulgence in homosexual activity by those who were, by nature, heterosexual. . . .
>
> As Norman Pittenger, an Anglican theologian, states, "For a man or woman whose sexual desire and drive is inevitably towards the same gender, acting in homosexual physical expression is in fact a way of glorifying God and opening the self to the working of the divine love in human affairs."[25]

Metropolitan Community Church elder, the Reverend Donald Eastman, writing in the *Gay Theological Journal,* asks, "What is 'natural?'" Regarding Romans 1:26-27, Eastman answers:

> "Unnatural" in these passages does not refer to violation of so-called laws of nature, but rather implies action contradicting one's own nature. In view of this, we should observe that it is "unnatural," para physic, for a person today with a lesbian or gay sexual orientation to attempt living a heterosexual lifestyle.[26]

The following excerpt is taken from the booklet "Homosexuality and the Bible," published by the National Gay Pentecostal Alliance:

> Romans 1:26, 27 are two verses frequently offered as condemnation of homosexuality. Below we have printed these verses. Please take careful note of the words we have capitalized.
>
> "For this cause God gave them up unto vile affections: for even their women did CHANGE the natural use into that which is against nature: And likewise also the men, LEAVING the natural use of the woman, burned in their lust one toward another; men with men

working that which is unseemly, and receiving in themselves that recompense of their error which was meet."

Remember, if you will, that Paul would have had little or no knowledge of exclusive homosexuality, but was familiar with the bisexual lifestyle of Rome. And remember, too, that this epistle was written to the bisexual Romans. He said the women CHANGED the natural use into that which is against nature. That is, women who were by nature heterosexual engaged in homosexual relations. Doing so was against their nature, but was expected by their culture. We know that the women in question were heterosexuals, rather than Lesbians, because it says they had to CHANGE in order to engage in homosexuality. A Lesbian would not have needed to change anything, since homosexual relations would be normal for her. In verse 27, the men LEFT the natural use of the woman. A person cannot leave behind something they've never had. Since these men did leave behind heterosexual relations, they were obviously heterosexual by nature.

The lesson of these verses is clear: God does not approve of heterosexuals engaging in homosexual activity. The greater message is also clear: God does not want people tampering with their sexual orientation. If it is wrong for a heterosexual to attempt to be a homosexual to satisfy cultural expectations, then it is equally wrong for a homosexual to attempt to be a heterosexual to satisfy cultural expectations.[27]

Aside from the fact that this statement and others like it are blasphemous, it would be tempting to laugh them off. Yet we dare not do so. In a Biblically illiterate culture, such statements can be used with great effect to convince individuals that God really does not condemn homosexual activity, but, in fact, He condones it and creates certain people to be homosexual. This does not change the fact that the argument made by the National Gay Pentecostal Alliance and others of their ilk is totally without merit and is a pure fabrication that has been desperately concocted by the homosexuals to convince themselves and others that all of Christendom and Western Civilization has been totally confused for almost two thousands years regarding homosexuality.

Let us critique the NGPA statement since it is very representative of all the examples that we have looked at and of the tactic used by those who try to discredit the Romans 1 condemnation of homosexual acts. The writer claims that "Paul would have had little or no knowledge of exclusive homosexuality, but was familiar with the bisexual lifestyle of Rome." This contention is pure nonsense for several reasons. First of all, bisexuals are by definition homosexuals. Any person who commits sexual acts with another person of the same sex is a homosexual, regardless of the fact that he may engage in "heterosexual" sexual activities from time to time as well.

Secondly, it is often taken for granted by the sexual libertines that the writers of the Scriptures were men when, in reality, the Scriptures were written by the Holy Spirit working through the agency of certain men selected by God.[28] Although he was certainly well-versed in the subject, Paul would not necessarily have had to know everything about homosexuality to write Romans 1. Moses wrote a detailed and precise account of the creation of the universe in spite of the fact that neither he nor any other human being was present at the time. There are numerous prophetic passages in the Bible which were written by men who did not fully understand what the Spirit was having them write. In addition to those passages, there are verses which reveal things about the natural creation which the writer could not have known about at the time. Isaiah wrote that the earth is a circle;[29] Job testified that God "hangeth the earth upon nothing."[30] Paul spoke of the four distinctly different types of flesh owned by men, beasts, fish, and birds.[31] The writer of Hebrews relates that God made the worlds by His word out of things which the naked eye cannot see as opposed to "things which do appear."[32] All of these statements reflect facts which scientists have discovered and verified centuries after the prophets had made them known by the inspiration of the Holy Spirit. It is foolish for the homosexualists to predicate the meaning of certain Scriptural passages on the limited knowledge of the writers. At any rate, Paul certainly knew what homosexuality was.

The NGPA would have us believe that all of Rome was bisexual during the time in which Paul wrote his epistle to the Romans. This is absolutely historical fallacy. Even if Rome would have been a totally bisexual city, which it was not, the book of Romans, just as the rest of the Bible, was written for all mankind for all time. The disputed passage begins by announcing that "the wrath of God is revealed from heaven against all ungodliness and unrighteousness of men, who hold the truth in unrighteousness" and then proceeds to speak of those individuals who reject God and follow after their own sinful lusts. This passage is not dated and applicable only to the church and inhabitants of Rome. The first chapter of Romans, and indeed the whole book, is a great treatise on God's eternal law and His great mercy.

If the condemnation of wickedness found in Romans 1:18-32 is applicable only to one time and one people in history, then is this also true of the comforting promise found in Romans 8:38-39?

> For I am persuaded, that neither death, nor life, nor angels, nor principalities, nor powers, nor things present, nor things to come, nor height, nor depth, nor any other creature, shall be able to separate us from the love of God, which is in Christ Jesus our Lord.

To brush aside passages of God's holy Scriptures which convict us of our sins by saying, "Oh, God is talking to someone else in that passage," can only be viewed as nothing less than sheer insanity when one takes into consideration the eternal consequences of such arrogance. Yet this is exactly what the homosexuals do with Romans 1:18-32. Unfortunately, the lunatics are increasingly running the asylum that America is becoming. As Christians, we must be equipped to refute their relentless assaults on "the faith which was once delivered unto the saints."

NGPA's change theory to explain God's condemnation of homosexual acts in Romans 1:18-32 may contain an element of diabolic cleverness, but it is a patently desperate attempt to wish away the obvious. What but vain imagination could concoct such a fable? The claim that Romans 1:26-27 condemns "orientation change" falls flat on its face within even the immediate context of the verses. The sexual activity which is condemned in these verses is homosexual activity. If verses twenty-six and twenty-seven simply condemn the changing of one's "orientation," why would only "heterosexual" to homosexual change be condemned and not vice versa? If it is only the change of "orientation," not any sexual acts themselves, which is condemned, then why are homosexual acts graphically described and then referred to as "unseemly," "not convenient [proper]," "vile," and "reprobate"? Romans 1:26-27 does condemn a change to be sure. The passage condemns those who violate God's natural law, those who would step outside His creation order to do that which is unnatural. This and the fact that homosexual activity is contrary to God's written law as well is why His revealed Word calls homosexual acts "lawless" in I Timothy 1:9.

The whole of Scriptures confirms that this is the precise meaning of Romans 1:26-27. This passage is in complete harmony with others which describe homosexual activity and condemn homosexual acts in a very similar fashion. Leviticus 18:22 and Leviticus 20:13 both graphically depict homosexual sex—men who "lie with mankind, as with womankind." Both passages appear in the middle of a list of sexual perversions which are forbidden by God. Neither relies on the "interpretation" of one word but rather describes the forbidden act directly and to the point as does Romans 1:26-27. Those who would attempt to explain away the Scriptural condemnation of homosexual acts really do not have a leg to stand on considering that the Bible categorically prohibits such activity not only by name but also by a vivid description of the acts themselves. Yet they try.

Hendrik Hart is on the staff of the Toronto, Ontario based Institute for Christian Studies. In an article titled "Romans Revisited" which appeared in the publication the *Other Side,* Mr. Hart takes six tortured, whimsical pages to arrive at the conclusion that Romans 1:18-32 was actually only written as an example of poor theology. Hart writes in part:

> Specific times call us to new interpretations, new understandings of what is biblical. I believe my questions about another reading of Romans 1:18-32 need to be addressed for the sake of all within the church who struggle with the issue of homosexuality. For if that passage was used rhetorically by Paul to describe his own pre-Christian tradition of judgment and condemnation, and if in 2:1 he

turns against that, then what is said about same-sex behavior in Romans 1 is not intended by Paul to invoke in us a condemnation of homosexuality. . . .

It is too early to plead for universal acceptance of the reading I have pointed out. But I believe scholars have established a need for evidence and discussion that helps us address the interpretation of this crucial passage anew. And such evidence and discussion can best be expected if the question that begs for it is shared with others.[33]

A desperate drug addict will sell her own body for a fix of her favorite drug. Pro-homosexual "Christians" are willing to prostitute their intellect and sell their souls to the devil for a theological fix for their favored perversion. The drug addict is more despised in this world, yet I would submit that she is the more honest of the two. God's holy Word prohibits and condemns homosexual acts. Though it may be articulately defended, dressed in Biblical language, crowned with "compassion," and animated by worldly logic, any other view on the subject is nothing less than a satanic subterfuge, a desperate deception, which must be exposed and resisted by God's people.

CHAPTER TEN

Friendly Fire

Et tu, Brute?
—Shakespeare

We Christians are frequently our own worst enemies. So often well-meaning, misguided members of the body of Christ will literally destroy the very foundational arguments upon which our success in any given battle depends. Because of confusion, fear, the desire to soften up our image or to avoid condemnation from the world, or for any number of other reasons, Christians sometimes take positions or preach messages which greatly hinder the cause of righteousness and their brethren who are striving to take a Biblical stand on the great issues of the day. This has certainly taken place in the context of the battle between the homosexualists and those who believe homosexual behavior to be wrong. Many of us have felt the frustration of doing our best to present a unified, Biblical front on this issue while at the same time being forced to compete with the unbiblical statements and positions sometimes taken by other Bible-believing leaders, pastors, and spokesmen. Like errant artillery shells fired from friendly guns, these well-meaning but misguided words and policies explode within our Christian lines, blasting away at our foundational breastworks thus making the body of Christ and, consequently, our nation more vulnerable to the advancing pro-sodomite host. It is my intent to deal with some of that friendly fire in this chapter. Please understand that I do so not out of malice nor with the intent of doing harm to anyone but simply out of a need to defend the truth and with a concern for my family, my nation, and the body of Christ.

An extremely damaging and currently very popular unscriptural concept which is being presented as Biblical truth by many Christians is this seemingly innocuous little slogan: "Homosexuality is a sin, but it's no worse than any other sin." There are very few Christian pastors or pro-family leaders fighting homosexuality who have not made that statement in public.

"Conservative," evangelical Christian Joe Dallas has, to his great credit, taken a public stand against the sin by which he was once enslaved. Unfortunately, Mr. Dallas's public positions on the issue sometimes weaken, rather than strengthen, the case against homosexual activity. For instance, in his book *A Strong Delusion,* Dallas makes this statement concerning the sinfulness of homosexual acts: "I think it's a sin, no worse or better than some of my own sins."[1]

Quite frankly, Joe Dallas is squarely within the mainstream of American evangelical Christianity with this egalitarian sin doctrine. It is a deception which has been embraced by some of Christendom's leading spokesmen. On his "Break Point" radio message, Chuck Colson has stated, "... homosexuality is no worse than many other sins—don't be judgmental; don't gay bash."[2]

During a May 2, 1997 interview with Hugh Downs on the ABC program "20/20," Rev. Billy Graham was asked his opinion on homosexuality. Graham answered:

> Yes, well, I think that the Bible teaches that homosexuality is a sin. But the Bible also teaches that pride is a sin, jealousy is a sin and hate is a sin. Evil thoughts are a sin. And so, I don't think that homosexuality should be chosen as the overwhelming sin that we're doing today.[3]

To portray homosexual acts as being a sin no worse than any other sin is unscriptural, minimizes the seriousness of these acts, sows confusion in the body of Christ, and jeopardizes the eternal destinies of many unsaved souls. Let us take a dispassionate, Biblical look at this egalitarian sin concept.

Certainly it is true that all human beings have sinned. "For all have sinned, and come short of the glory of God" (Romans 3:23). It is likewise true that "the wages of sin is death"[4] and "the soul that sinneth, it shall die."[5] As Christians we know that any sin, any imperfection in our thoughts, words, or deeds is enough to separate us from our perfect Creator Whose holy eyes cannot bear the sight of sin. Any sin—whether of omission or commission, large or small, vicious or simply foolish—any sin not covered by the blood of Christ will condemn the sinner to eternity in the lake of fire. We know that it is only by the blood of Jesus that we can be washed, sanctified, and justified before God. Christ's death is the only atonement that God accepts for our sins. If we are not in Christ, we are in our sins and we stand condemned.

Yet this does not mean that God views all sins equally. Certain sins of open rebellion especially stir God's wrath and bring His righteous judgment upon not only the rebel committing the act but also upon the people who permit such evildoers free reign.

Innocent bloodshed is one such case. The Scriptures are clear regarding God's position on the shedding of innocent blood and what He does to nations which permit the murder of the innocent. Sooner or later, God reacts with great fury against the cold-blooded murder of innocent people, including unborn people, made in His image. It is safe to say that God views and reacts to murder in a different way than He reacts to a Christian uttering an impatient word in a pressure-packed situation. The former sin is a cruel, gross act of rebellion against the Creator; the latter is a momentary failing of the flesh. Most murderers never repent of their violent rebellion. The nations which permit murderers to go unpunished are destroyed. Murder snuffs out innocent human life and devastates whole families while denying God's sovereignty and His image in mankind. By contrast, impatient words can be emotionally hurtful, but that is about it. There is certainly no record of the Lord destroying whole cultures for such minute transgressions. Again, any sin of any magnitude, any imperfection not atoned for by the blood of Christ, condemns the sinner. As Christians it is wrong and dangerous to operate under the false assumption that we have *carte blanche* to engage in sins of a less serious nature. Sanctification is the command of the Scriptures. Nevertheless, it is clear that God does not view all sin in the same light.

But what about homosexual sin? How does God view such transgression? There is plenty of Scriptural proof that adds weight to the contention that God does not view all sins as equal and that He does hold homosexual acts to be especially repugnant and worthy of His wrath. Homosexual acts are labeled an abomination by God in several passages of Scripture.[6] The word *abomination* is derived from the Hebrew word *toebah* (tôw 'êbâh). *Toebah* has the meaning of loathsome or detestable even to the point of being sinister or repulsive. The Lord views homosexual acts so evil as to be repulsive and sinister! Considering all the temporal and eternal repercussions of such acts as well as the simple mechanics of homosexual activity, there is no need to expound on why God would label them repulsive. Homosexual acts certainly are also sinister in that they are an extreme "counter-culture" activity diametrically opposed to God's created order.

Elsewhere in this book we have listed the very strong adjectives which God uses to describe homosexual activity, adjectives which make very clear His loathing and hatred for such rebellious acts, the committing of which so arrogantly transgresses and mocks His created order and stated law. The Bible contains graphic accounts of the divine anger and judgment which homosexual activity provokes. In Genesis 18:20, God calls the sin of Sodom and Gomorrah, which is sodomy, "very grievous." The Lord destroyed those cities along with several surrounding towns because their inhabitants had freely engaged in homosexual activity. The book of Jude informs us that those cities are an example of God's vengeance. II Peter 2:6 tells us that God condemned and turned them to ashes for "an example unto those that after should live ungodly." Obviously, it is an example which many today are anxious to minimize, explain away, or just plain ignore.

Chapter nineteen of Genesis carries this account of God's wrath being poured out on Sodom and Gomorrah: "And Abraham gat up early in the morning to the place where he stood before the Lord: and he looked toward Sodom and Gomorrah, and toward all the land of the plain, and beheld, and, lo, the smoke of the country went up as the smoke of a furnace."

The same passage documents the danger of peacefully co-existing with perversion. Certainly Lot was righteous in that the lawlessness and perversion of the sodomite culture in which he lived "vexed his righteous soul from day to day." Unfortunately, the vexation of his heart apparently did not translate into action against the evil around him. Sodom was literally overrun and controlled by militant sodomites. If Lot had been forcefully speaking and acting against the dominant culture of the town in which he lived, the sodomites would have either destroyed him or kicked him out of town long before the angels arrived to rescue him and his family from the wrath to come.

Christians today can learn much from Lot's experience. When we "roar all like bears, and mourn sore like doves"[7] but do not act against the great wickedness of our day, we are in danger of being desensitized by the filth around us and having our own fidelity to the Lord's standards eroded. We may say that we love God and His law. Yet if we are not living out this conviction daily, when push comes to shove, we may not act in a way consistent with our once righteous souls. Living in peace with God's enemies can subtly and gradually lower one's standards.

Co-existing with extreme wickedness had apparently perverted Lot's value system, to say the least. When the heat was on, he offered his virgin daughters to a mob of howling perverts. Lot evidently saw the rape of his daughters as a lesser-of-evils solution to his visitors' immediate peril. In the end, Lot not only lost his wife during the destruction of Sodom and Gomorrah, but he also lost all his possessions and eventually he lost his daughters to perversion—perversion in which he was an accomplice (Genesis 19:30-38). But of course, Lot had not exactly set a good example for his daughters. They had no doubt heard him privately condemn the sodomite culture of their town, but had apparently not seen much public witness or action by their father against that same culture on behalf of righteousness. Such a situation can certainly cause a young person to wonder how vile the sin at issue actually is and thus can tend to desensitize him toward other sins which seem even less serious by contrast. Lot's daughters had seen their father choose economic pragmatism over righteousness. For what other reason did Lot settle and stay in the region of Sodom and co-exist with its perverted citizens except that it was "well watered everywhere"? The girls had seen the moral weakness of their father come to fruition when he extended them as a peace offering to the perverts whom he had been privately condemning but publicly condoning with his inaction and silence. Is it surprising that Lot's daughters ultimately committed an abominable act with their own father when they felt that it was their only hope of attaining their goal of having children? Perhaps "heterosexual" incest seemed mild to a couple of young women raised to tolerate homosexuality. Such are the dangers of placidly living in the midst of godless rebellion. The question must be asked, What lesson are Christian young people today learning from their parents' interaction with the wicked culture which currently predominates America? Is it not true that many Christians have quietly offered their own children to the evil people around us rather than fight for what is right? After all, what are we doing when we peacefully co-exist with abortionists, sodomites, pornographers, and a God-hating culture which is determined to take our nation into the pit of hell? What, for that matter, are we doing when we put our children into the public (government) schools?

The existence of an open homosexual subculture within a nation is analogous to the existence of one rotten apple in a barrel of apples. That homosexual subculture, like the apple, will eventually putrefy everything around it. The subculture will become the dominant culture. Lot discovered that the hard way, just as the American church will one day soon, short of a great awakening. Homosexuality is a stench in God's nostrils, a stench which He will only bear for so long before pouring out His wrath on the source of the odor. Those who commit or condone homosexual acts are breaking God's holy law and directly assaulting His created order. Meanwhile, those modern-day Lots who quietly co-exist with the sodomite nation in our midst are, quite frankly, running the same risks which Abraham's nephew ran. They are co-existing with a sin which God has said must not be tolerated.

Throughout the Old Testament, homosexual acts are listed with such grievous sins as idolatry, adultery, and murder. This is a pattern which is repeated throughout the New Testament. Under the Law of Moses, God demanded execution as the punishment for homosexual acts (Leviticus 20:13). We see God commending the Hebrew kings who refused to tolerate sodomites in the land. Speaking of homosexual acts, Romans 1:32 says that persons "which commit such things are worthy of death."

Perhaps this would be a good place to interject that yes, any sexual acts between two women most certainly are transgressions of God's law just as surely as similar acts between men are. "Lesbianism" clearly violates God's dictated law as revealed in nature as well as it does His written law. Again, the only sexual relationship which God has allowed and sanctified is the union of one man and one woman within the bounds of holy matrimony.[8] Romans 1:26-27 contains this clear condemnation of "lesbianism," saying, "For this cause God gave them up unto vile affections: for even their women did change the natural use into that which is against nature." In another passage dealing with sexual sin, including all forms of homosexuality, the Scriptural command is:

> Flee fornication. Every sin that a man doeth is without the body; but he that committeth fornication sinneth against his own body. What? know ye not that your body is the temple of the Holy Ghost which is in you, which ye have of God, and ye are not your own? For ye are bought with a price: therefore glorify God in your body, and in your spirit, which are God's (I Corinthians 6:18-20).

Sexual activity between two women is homosexual fornication and therefore condemned by God. This passage also again testifies that all sin is not equal in God's eyes by pointing out that sexual immorality, in addition to being a sin against God and other people, is a sin against one's own body.

One consistent feature of violent, judgment-bound societies has been the toleration of open homosexuality. Rome and Greece did not survive the proliferation of homosexuality. In modern times, a rising homosexual subculture in Germany in the first half of the twentieth century was one marker which signaled an approaching cataclysmic disaster for that nation. Obviously, God views homosexuality as an especially vile sin, a sin which He judges not only eternally but in the temporal sense also, a sin which merits not only individual punishment but corporate chastisement of whole nations and cultures as well.

In light of all of this, why do so many Christians use the homosexuality-is-a-sin-but-it's-no-worse-than-any-other-sin approach? No doubt they do so for numerous reasons, not the least of which may be to avoid being labeled as self-righteous or judgmental. Others may adopt such a posture simply out of misunderstanding. Whatever their reasoning, those who espouse such an unbiblical doctrine should give serious thought as to the consequences of their stance. God expects us to use His Word carefully and accurately. "Study to shew thyself approved unto God, a workman that needeth not to be ashamed, rightly dividing the word of truth" (II Timothy 2:15). The all-sins-are-alike approach not only misrepresents God's holy Word, but it also lowers the resistance of individuals who are being tempted to commit homosexual acts; and it neutralizes Christians in their defense against sexual perversion while actually leading to the acceptance of open homosexuals in the church.

That last assertion calls for a short explanation which can be given in the form of a hypothetical scenario. Those eager to mainstream homosexual activity, including and perhaps especially in the church, can seize the unbiblical egalitarian sin doctrine and take it to the logical conclusion that homosexuals have every right to be members of the body of Christ.

Here is how they do it. The prospective sodomite church member begins by posing this question, "Are all men sinners?" The answer is rightfully "yes." "Does this mean that even Christians, including pastors, are sinners?" Again the answer must be "yes," but here is where the deception of no sin being worse than another sin bears bitter fruit. "Is my sin of homosexuality any worse than the sins of the pastor or of the sins of anyone else in this church?" The answer to that question, to be consistent with the egalitarian sin doctrine, would have to be "no." "Then why can I not become a member of this church and perhaps even an officer of it?"

Why not indeed? If all sins are the same, then why should homosexuals be thrown out of churches? In fact, if all sins are equal and all pastors are sinners, then why should homosexuals not be allowed to pastor? If we accept the proposition that all sins are equal, then why should society discriminate against individuals engaged in homosexual behavior? Why have Christian cultures always outlawed and punished such activity, and how in the world could any society justify doing so today? After all, if all sins are the same, then all sins should be treated equally. If pastors and church leaders are going to condemn sodomy or, for that matter, murder, rape, adultery, fornication, or pedophilia, then they had better spend equivalent time and fervor condemning grouchiness and impatience. If the g/l/b/t crowd is going to be excluded from holding church offices and disfellowshiped for its sin, then should not every church member who is less than perfect be treated the same way?

It is easy to see how the unbiblical stance that all sins are the same can lead to vast confusion and a minimizing of abominable sins such as homosexuality, adultery, and abortion. As Christians we must present the truth as God has delivered it to us. Homosexuality is an especially destructive, rebellious sin which kindles the wrath of God and provokes His judgment. This judgment is not restricted only to those individuals who practice homosexuality, but it is also visited upon those nations which allow such abominable activity to proliferate unhindered, unpunished, and even protected by the civil government. Yes, we must strive to avoid all sin and repent when we fall short. "Because it is written, Be ye holy; for I am holy" (I Peter 1:16). Still, all sins are not equal. Homosexual acts are especially sinister, detestable sins of open rebellion, the results of which must not be minimized.

This brings us to another volley of friendly fire with which those of us who have taken an aggressive public stand against homosexuality must often deal. A number of times I have been confronted by true Christians, even pastors, who have condemned the prioritizing of the homosexual issue. These individuals (yes, it does enter my mind that perhaps they are looking for an excuse to do nothing) will state something to the effect of "Homosexuality is a sin, but there are other serious sins such as adultery. Why are you putting such emphasis on this one sin?" This particular argument has some limited merit in that the church should be speaking out strongly against adultery and demanding a return to the days when it was punished by the civil government. On the other hand, at least at this point in time, there is no well-funded, powerful adultery movement with a political machine stretching from Washington, D.C. to every state capital and many of the smaller units of government. There are no "Christian" adulterer organizations cranking out literature and Bible studies which claim that the Bible condones adultery. I know of no church denominations or pastors who champion such a cause. I am unaware of any adulterer teacher organizations, adulterer pride marches, or adulterer non-discrimination legislation pending. It does not take much discernment to reach the conclusion that the homosexual movement, like the pro-death movement, must be met head-on by the body of Christ. The homosexual lobby is the vanguard; the sodomites are the shock troops of a culture which fully intends to overwhelm, crush, and silence the Christian nation which still exists within America. The church must place a priority on confronting and defeating the homosexual juggernaut. Unless we deal decisively and Biblically with both the homosexual and pro-death elements of the enemy's forces, we will not experience much success anywhere else.

Let us move on and take a look at another facet of friendly fire which has caused immense damage to the church and pro-family movement's capability to defeat the homosexual lobby in the political arena and everywhere else. In my estimation, one of the most destructive statements concerning homosexuality which has ever escaped the lips of a pro-family leader is this: "We believe in full civil rights for gays and lesbians—just not *special* rights."

As usual, Dr. Tony Campolo goes beyond his more conservative brethren and frames working to end discrimination against homosexuals as a ministry of the church! In his book *20 Hot Potatoes Christians Are Afraid to Touch,* Campolo preaches:

> Love requires justice. I believe that if Jesus were in our shoes, He would reach out in love to His homosexual brothers and sisters, and His love would be translated into a call for them to be justly treated by others. That call for justice would require that we work to end the discrimination that has made homosexuals into second-class citizens and denied them their constitutional rights. His love would lead Him to work to create an atmosphere in society wherein homosexuals could be open about who they are and no longer live in fear of oppression and persecution.[9]

While most conservative and Christian leaders do not take such a pro-active stance regarding anti-discrimination statutes for "gays," many publicly espouse the position of full civil rights for homosexuals minus so-called special rights—a position which leads to the same disastrous conclusion in the long run. I do not doubt that such an expressed opinion on the part of many Christians springs from the desire to be compassionate. Nevertheless, this does not negate the fact that it is a position which is wholly unbiblical and extremely detrimental to the cause of Christ and the defense of righteousness. In the next chapter, we will deal more in depth with homosexuality and the law. For now, let us take a look at this concept of just no special rights and where it leads.

Until 1961, homosexual acts were outlawed in all fifty states. Those laws were a great incentive for individuals who were determined to commit homosexual acts to at least stay "in the closet." With such statutes in place, no decent American had to worry about being charged with a violation of law for discriminating against sexual deviants. No one faced the prospect of having to choose between diversity classes or jail for refusing to rent to homosexuals or for slighting one of those individuals now belonging to America's perverted *prima donna* class. No American taxpayer was faced with the prospect of subsidizing pro-homosexual curriculum in state-financed public schools and universities. There were no gay pride events or parades featuring semi-nude sexual libertines. Sodomites were never seen on television; the only homosexuals in the movies were naturally cast as perverts. An open homosexual being elected as a congressman, state legislator, city councilman, or mayor was such a remote possibility that it did not rate any more consideration than did the prospect of an out-of-the-closet "gay" child care worker, police officer, judge, school teacher, or EMT. There were no open sodomites serving as Big Brothers or Big Sisters. The Boy Scouts was not under siege by sexual perverts wanting to be Scout leaders. And there was no AIDS epidemic.

All of the unthinkable things mentioned have now come to pass all across America. Why has this happened? This has happened because laws banning homosexual acts have generally not been enforced and have even been repealed in many states. Since the early 1960s there has been a sea change in the strategy of the conservative pro-family movement, including the strategy taken by most Christian leaders, with regard to homosexuality. It is a monumental shift which has borne bitter fruit and is increasingly reflected in the laws of our land. Whereas the vast majority of Christian leaders and pastors once understood the importance of the civil government's inclusion of sodomy and other perverted sexual acts in the category of sexual crimes, precious few today seem to grasp this and even fewer are willing to take such a stand publicly. The bench mark which now identifies one as a "hard-core" pro-family leader is the position that open homosexuals should be denied "special rights." It is said that "we believe homosexuals should have full civil rights like everyone else. We don't believe in discrimination. We just do not believe homosexuals should have special rights." Quite frankly, I would submit that such a position is disingenuous, untenable, unconstitutional, and unbiblical, as I will share in chapter eleven. For now, let us simply look at the logical conclusion of the just-no-special-rights argument.

One might ask, If the homosexual is doing nothing illegal and if he should be granted all the same rights that law-abiding moral citizens are recognized as having, then why should he not be allowed to run for political office, operate a day care center, be a school teacher, be a policeman, serve in the military, or be an EMT? Why is it a special right for a law-abiding citizen to be afforded the opportunity to have any of the above occupations as long as he can fulfill the immediate requirements of the job? If we do not believe in discrimination against open homosexuals, then how do we justify not protecting them under various non-discrimination laws concerning employment and housing, if we are going to have such laws on the books?

The sad fact is that many in the pro-family movement want to win the war against the homosexual movement, but they want to do so without taking any causalities on our side. Pro-family and Christian leaders must be willing to bear the anger and ridicule that is leveled against those of us who take the only position on the homosexual issue which will eventually bring our efforts to roll back the "gay agenda" to a successful conclusion. That position is this: Individuals who commit homosexual acts are sexual criminals who should be punished by the civil government. Any other position than this is foundationally flawed, Biblically and constitutionally, and doomed to failure. The homosexuals love the pro-family's just-no-special-rights argument because they know that it is a position built on rapidly eroding sand.

It is time that Christian and pro-family leaders begin to take a defensible position regarding homosexual acts. We must frame the argument by insisting that such acts be outlawed again. Invariably, when I take this position in a debate, my opponent must shift from the offense to the defense and attempt to explain why sexual perversion should not be punished. Instead of desensitizing the audience to the prospect of some new stride by the homosexuals, thus institutionalizing past gains, the discussion now becomes: Should homosexual acts be outlawed? The underlying constant becomes that homosexual acts are perverted with the point of contention being: Do people have a right to commit all manner of sexually perverted acts, or should the civil authorities penalize them? This is called framing the discussion, and

Christians and pro-family leaders must begin doing that framing instead of letting our antagonists do so. Ultimately, he who effectively frames the discussion, wins the argument. Pro-family spokesmen must return to a constitutional, Biblical framework regarding homosexual acts. Any other position will doom us to failure at the hands of a queer nation which is more than able to exploit timidity and inconsistency. Quite frankly, it is critical that Christians stop shying away from the truth that homosexual acts must be outlawed once again. Cowardice cannot earn us anything but disastrous defeats. Unfortunately, many Christians cannot even get past the fear of being accused of supporting discrimination.

In recent years, the concept of discrimination has been misused as a club to bludgeon into silence those who oppose homosexuality. Today anyone who takes the position that American citizens should have the option of not renting to, hiring, or associating with homosexuals is demonized for discriminating and portrayed as being equivalent to a Nazi or Ku Klux Klansman. In an effort to avoid such character assassination, many people shrink away from any possibility of being accused of practicing discrimination. While this has been a very effective tactic for the sodomites, it is not an honest one. The reality is that in certain instances, discrimination is not only right but it is also essential for obedience to God, the maintenance of morality, and the very survival of society! As for Christians, while we are to reach out to sinners with the gospel of Jesus Christ, the Scriptures also teach us to discriminate against evil. Passages such as Ephesians 5:11 command as much: "And have no fellowship with the unfruitful works of darkness, but rather reprove them."

One definition of the word *discriminate* is "to use good judgment."[10] There was a time when responsible people were encouraged to use good judgment, to be discriminating in their choices. To be a discerning, discriminating person was considered a very good thing. Wise employers took into account a potential employee's character before hiring him and rejected thieves; liars; drunkards; and sexual perverts, including homosexuals. Voters considered sound moral character a prerequisite for any political candidate. When leasing a dwelling, it was thought to be a private property owner's right and responsibility to refuse to rent to individuals involved in immoral behavior. In other words, there was a time when it was rightly understood to be a good and necessary thing to discriminate against persons lacking moral character. Most people once realized that renting to, hiring, doing business with, and voting for immoral people only legitimize and encourage immorality.

But not anymore! Now the official party line of the media and the immoral elite of our nation is "As long as the person can do the job, what he does in his own time is irrelevant." Those who dare to suggest that men sodomizing other men and women engaging in degrading unnatural sexual acts with each other is perversion which should be discriminated against are labeled bigots. Good, decent citizens who attempt to adhere to a certain moral code in their lives and business transactions are even subject to prosecution by the civil government in many states! In short, evil is now called good and good is called evil.

Almost no one would condone a law which would force landlords to rent to those who engage in bestiality or a statute which would require employers to hire drug addicts. In fact, it is considered to be good judgment to discriminate by refusing to employ or rent to such individuals, even though the acts in question are committed by consenting partners in private. Why should there be a different standard applied with regard to sodomites? Character does count, and persons who engage in sodomy and other perverted homosexual practices are obviously of very low moral character regardless of maintaining in public a veneer of niceness. Decent citizens should not be prohibited from exercising good judgment by refusing to hire, rent to, or associate with homosexuals.

"But that's discrimination," snarl the sexual libertines. Of course it is! It is godly discrimination, and it is time that Americans begin to practice it once more. Almost everyone believes in and exercises some sort of discrimination. The legitimate question is what behavior is proper to discriminate against? Homosexuals are sexual outlaws. When society's laws do not uphold that truth, the weak and the innocent suffer and even the most basic of liberties are put at risk.

Until 1982, Wisconsin's state statutes allowed citizens to practice good judgment when it came to dealing with individuals engaged in homosexual acts. Wisconsin is currently one of a handful of states which forbid discrimination against the perversion of homosexuality. Ask Ann Hacklander what happens to those who attempt to discriminate against homosexuality in the Badger State. As a college student living in Madison in the 1980s, Miss Hacklander refused to share her apartment with an open lesbian who answered her advertisement for a roommate. That exercise of good judgment cost Ann a fine, thousands of dollars in legal fees and court costs, as well as the humiliating experience of being ordered to undergo sensitivity training conducted by a homosexual rights group. Such are the results of state protection of the sexually perverted acts which every state in the Union held to be criminal until 1961.

For the past several decades, the homosexual movement has engaged in a massive public relations campaign aimed at demonizing anyone who dares to suggest that American citizens should have a right to discriminate, to use good judgment, when dealing with persons involved in homosexual activity. That campaign has borne bitter fruit. Open homosexuals, bisexuals, cross-dressers, and transgenders now serve as legislators, judges, policemen, medical technicians, food service workers, teachers, and adopters of children. This is a tragic situation given the fact that the homosexual community is the source of a greatly disproportionate amount of violence, sexual assault, and disease; and it brings the judgment of God upon our land. It is doubly tragic that so many Christian leaders reinforce the "right" of open homosexuals to be free from all forms of discrimination.

In their determination to mainstream their sexual deviancy, homosexual activists have no qualms about equating discrimination against homosexual activity to hate and violence directed against bona fide ethnic groups. This is a campaign in which truth, decency, and history are deemed irrelevant. For instance, in recent years, homosexual strategists have launched a well-constructed campaign to exploit the suffering of Hitler's holocaust victims by claiming that tens of thousands of homosexuals were exterminated in Nazi death camps.

Well-heeled "gay" groups have lobbied vigorously and committed a vast amount of resources to securing a spot, literally buying a place, in holocaust museums around the nation in order to perpetuate the hoax of a "gay holocaust." The Union of Orthodox Rabbis of the U.S. and Canada has publicly protested these shameful, dishonest tactics, as has the Rabbinical Alliance of America.[11]

While it is true that several thousand "fem" homosexuals may have died in labor camps (not death camps), just as did other criminals and political prisoners, "butch" homosexuals were at the very center of the Nazi power structure; in some cases they even served as concentration camp guards. One of the most notorious, Auschwitz executioner Ludwig Tiene, sodomized hundreds of boys and young men even as he strangled and gnawed them to death.[12]

To this day, homosexual influence in the German neo-Nazi movement remains strong. Michael Kuhnen, a major German neo-Nazi leader who recently died of AIDS, was openly homosexual.[13] The militant homosexual movement in America also has its roots in the Nazi Party.[14] The National Socialist League is a homosexual branch of the American Nazi Party.[15] The infamous American Nazi leader Frank Collin was a homosexual.[16] The homosexual aspect of Hitler's Nazi Party has been documented by a number of historians, including the well-respected William Shirer in his famous volume *The Rise and Fall of the Third Reich* and Scott Lively and Kevin Abrams in their book *The Pink Swastika: Homosexuality in the Nazi Party.*

For homosexuals to exploit the suffering and death of millions of people in an attempt to shame Americans into accepting non-discrimination policies inclusive of gross sexual perversion is despicable. Likewise, it is despicable and dangerous for Christians to support "full civil rights, just no special rights" for homosexuals based on a desire to avoid being tarred with the sodomite hate brush. No nation can long survive whose people do not have the moral fiber and good sense to support discrimination against and even criminal penalties for those who commit certain acts of violence and perversion.

Let us deal with another unbiblical concept often touted by individuals who are certainly on the right side of the issue that we are discussing but are promulgating the wrong message. It seems to be all the rage today to urge Christians to refrain from interjecting Biblical truth into public debate.

Dean Merrill is an author and a Christian media veteran who has worked as an editor for a number of Christian publications. Merrill is currently the vice president and publisher of International Bible Society. In his book *Sinners in the Hands of an Angry Church,* Merrill makes a number of statements with which I certainly take issue, including this one on the use of God's Word in public dialogue:

> Christians who understand their minority status but still want to influence the culture for good engage in reasonable dialogue about the issues. They control their voice level and even keep a smile on their faces while they present common-sense reasons why A might be a better option than B or C for all concerned. The source of their common sense, of course, is God's wisdom as revealed in the Bible. But Christian apologists don't bring that up, because it would serve only to polarize the listeners into a side debate about whether the Bible is reliable, is allowable in the public square, etc., etc., etc.[17]

Dean Merrill is so paranoid about using the Bible in public discourse that he even counsels Christians against using the words *moral* and *immoral* to justify a position! According to Merrill, this may cause our opponents to inquire what authority we are using to define the morality or immorality of the given issue, which in turn may force us to admit "the Bible."[18] As stated by Mr. Merrill, "Thus the word *moral* is little more than code language for *Biblical* and suffers the same limitations."[19]

If we cannot use the Bible and if we cannot appeal our issues on the basis of morality, what is left? Merrill advises, "We are likely to get further if we speak of policies, laws, and programs that are *effective, useful, helpful, a good example, beneficial in the long run.*"[20] I suppose Dean Merrill's strategy makes a lot of sense if one believes that man is basically good and that America is better off as a pluralistic society in which any and all belief systems, other than Christian, have equal weight in relation to the governance of our nation. Personally, I believe his approach is morally, intellectually, and spiritually bankrupt.

In one of his "Break Point" radio messages titled "Arguing Against Gay Marriage: How Not to Sound Homophobic," Chuck Colson made this statement regarding the 1996 debate over the Defense of Marriage Act in the U.S. House of Representatives:

> Several representatives responded to Gunderson [an open homosexual Congressman from Wisconsin] by opening their Bibles and reading from them. One lawmaker bluntly described homosexuality as "perversion." But these are perfect illustrations of how *not* to argue this issue.
>
> The vast majority of Americans no longer believe in the authority of Scripture. So how *do* we argue against gay marriage in a way that our neighbors can understand? The answer is, we have to argue in a way that appeals to the common good.[21]

Colson's remark about not using the Bible but rather simply appealing to the common good in order to turn back the homosexual tide, quite frankly, smacks of subjective humanism. The very reason that America is caught up in moral anarchy is rooted in an eroding respect for the Bible as the true source of law and liberty. Colson is using apparent effect to dictate method without considering cause, regardless of what is right.

Certainly most Americans do not believe in the authority of Scripture, and many appear to brush off any reference to God's holy ordinances as irrelevant. That is not at issue here. The issue is right and wrong. It is only right that Christians expound and use God's eternal truth boldly and publicly at every possible opportunity. That the world may not respond in a visibly favorable manner is irrelevant and no surprise. Why do Americans not give the Scriptures proper respect? Is it not because for so long the Scriptures have not been publicly referenced, proclaimed, and defended? The cause of America's drift from a Biblical worldview is that the body of Christ has not wielded the sword of God's Word effectively and authoritatively in the public and political arenas. The solution is to use the Word of God more, not less. Mr. Colson should have been praising God to see a U.S. congressman using the law of the Lord to confront an act which violates the very laws of nature and of nature's God upon which this nation was founded. After all, as our first President put it, it is literally impossible for a government official "to rightly govern the world without God and the Bible."[22]

Why do the American people treat the law of God as if it were a dead letter? Because so many Christians, including pro-family leaders, government officials, and pastors, do. We must lift up the Word of God and defend it for what it is—the eternal, perfect, immutable source of all truth and all true law. The longer we shy away from doing so, the less respect our nation's people will have for the only standard which can successfully govern a country.

I always use the Word of God in the debates on homosexuality in which I am involved. I use the Bible within the context of the laws of nature and of nature's God when speaking of civil government. I use Scriptural passages relating to God's judgment when speaking of the results of a nation's rebelling against His perfect precepts. Finally, I turn to the Bible verses which show the way of salvation in Christ when speaking of the only answer for the individual homosexual.

Unfortunately, it seems it is becoming increasingly popular among some Christian leaders to counsel their brethren to refrain from using the Word of God during public debate over "political issues." This is a very wrong and, quite frankly, treasonous strategy. First of all, it is wrong to be ashamed of the Word of God.[23] This assertion should need no defense. Secondly, it is tactically wrong not to use the Word of God. There is only one way by which we Christians will see our beloved nation won back from the reprobate forces which are destroying her. That way can be summed up by repeating the words of George Washington: "Let us raise a standard to which the wise and honest can repair; the event is in the Hand of God."[24] The only hope for our nation is that God will have mercy on our efforts. This nation will have to experience a spiritual revival, or all is lost.[25] Why do we think that the Lord will grant us a spiritual revival and political reformation if we are not willing to publicly and consistently use His Word in a manner appropriate to the occasion? The very institutions we are trying to change were founded upon God's law. The hearts which we are trying to reach will be transformed only by God's Word. The Scriptures tell us that the Word of God does not return void.[26] Hebrews 4:12 says:

> For the word of God is quick, and powerful, and sharper than any two edged sword, piercing even to the dividing asunder of soul and spirit, and of the joints and marrow, and is a discerner of the thoughts and intents of the heart.

Is this Scripture verse and the rest of the Bible simply quotable quotes, or do we really believe that they are eternal truth? If the Bible is eternal, immutable truth, then we must base our words and actions upon it.

This great nation was built upon an unabashed loyalty to the law of God and the gospel of Jesus Christ. If we are serious about making progress against the forces of darkness loose in our land, then we must be willing to disseminate the light of God's Word with the knowledge that He will bless our steadfastness and that men will be saved by exposure to His truth. That is the only strategy which will rescue America and her people from total destruction. Jesus did not shy away from the use of Scripture when preaching to a "wicked generation."[27] Certainly the prophets did not subscribe to Mr. Colson's contention and the insistence of many other contemporary Christian leaders that it is useless to preach the Word of God to people who do not respect that authoritative Word. Instead, they simply took a stand for righteousness and left the results in the Lord's hands. We are wrong and foolish to do anything less.

This is not to say that we should jettison all other persuasive arguments. With regard to the homosexual issue, the empirical evidence showing the violence, destruction, and health risks that the homosexual life breeds is very powerful and certainly should be employed. However, all of our arguments must be built upon the solid and trustworthy foundation of God's holy Scriptures. We will have no security or hope of success building on any other foundation.

Let us also remember that we are planting seeds. During these times of luxury and ease, those seeds may not take immediate root, but in coming times of turmoil and judgment, we may trust that some of them will grow and bear good fruit.

The final, but in some ways the most damaging, friendly fire concept with which we will deal is the fallacy that one can live simultaneously and indefinitely as a homosexual and a Christian. Obviously, the pro-homosexual crowd thinks that this is entirely possible.

Dr. Tony Campolo is one of those evangelicals who tries to create a murky middle on this issue. I am talking here about those who do call homosexuality a sin, but then turn around and support much of the homosexual agenda, even to the point of maintaining that a person can be a homosexual and still be a Christian. In an impromptu sidewalk debate I had with Dr. Campolo one winter night in 1997, he was adamant that while homosexual acts are a sin, there are many "gay Christians." Dr. Campolo has often spoken in his writings of our "homosexual brothers and sisters."[28] Unfortunately, Campolo's philosophy is too often echoed by individuals who are considered to be among the front ranks of the so-called conservative, Bible-believing church. In *A Strong Delusion,* Joe Dallas also speaks repeatedly of "gay Christians." But is not the term "gay Christian" an oxymoron? Not according to Dallas who writes:

A Christian may, indeed, be openly homosexual. . . .

Most of the people I knew, while working at the Metropolitan Community Church [a "gay" denomination], were from conservative backgrounds like mine. They had come from Baptist, Pentecostal, or fundamentalist churches where they'd had a genuine conversion experience. Yet we all had decided that homosexuality was acceptable and, to the best of my knowledge, we did not become non-Christians the moment we made that decision. . . . For all intents and purposes, we were Christians, and we were homosexual.[29]

How we confront the gay Christian movement is crucial. Paul's instruction—"Yet count him not as an enemy but admonish him as a brother"—should be kept in mind. The members of the gay Christian movement are not our enemies. They claim Christ as their own. . . .

It would take unusual arrogance to think that we, the Christian community, can approach the gay Christian movement as righteous folks approaching degenerates. . . .[30]

In 1981 Professor Richard Lovelace at Gordon-Conwell Theological Seminary commented, in *Christianity Today* magazine, "Most of the repenting that needs to be done on the issue of homosexuality needs to be done by straight people, including straight Christians. By far the greater sin in our church is the sin of neglect, fear, hatred."

Many Christians, of course, and many churches, have opened their doors and hearts to homosexuals. They have loved them, without compromising the Bible's standards, and by speaking the truth in love, they've seen gays and lesbians won into the kingdom of God.

But not all pastors and congregations can say the same, which brings us to a crucial point: If homosexuals have found rejection and isolation in society, then come into our sanctuaries, only to find no sanctuary at all but more rejection, then the judgment we so eagerly pronounce on them for their perversion of sex will no doubt fall on us as well—perhaps a hundredfold—for our perversion of the gospel.[31]

With friends like Joe Dallas who needs enemies? Since when is the church of Jesus Christ a sanctuary for rebels? I have no reason to doubt that Mr. Dallas is a sincere, loving Christian doing his best to confront the sin of homosexuality. The tragedy is that he has taken a very unscriptural position when he promotes the concept that open homosexuals can be considered part of the body of Christ. In fact, he has taken a position which must make the devil leap for joy!

Rather than systematically critiquing any individual's statements regarding this "gay Christian" contention, I will simply lay out the Biblical model for dealing with sexual outlaws within the church. The Scriptures which will be given apply to persons engaged in any sort of sexual perversion, including fornication and adultery. The church of Jesus Christ is *commanded* by the Word of God to severely discipline those who are involved in open rebellion against God's Word. Those who speak of welcoming such individuals into the church as members of the body of Christ are minimizing the grievousness of the sin and joining in the rebellion. It is one thing to invite a "seeking" homosexual to church to hear the Word of God preached. It is quite another thing to allow that same person to sit in church week after week as an open homosexual. It is even worse to admit such a person as a member of the congregation or to allow him to be as a de facto member of the church through inaction on the part of church leadership.

I Corinthians 5 gives us very plain instruction regarding how to deal with a sexually immoral person within the body of Christ, as well as with those involved in other acts of open rebellion against God's law. In this passage, Paul is writing to a people who tolerated open immorality in their ranks. The Corinthians apparently thought that they were being very loving, very Christian by allowing such rebels to remain in fellowship. Paul rebukes them for being "puffed up." How many churches in America today are governed by similarly puffed-up leaders who take pride in being "Christlike" by tolerating open rebellion against God in their congregations?

Regarding the sexually immoral, we are told along with the Corinthians "to deliver such an one unto Satan" and to "put away from among yourselves that wicked person." The word *purge* is also used. We are warned that "a little leaven leaveneth the whole lump." I Corinthians 5:11-13 says this:

> But now I have written unto you not to keep company, if any man that is called a brother be a fornicator, or covetous, or an idolater, or a railer, or a drunkard, or an extortioner; with such an one no not to eat. For what have I to do to judge them also that are without? do not ye judge them that are within? But them that are without God judgeth. Therefore put away from among yourselves that wicked person.

The question may be asked of Joe Dallas and others who insist that the body of Christ should keep fellowship with "gay Christians": What part of I Corinthians 5 do you not understand? Here we are clearly told that the church has the responsibility to judge its own members who have been caught in sexual immorality and other unlawful acts. Those involved in sexual immorality and other open violations of God's law are to be disfellowshiped and shunned unless and until they repent. The hope of the church in taking such an action is that the offender will repent as explained in verses four through six:

> In the name of our Lord Jesus Christ, when ye are gathered together, and my spirit, with the power of our Lord Jesus Christ, to deliver such an one unto Satan for the destruction of the flesh, that the spirit may be saved in the day of the Lord Jesus. Your glorying is not good. Know ye not that a little leaven leaveneth the whole lump?

The body of Christ is commanded to remove from our ranks immoral individuals who refuse to repent. Such judicial action taken by the church does not preclude additional judgment and punishment of the ejected offender by the civil courts.

As explained in chapter eight, it is important to understand that the word *judge* as used in I Corinthians 5 transcends making a simple judgment of an action as right or wrong. Verses twelve and thirteen should not be misunderstood to mean that Christians do not have a duty to judge whether or not actions of non-Christians are right or wrong. These verses do not negate the many Scripture verses which command Christians to confront the forces of darkness. Here the use of the word *judge* involves, in a judicial sense, the bringing of charges and punishment. That is why Paul tells us that church officials, using himself as an example, have nothing to do with judicial actions outside the church; that is the responsibility of the civil authorities (Romans 13:1-6).

To insist that the body of Christ is to be a sanctuary for professing homosexuals is truly a gross distortion of the gospel. Lawlessness begets lawlessness. The church must not tolerate open rebellion against God's Word. Rebels must be promptly confronted and, unless true repentance takes place, removed from all fellowship and shunned. To do less is to encourage lawlessness, put a stumbling block in the path of weaker brothers and sisters,[32] and show utter contempt for God's clear commands. To insist that open homosexuals should be embraced as part of the body of Christ is a perversion of the love of Christ.

Such a policy may play well with the world, but it does not please the Lord.

Certainly until Christ returns, His church will be composed of less-than-perfect people. However, let us differentiate between a less-than-perfect people daily striving to be more like Christ and a body of believers which includes outright rebels. I Corinthians 6:9-11 makes that clear distinction. The passage lists persons involved in open rebellion to God and very succinctly states that such persons "shall not inherit the kingdom of God." Dr. Campolo, Mr. Dallas, and others speak of "gay Christians," but the Scriptures tell us that homosexuals are condemned to hell unless they repent of their sexual sin by confessing it, renouncing it, and experiencing a new birth in Christ. We could spend hours arguing over whether or not a truly born again Christian could turn to homosexuality, thus igniting a divisive once-saved-always-saved debate; but why is this necessary? The bare facts are that no matter what other label he may claim, if an individual is living as a homosexual committing perverted sexual acts, that individual *will not inherit the kingdom of God unless he repents.* That is the Word of the Lord. To die a homosexual is to die condemned. This fact alone should be enough to expose the danger and the deceit of speaking of "gay Christians."

Would Mr. Dallas and others who espouse a non-exclusionary doctrine for homosexuals be willing to embrace known, unrepentant child molesters, rapists, adulterers, or murderers as fellow members in Christ's church? Do we ever hear talk of "Christian" rapists or "Christian" pornographers? Yet they speak of "gay Christians." So much for the body of Christ being "a chosen generation, a royal priesthood, an holy nation, a peculiar people; that ye should shew forth the praises of him who hath called you out of darkness into his marvelous light."[33] So much for the many other verses dealing with the purity of the body of Christ such as II Corinthians 6:14-16:

> Be ye not unequally yoked together with unbelievers: for what fellowship hath righteousness with unrighteousness? and what communion hath light with darkness? And what concord hath Christ with Belial? or what part hath he that believeth with an infidel? And what

agreement hath the temple of God with idols? for ye are the temple of the living God; as God hath said, I will dwell in them, and walk in them; and I will be their God, and they shall be my people.

While it is one thing to be gentle and understanding regarding each other's struggles and failures which have been repented of, it is quite another thing for the body of Christ to embrace sin which our God has condemned in the strongest of terms and to link the name of Christ to a gross sexual perversion. To do so is a distortion of the Scriptures, an abdication of duty, and surely an abomination in the eyes of the Lord. Yet that is exactly what we do when we allow persons involved in homosexual acts to be considered as part of the church of Jesus Christ and pay them the high honor of addressing them as "Christian."

Ephesians 5:11 commands Christians to "have no fellowship with the unfruitful works of darkness, but rather reprove them." Homosexual activity is truly an unfruitful work of darkness. The church of Jesus Christ has been commanded to reprove such activity, yet some are adamant that we should allow the darkness of homosexuality to exist within the body of Christ. Those who counsel such an approach truly are living under a strong delusion!

CHAPTER ELEVEN

Answering Sodom

*Thus saith the LORD, Stand ye in the ways, and see,
and ask for the old paths, where is the good way, and walk therein,
and ye shall find rest for your souls. . . .*
Jeremiah 6:16

These days conservative Christians spend much time fretting that subjective philosophy has become rooted in our society. We are told by Christian pastors, talk show hosts, and group spokesmen that the problem is that very few Americans are guided by objective, immutable standards. I would be the first to agree with this assessment. Our politicians, the mainstream media, heretical church denominations, and the American people in general live and make decisions based upon whim, emotion, perception, and experience; hence, the appalling situation in which we now find ourselves. Because we have departed from God's immutable, unchanging truth, America is on a fast-track to destruction. None of this is alarmist rhetoric; it is all true.

However, the real problem is that it is not only the liberals, the immoral left, the intellectual elite, the neo-fascists who approach the great issues of our day in a subjective, utilitarian fashion. The real factor destroying our nation today is that many Bible-believing Americans and their leaders do the same to a lesser degree! Too often, those who ought to be holding the line against the haters of Biblical absolutism take positions which, in reality, are pale imitations of the ungodly deceptions which they are fighting. In previous chapters, this has been pointed out in a number of ways. While we have spent much time examining the rhetoric and doctrines of the homosexual movement, we have also examined some of the well-meaning, but wrong-headed, rhetoric and doctrines which have tragically become so popular among Bible-believing, pro-family leaders, pastors, and spokesmen. Policies and rhetoric do have consequences, especially when those policies and words are at odds with God's eternal standards. If the body of Christ is not willing to preach the Scriptures as written when addressing flagrant violations of God's law, including homosexual acts, the seriousness of the violation is diminished in people's minds. Consequently, many individuals begin to feel quite comfortable with the open promulgation of a heinous sin while vulnerable people are more easily seduced to commit abominable acts and are less likely to repent of those acts. The end result is tragedy and judgment. In recent years, the unbiblical, subjective approach employed by many of the leaders in the body of Christ with regard to the spread of homosexuality in our land has borne bitter fruit.

A homosexual tidal wave has crested and crashed over our nation. By the late 1960s and early 1970s, the homosexuals had gotten their act together enough to launch sustained, cohesive frontal attacks against the professional, societal, civil, and religious structures which had previously held the sodomites' influence in check, kept their perverse behavior behind closed doors, and hence, their political clout and proselytizing activity to a minimum.

In the 1990s the homosexual lobby is relentlessly advancing virtually everywhere. The sodomites and their allies have not only established beachheads in every realm of society, including the civil government, but they are also rapidly expanding those beachheads and blitzkrieging into the very heart of America. Their highly aggressive invasion forces are helping themselves to the victor's spoil, including taxpayers' subsidies, children's minds, and confused souls. Day after day, the homosexualist forces achieve more objectives. Day after day, they consolidate their gains and fortify their positions, making the prospects that much dimmer for a reversal of the tide of battle in favor of the forces of righteousness.

Standing against this perverse juggernaut has been a too feeble, often timid, easily embarrassed pro-family movement which had counted on a just-no-special-rights Maginot line to stop the invaders, an ineffective defensive line long ago by-passed by the depraved storm troopers of the sexual libertine army which now occupies much of America. The simple truth is that the pro-family movement in this nation has come to its Dunkirk. It is time to evacuate the troops from the indefensible and incredibly dangerous pocket into which they have been pushed, rearm with an appropriate battle plan, and launch our own offensive.

Although there is currently considerable noise and fury coming from conservative Christian leaders and pro-family spokesmen concerning the danger to family, church, and nation posed by the homosexual movement, no national high profile leader on our side—as of this writing and to my knowledge—has had the courage or the foresight to openly take the only principled position which holds out any hope of victory for those who adhere to a Biblical worldview of man, morality, and civil government. That position, simply stated as it has been repeatedly throughout this book, is that homosexuals are sexual outlaws who should be punished by the civil government, even as they are evangelized by the church. Unless we Christians are willing to stand on a solid foundation of objective Biblical truth, we have absolutely no prospect of turning back the homosexual onslaught. The Scriptures tell us that "the battle is the LORD'S."[1] Most Christians love to quote that verse; yet many turn around and fight as if it were not true.

Throughout this book we have examined the necessity of taking an unabashedly Biblical approach when publicly witnessing against the sin of homosexuality and when privately witnessing to the sinner. Much of the church has not done that. Rather, a plethora of subjective doctrines have sprouted up, doctrines which may make the gospel less offensive to the world but which also distort the Word of God to the ruination of many and, ultimately, our nation.

A similar subjective approach has been taken by Christians and pro-family leaders with regard to homosexuality and the law. In the last chapter we touched on the concept of civil rights but just no special rights, which has been at the heart of the pro-family movement's fight against homosexuality. That concept is likewise a subjective rather than an objective approach to dealing with the homosexual movement. There simply is no Biblical, historical, or legal precept which justifies such a position. None! Consequently, trying to defeat the homosexual agenda with such an argument is about as effective as trying to disable an Abrams tank with snowballs. What is even worse is that it is an approach which actually violates the very law upon which this nation was founded and to which all nations are ultimately subject, the laws of nature and of nature's God. In plain English, the just-no-special-rights approach is in itself a sin as it is the promulgation of a policy which is at odds with God's will and His commands. As such, it is a sure recipe for defeat and judgment!

In 1996, pro-family forces were outraged by the U.S. Supreme Court decision *Romer v. Evans*. In this decision, the Court held that Colorado's Amendment 2 violated the Equal Protection Clause of the Fourteenth Amendment to the U.S. Constitution. Amendment 2 was a statewide referendum which was approved by Colorado voters and adopted to that state's constitution. Amendment 2 precluded "all legislative, executive, or judicial action at any level of state or local government designed to protect the status of persons based on their 'homosexual, lesbian or bisexual orientation, conduct, practices or relationships.'"[2] The U.S. Supreme Court's decision in *Romer v. Evans* was no doubt a travesty and a complete mockery of law. At the same time, it was a logical conclusion, a virtual echo of the just-no-special-rights strategy which conservatives have been pursuing. Justice Anthony Kennedy, speaking for the majority, wrote in part:

> The State's principal argument in defense of Amendment 2 is that it puts gays and lesbians in the same position as all other persons. So, the State says, the measure does no more than deny

homosexuals special rights. This reading of the amendment's language is implausible. . . .

The amendment withdraws from homosexuals, but no others, specific legal protection from the injuries caused by discrimination, and it forbids reinstatement of these laws and policies. . . .

[W]e cannot accept the view that Amendment 2's prohibition on specific legal protections does no more than deprive homosexuals of special rights. . . . We find nothing special in the protections Amendment 2 withholds. These are protections taken for granted by most people either because they already have them or do not need them; these are protection against exclusion from an almost limitless number of transactions and endeavors that constitute ordinary civil life in a free society.[3]

Justice Kennedy's decision is a stark witness to the suicidal nature of clinging to a just-no-special-rights approach to homosexuality. What Kennedy said, in essence, is that while Colorado voters and state officials may claim that Amendment 2 simply mandated that homosexuals be treated like every other law-abiding citizen and only be denied "special rights," such would not be the result. In that sense, Kennedy was right. After all, if the sexual acts which homosexuals commit are deemed to be legal, then why should discrimination based on those acts be allowed? Discrimination against "heterosexuals" is not allowed on such a basis.

Imagine a married man being fired from his job due to his employer's decision that intimate relations between the man and his wife are immoral. Imagine a married woman being denied an employment position at a day care center for the same reason. It would not be deemed "special rights" for "heterosexuals" to allow them to seek a legal remedy, and even damages, in such a situation. Intimate relations between a man and a woman within marriage is legal. If intimate relations between two homosexuals is also legal, then on what grounds can we insist that homosexuals be banned from pursuing legal remedy when they are discriminated against on that basis? There is none because we have cut the ground from under our feet.

The U.S. Supreme Court should have allowed Amendment 2 to stand because states have the right to pass legislation allowing, even mandating in some cases, discrimination against persons committing immoral acts which violate the laws of nature and of nature's God. As Justice Antonin Scalia wrote in the minority dissent:

> If it is constitutionally permissible for a State to make homosexual conduct criminal, surely it is constitutionally permissible for a State to enact other laws merely disfavoring homosexual conduct. . . .
>
> I had thought that one could consider certain conduct reprehensible—murder, for example . . . and could exhibit even "animus" toward such conduct. Surely that is the only sort of "animus" at issue here: moral disapproval of homosexual conduct, the same sort of moral disapproval that produced the centuries-old criminal laws that we held constitutional in Bowers.[4]

The decision to strike down Amendment 2 outraged pro-family and Christian leaders; yet the reasoning used to justify the *Romer v. Evans* decision is the exact same philosophy trumpeted by most pro-family and Christian leaders, that philosophy being that open homosexuals should be guaranteed every right and freedom law-abiding citizens are guaranteed. Again, unless we fight the homosexual scourge God's way, we are doomed to defeat. Just no special rights is not God's way. We have seen where such a corrupt position naturally leads.

The truth is that homosexuals are sexual outlaws. Sodomy and other same-sex acts are actions which the civil government should and must outlaw if the dark veil of sexual perversion descending across this nation is to be torn away. Those states with anti-sodomy laws still on the books should enforce them. Those states without such laws should reinstate them. If the perverted acts in which the homosexual is involved are not considered worthy of censure by the civil government by way of negative legal sanctions and punishment, why should such individuals not be protected from class discrimination just as are other law-abiding Americans?

Why do we say "just no special rights" for homosexuals when we would never say the same for pedophiles, necrophiles, rapists, the incestuous, or for that matter, thieves, drug users, or murderers? These are all people who have broken civil laws which have been rightfully put in place to punish destructive behavior which violates the same laws of nature and of nature's God which homosexual acts violate. It is possible to bar a pedophile from child care employment because his behavior is illegal. Merchants may discriminate against a thief when hiring because stealing is illegal. When a person engages in activity which makes him a criminal in the eyes of civil government, citizens do not have to worry about how to interact with such a person or the negative impact he may have on them or their loved ones. Why? Because the person is either in prison, has been executed, or has paid the price for his crime and has agreed to live as a law-abiding member of society. At any rate, that is the way our justice system is supposed to work.

But on what basis can homosexuals be banned from any employment position or government post when by civil law the sexual acts which they are committing are held to be entirely legal? Furthermore, what statement does it make to the citizenry as a whole, especially to the young, when homosexual acts are deemed appropriate, a matter of legitimate choice, by the civil government, and when even Christian leaders for all practical purposes take the same position?

To base opposition to the homosexual agenda on the just-no-special-rights paradigm is to guarantee victory for the purveyors of perversion, as recent history amply attests. The homosexuals know this, even if our side does not. Franklin E. Kameny, Ph.D., is revered by homosexual activists as the father of gay activist militancy. In his younger days as the leader of the militant Mattachine Society, the Harvard scientist was on the cutting edge of a social and political "reform" movement that laid the groundwork for the sweeping victories which have been won by the sodomite movement in the last three decades. In an interview which appeared in the February 26-March 11, 1998 issue of the *Wisconsin Light,* the seventy-two-year-old Kameny gave his perspective vis-à-vis several political setbacks recently suffered by the homosexual movement as opposed to the essential strategy for eventual victory:

> "Ultimately," according to Kameny, "of course most, if not all of these battles will be trumped by the enactment of ENDA (the Employment Non-discrimination Act pending in Congress) and so it is there that we must continue to direct our efforts in full force and relentlessly. While ENDA deals only with employment discrimination, once it has become law, additional protections in housing and public accommodations will probably be relatively easy to enact."[5]

What Kameny was saying is true. This is what has happened in my home state of Wisconsin. In 1982, Republican Governor Lee Dreyfus signed the Wisconsin Fair Employment Act which outlawed discrimination in employment based upon "sexual orientation." Once that act was signed into law, it was a foregone conclusion that all subsequent legislation would contain sexual orientation in any included non-discrimination clauses. Wisconsin statutes are now laced with the sexual orientation language. Under Wisconsin Statute 21.35, even the Wisconsin National Guard is forbidden to discriminate against known homosexuals. Statute 21.35 states in part:

> Notwithstanding any rule or regulation prescribed by the federal government or any officer or department thereof, no person, otherwise qualified, may be denied membership in the Wisconsin national guard because of sex, color, race, creed or sexual orientation and no member of the Wisconsin national guard may be segregated within the Wisconsin national guard on the basis of sex, color, race, creed or sexual orientation.

Such are the results of letting the homosexual camel's nose under the tent simply because the beast is dressed in the cloak of non-discrimination.

The homosexuals know that the key to total victory for their movement lies in getting Americans as a whole to accept the proposition that homosexuals are just average citizens who may engage in certain acts with which not everyone agrees, but which, nevertheless, should certainly not be treated as criminal, for heaven's sake! Yes, the Employment Non-Discrimination Act (ENDA) must be stopped as it would use the 1964 Civil Rights Act to bring the full weight of the federal government down on the head of any American who would discriminate against homosexuals. On the other hand, the just-no-special-rights position of many in the pro-family movement is on a collision course with itself as it points toward the same practical conclusion as ENDA, but without the federal coercion! What the homosexuals are working for are laws which would guarantee that a person would never be discriminated against in any way due to the fact that he commits homosexual acts; and thus the homosexual lifestyle would be considered as perfectly legitimate by civil authorities when formulating legislation and policies. Ironically, many Christian leaders and pro-family spokesmen are espousing the exact same policy in a different package with their full-civil-rights-but-just-no-special-rights rhetoric!

Former Christian Coalition leader Ralph Reed has said he is against ENDA and other so-called special rights legislation for homosexuals. In his book *Active Faith,* Ralph Reed summarizes what he believes to be the correct policy to which the civil government should adhere concerning homosexuality. In so doing, he captures the essence of the position most Christian and pro-family leaders (and homosexuals) currently hold on this issue:

> [T]he government should tolerate but not encourage homosexual conduct. . . .

> [W]e allow for deviations from our own moral code as a matter of course. This is true not only of gays and lesbians, but of those who divorce the wives of their youth, those who disrespect their parents, and those who cheat on their spouses. Religious conservatives are not seeking as part of their political agenda to arrest those engaged in homosexual practices. But tolerance of homosexuality does not mean approval or government affirmation. . . .

> Gays should be afforded the same protections that other citizens enjoy: to register to vote, turn out at the polls, run for office, and affect the public-policy process.[6]

And so it goes. Christian "conservatives" such as Ralph Reed talk tough about not allowing homosexuals to have "special rights" in the form of specific statutory protection from discrimination based on "sexual orientation" but then turn around and say it is wrong to discriminate against homosexuals and, in fact, such discrimination should not be allowed! The "gay" Brer Rabbit is laughing up his sleeve as he begs not to be thrown into the protective just-no-special-rights brier patch which has been planted by Reed and other pro-family leaders. The just-no-special-rights strategy implicitly presupposes that homosexuals have a right to engage in sodomy and other acts free from any negative sanctions from civil government. This is a godless libertarian doctrine and certainly not a Biblical or constitutional principle. Of course, it is the very supposition which Justice Byron White correctly labeled "facetious,"[7] or to use a synonym, *laughable,* in the *Bowers v. Hardwick* decision. Today, it is the homosexualists who are having the last laugh as "anti-homosexual" leaders base their strategies against the homosexual agenda on the very principle which will ensure the sodomites ultimate victory. How strange and disturbing to see people who rail against the moral relativism of our day simultaneously promulgate a doctrine which can only be thought to originate out of a perceived necessity to be accepted as relevant within the amoral, nihilistic culture of the '90s. What else can explain this just-no-special-rights policy?

Luke 6 contains a warning from Christ to those who would attempt to build without a solid foundation. The Lord tells of a man who built his house bereft of such a foundation and relates that "the stream did beat vehemently, and immediately it fell; and the ruin of that house was great." Those Christian and pro-family leaders who refuse to build their arguments against homosexuality on a proper foundation may see some temporary success, but in the long run they will see the utter collapse of all existing barriers to a complete victory by the homosexualists! To avoid certain disaster, we must fight the homosexual movement from a correct foundation.

We Christian Americans often speak of our great heritage and of how "it is impossible to rightly govern the world without God and the

Bible."[8] Then why is it that we ignore that same heritage and attempt the impossible when it comes to staking out our position on such a critical issue as homosexuality? The Great Lawgiver has declared homosexual acts to be criminal in His Lawbook, the Bible. It is for this reason that, until recently, the treatment of homosexual acts as criminal was taken for granted in our Western legal jurisprudence.

Sir William Blackstone (1723-1780) was a British author and judge who systematized nearly six hundred years of English common law dating back to the Magna Carta into a four-volume *Commentaries on the Laws of England.* America's own common law was birthed out of English common law. Until recent years, Blackstone was required reading for would-be attorneys. Under English common law, homosexual acts were a capital offense. In his *Commentaries,* William Blackstone wrote that sodomy is an "infamous crime against nature . . . A crime, which ought to be strictly and impartially proved, and then as strictly and impartially punished."[9] Blackstone called homosexual acts "an offence of so dark a nature . . . the very mention of which is a disgrace to human nature. . . . a crime not fit to be named."[10]

In America, the Puritans mandated the death penalty for homosexual acts. America's founding generation of statesmen and lawmakers likewise detested and outlawed homosexual activity as a violation of God's dictated and revealed law. Thomas Jefferson held that sodomites should be castrated.[11] General George Washington's order book includes a directive concerning the punishment of one of his soldiers for attempted sodomy. The order, issued March 14, 1778, reports that the Commander in Chief of the Colonial Army not only approved the sentence of the offender but that he also did so "with Abhorrence and Detestation of the Infamous Crimes . . ."[12]

Our national and state founding fathers viewed homosexual acts with the same abhorrence and disgust with which they viewed lewd acts between humans and animals. To this day, state statutes forbidding sodomy which are still on the books can usually be found grouped with statutes forbidding bestiality.

America's founders read, studied, and cited Blackstone as an authoritative source when formulating laws for this nation and the various states. They agreed whole-heartedly with Blackstone and the English common law's categorization of homosexual acts as criminal. Justice Byron White summarized the historical legal status of sodomy relative to American law in writing for the majority in the United States Supreme Court's decision *Bowers v. Hardwick* of 1986. In *Bowers v. Hardwick,* the court correctly upheld the right of the states to outlaw and punish acts of sodomy. Speaking for the majority and responding to those who had claimed a constitutional "right" to engage in sodomy, Justice Byron White wrote this:

> Sodomy was a criminal offense at common law and was forbidden by the laws of the original thirteen States when they ratified the Bill of Rights. In 1868, when the Fourteenth Amendment was ratified, all but 5 of the 37 States in the Union had criminal sodomy laws. In fact, until 1961, all 50 States outlawed sodomy, and today, 24 States and the District of Columbia continue to provide criminal penalties for sodomy performed in private and between consenting adults. . . . Against this background, to claim that a right to engage in such conduct is "deeply rooted in this Nation's history and tradition" or "implicit in the concept of ordered liberty" is, at best, facetious.[13]

In spite of the plain facts which prove otherwise, those who defend the indefensible continue to argue that homosexuals have a constitutional right to engage in sodomy and other perverse same-sex activity. Tragically, the homosexualists are supported in that position by those Christian and pro-family leaders who insist on promulgating the just-no-special-rights argument. We modern Christians are apparently much more civilized and intelligent than the generations before us who defended our faith and built our nation. In reality, we have become law-breakers!

American Christians have the privilege and the obligation to frame our arguments and base our actions within the arena of civil government—state and national—upon the Biblical precepts codified in the charter of our nation, the Declaration of Independence. The man known as the Father of the United States Constitution, James Madison, insisted that the original intent of the framers of the Constitution must be followed if Americans were to avoid the very dangerous situation in which we now find ourselves. Madison said this: "If the sense in which the Constitution was accepted and ratified by the nation be not the guide in expounding it, there can be no security for a consistent and stable, more than for a faithful, exercise of its powers."[14]

America's founders made it very clear that America's bylaws, the Constitution, are to be interpreted and expounded only in harmony with the charter upon which it is predicated. The Declaration is more than just a poetic-sounding statement filled with lofty ideas. The Declaration is law. The Supreme Court has recognized this truth. The Declaration is also listed under the heading of "The Organic Laws of the United States of America" in the *United States Code Annotated*. While nowadays very few people have a clue as to the significance of the Declaration and its relation to the U.S. Constitution, this was obviously not always so.

On April 30, 1839, President John Quincy Adams delivered a speech in New York City on the fiftieth anniversary of the inauguration of George Washington as President of the United States. The title of Adams's message was "The Jubilee of the Constitution," the year also being the fiftieth anniversary of that document. John Quincy Adams lived through America's founding era. The son of John Adams who was a signer of the Declaration of Independence and the second President of the United States, John Quincy Adams was a brilliant man. Throughout his address, Adams reaffirmed for his fellow Americans the significance of the Declaration of Independence as the charter of our nation. Commenting on the successful conclusion of the Constitutional Convention, Adams declared:

> And thus was consummated the work, commenced by the Declaration of Independence. . . .
>
> The revolution itself was a work of thirteen years—and had never been completed until that day. The Declaration of Independence and the Constitution of the United States, are parts of one consistent whole, founded upon one and the same theory of government . . .[15]
>
> And this is the day of your commemoration. The day when the Revolution of Independence being completed, and the new confederation Republic announced to the world, as the United States of

America, *constituted* and organized under a government founded on the principles of the Declaration of Independence.[16]

America's people and statesmen once understood and accepted the precepts in the Declaration of Independence as the foundation of our nation's laws. There are a number of crucial principles delineated in the Declaration, but I believe the most important is that document's reference to the laws of nature and of nature's God. The writers of the Declaration of Independence cited the laws of nature and of nature's God as the supreme authority which gave the American colonies permission to separate from their highest civil authority, the English Crown. In so doing, they identified God's dictated and revealed law as being superior to any legislation, decision, or edict of man, and therefore as being the highest legal authority upon which America was founded and with which all her laws must be in harmony.

America was founded as a republic, a nation under law. Likewise, all state governments were required to be republican in form in order to be admitted into the Union. In other words, the state governments, like the national, are to be governments of law, not of men. But of what law are we speaking? Pertaining to the national government, that answer is easy: the law identified in the charter of our nation, the Declaration of Independence. But what of the states? The same standard applies. For instance, the state statutes which contain the Enabling Act allowing my own home state to become part of the Union, *The Revised Statutes of the State of Wisconsin,* passed January 10, 1849, have prefixed to them the Declaration of Independence and the Constitutions of the United States and of the State of Wisconsin. The preamble to the Wisconsin Constitution also identifies "Almighty God" as the Author of man's freedoms and, consequently, the laws governing those freedoms. Even apart from such empirical evidences, it is simple common sense that the founders of our nation would define republican the same for the state governments as for the national government. In other words, the rule of law would have the same definition and source.

It is evident that our national government and each state government are to be governed only in accordance with the laws of nature and of nature's God, which are, in reality, God's creation and revealed laws—regardless of how badly many unbelievers would like to have it otherwise.

At the time of the writing of the Declaration of Independence, the phrase *laws of nature and of nature's God* was in settled use in the Colonies and had been in the Western world for centuries. This is simply well-documented truth. The founding fathers' ancestors, the Puritans, used the phrase to denote the creation laws and revealed laws of the God of the Bible. The political theorists and legal scholars whom the founding fathers studied and emulated used that phrase in the same way. In his treatise *Of Civil Government,* a treatise much studied and quoted by America's founding fathers, John Locke (1632-1704) wrote:

> Human laws are measures in respect of men whose actions they must direct, howbeit such measures they are as have also their higher rules to be measured by, by which rules are two—the law of God and the law of Nature; so that laws human must be made according to the general laws of Nature, and without contradiction to any positive law of Scripture . . .[17]

In his *Commentaries on the Laws of England,* William Blackstone identified the supreme laws by which all men are bound: "Upon these two foundations, the law of nature and the law of revelation, depend all human laws; that is to say, no human laws should be suffered to contradict these."[18] Blackstone identified the law of nature as the rule of action dictated by God to which His entire creation is conformable. Blackstone wrote:

> This will of his maker is called the law of nature. . . .[19]

> It is binding over all the globe, in all countries, and at all times: no human laws are of any validity, if contrary to this; and such of them as are valid derive all their force, and all their authority, mediately or immediately, from this original.[20]

Concerning the other supreme law of which he spoke, the law of nature's God, Blackstone stated, "The doctrines thus delivered we call the revealed or divine law, and they are to be found only in the holy Scriptures."[21]

When America's founders acknowledged the laws of nature and of nature's God as the supreme law of our land, they were speaking of none other than God's creation law and His revealed law.

Every American Christian should understand the full significance of the Declaration of Independence and how it applies to the U.S. Constitution and the state laws of our land. Of course, we should also understand that even if America were not blessed with such a founding document, we Christians still have an obligation to work to see God's law codified into civil law. Psalm 103:19 tells us that God's "kingdom ruleth over all." Psalm 47:8 reads, "God reigneth over the heathen . . ." Daniel 4:17 affirms that "the most High ruleth in the kingdom of men." Romans 13 makes it clear that civil rulers are to act as "God's ministers." Within the jurisdiction which God has granted, civil government rulers are to uphold His true law. Numerous Scripture passages command Christians to be a people who seek justice. Apart from God's law there is no justice! Yet many Christians have bought into the fantastical notion that it is somehow wrong to insist that man's law be in conformity with God's law. In due time, the Supreme Judge of the Universe will make it abundantly clear to all humans that they were, and are, under His law.

Meanwhile, in light of our nation's founding documents and our Biblical mandate to work to bring our nation's laws back into conformity with true law, why is it that modern Christian and pro-family leaders have refused to take a truly lawful stand against homosexuality by declaring such acts to be not just immoral but also unlawful in the truest sense of the word? Why do they prattle on about just-no-special-rights rather than simply state the truth that homosexuals are sexual outlaws who should be not only disciplined by the church, when applicable, but also punished by civil government? Is such a position considered too archaic or unloving? Are Christian leaders and statesmen horrified by the prospect of having to answer questions by referencing the "textbook of the patriots," the Bible, during public debate? What in the world is behind the pro-family movement's desertion of God's immutable truth when it comes to the volatile issue of homosexuality? Perhaps it is terror at the thought of being asked the inevitable questions: "Are you trying to organize a state-sponsored witch hunt? Are you proposing a police state where the authorities peer into bedroom windows?"

The outlawing of homosexual acts has nothing to do with witch hunts or police states. Certainly unconstitutional enforcement of any statute is always possible, but that is no reason to not legislate and enforce just law. Whenever the prospect of criminalizing homosexual acts is raised, a hue and cry goes up that the government has no business concerning itself with activity engaged in by consenting adults behind closed doors. Yet even today in post-Christian America, there are immoral acts done between consenting adults in the privacy of their homes which are rightfully criminalized by the civil government. Very few Americans raise the specter of a police state or witch hunt when asked if laws prohibiting prostitution, incest, bestiality, necrophilia, and drug use should continue to be on the books and even enforced. Maintaining laws against those activities has not precipitated a police state. Those laws have, in fact, helped to suppress such actions while also convincing citizens that such activity is wrong and immoral. Beyond that, life, liberty, and certainly children and families have been well-served by those laws which reflect the laws of nature and of nature's God. No American citizen is required to hire a drug user or to rent to a known prostitute. Individuals proven to be involved in the activities named can be freely and immediately banned or removed from important positions of trust and responsibility. Such persons are, in fact, subject to arrest and prosecution. This should also be the case with homosexuals.

How would laws against homosexual acts be enforced? They would be enforced the same way any other law is enforced. If a person confesses to committing homosexual acts or is caught in a homosexual act by police or credible witnesses, such a person would be charged and would have his day in court. The suspect would be considered innocent until proven guilty, and it would be the prosecutor's responsibility to prove that a violation of the law took place. Perjury by a witness would be punished, and government officials would be held legally accountable and even open to civil lawsuits if those authorities engaged in "witch hunts" or violations of a citizen's constitutional rights. In short, the accused would be guaranteed all his rights of due process and constitutional safeguards. Homosexual crime would be treated as any other crime is treated. Police would not be peaking into bedroom windows to catch sodomites any more than they now peak into bedroom windows to catch other criminals. Trespass, including trespass by government officials, is unlawful, as are warrantless searches. It is also unlawful to entrap individuals into committing a crime.

In light of the hesitancy of the Christian community to take the appropriate stand that homosexual acts must be outlawed by the civil government, one has to wonder how long Christian support for prostitution laws will hold up once the general public begins to ridicule those laws in the same manner as they now attack anti-sodomy statutes. How far is America from the Amsterdam model of anything goes, including storefront prostitution? If we do not take a righteous stand against homosexuality, such an appalling environment in America is just around the corner. Either we fight lawfully, God's way, or we lose. It is just that simple. Our strategy must be to repeal all non-discriminatory and hate crime laws and once more outlaw homosexual acts.

On what basis dare we take this position? Solely on empirical evidence of harm? No, such a strategy in itself is dishonorable and will never be successful. Homosexuals can always claim that the harm done by their acts is self-inflicted between consenting adults and any harm done to others is the result of extremists in their community. If the truth is finally generally accepted that homosexuals commit a disproportionate amount of child abuse, they will then say, "Just punish the offenders, not all of us." The spread of disease from the sodomite community will simply be cast as the afflictions of a misfortunate minority, and the emphasis will be put on finding a cure for the disease by spending more taxpayer dollars rather than changing the behavior which is spreading it. This is, in fact, what we have already been seeing with regard to AIDS.

Certainly empirical evidence of harm should and must be used in the fight to outlaw homosexuality, but such proof should be used as corroborating evidence, not as a primary argument. Such evidence should also be employed to prove that man truly does reap what he sows. God's law bans homosexual acts. Those who choose to violate that law will suffer various afflictions. A people who tolerates such outlawed behavior will suffer increased health risks, an ever increasing spiral of violence of all kinds, a general unraveling of their society, and the judgment of God upon their heads. I firmly believe it is very important to showcase the effects of homosexuality left unchecked. However, it is much more vital to document the true cause of those effects, which is that homosexual acts violate the laws of nature and of nature's God, the very laws this nation was founded upon and meant to be forever governed by. That is the pre-eminent reason why the civil government should outlaw homosexual acts.

Many Christian pro-family spokesmen feel uncomfortable referring to God and the Bible when dealing with an issue in the arena of civil government. This is more than unfortunate. This is dangerous and sinful, as we spoke of in a previous chapter. Here in America we are blessed that our governmental institutions are founded upon, and meant to be in harmony with, the laws of nature and of nature's God. Many Christians do not realize this; obviously many politicians do not want to admit it. All of that notwithstanding, all nations and all people are under God's law. Refusing to recognize this fact does not change it anymore than refusing to believe in God causes Him to not exist. After all, if men are not under God's law, whose law are they under? Man's law? Man is sinful and when he turns inward to his own intellect and emotion as the authoritative source as to what is right and wrong, lawful and unlawful, the results are predictable, horrible, and bloody. God's law, as found in the Holy Scriptures, is the legitimate source to which our governing officials must look when constructing the statutes and ordinances by which our society is governed.

Romans 13:1-7, among other Scripture passages, makes it abundantly clear that civil government does have the power and the obligation "to execute wrath upon him that doeth evil." This does not mean that civil authorities have the power to punish thoughts or to try to coerce people to convert to Christianity. Faith in Christ is a matter of the heart and strictly between an individual and the Lord (Romans 10:9). God has given the civil government no jurisdiction over opinions, political beliefs, or religious convictions. These are all matters of the heart. On the other hand, God has clearly given the civil government jurisdiction over some physical activity, specifically the authority to punish certain acts which clearly violate His dictated law and revealed law. Throughout the Bible, acts of homosexuality are defined as being unlawful acts punishable by the civil government. The government of the nation of Israel was constrained by God to severely punish such acts. Civil government today is likewise constrained.

I Timothy 1:8 reads, "But we know that the law is good, if a man use it lawfully." Law is good if properly used, and the next verse informs us exactly what this means: "Knowing this, that the law is not made for a righteous man, but for the lawless and disobedient, for the ungodly and for sinners, for unholy and profane ..." Law is not to be used to deprive persons of inalienable liberties or to thrust the long arm of government into spheres of jurisdiction where it has no God-given authority. No, law is meant to be used for the punishment of persons who violate God's eternal statutes—the lawless and disobedient.

Some may argue here that these verses cannot be speaking of civil law by virtue of the fact that sinners, unholy and profane people, are mentioned. After all, even thoughts can be sinful, unholy, and profane. Certainly civil government has no jurisdiction with relation to the thoughts, attitudes, and in most cases, even the words of citizens. However, these verses are actually referring to the civil government's punishing lawbreakers, and verses nine and ten make that clear by defining the type of sin indicated:

> ... for murderers of fathers and murderers of mothers, for manslay-
> ers, for whoremongers, for them that defile themselves with

mankind, for menstealers, for liars, for perjured persons, and if there be any other thing that is contrary to sound doctrine.

Verse eight makes it evident that the law mentioned is a law exercised by man. What man? Verses nine and ten, by delineating some of the crimes to be punished by "good law" clarifies which "man" is granted the jurisdiction to exercise the law relative to the acts in question. Certainly the church has no grant of authority to punish murderers, kidnappers, liars, or whoremongers who are outside the church, and certainly no authority to go beyond disfellowshipping those within the church. I Timothy 1:8-11 is obviously stating that the civil government has the duty and that it is, in fact, a good thing for civil authorities to exercise the law in order to punish lawbreakers, including homosexuals, those who "defile themselves with mankind."

There is no need for Christians to argue whether or not this is a legitimate use of law within the context of the New Covenant. We do not have to get into heated discussions regarding the authority of the Mosaic Covenant relative to the New Covenant. First of all, the passage appears within the context of the New Covenant; and secondly, verse eleven pre-empts any such discussion by clearly stating that the law spoken of is "according to the glorious gospel of the blessed God." God's law, spoken of in I Timothy 1:8-11, is a part of the glorious gospel by which we were saved and under which we live. The simple truth is that God has legislated, mandated, commanded, insisted, and authorized that the civil government punish homosexual acts. A civil government which will not do so is acting unlawfully. A church which fails to support civil sanctions against sodomites is bestowing its blessing on unlawful activity by both the civil government and the sodomites. This is hardly appropriate for the church of Jesus Christ!

In spite of that, many Christian leaders and politicians refuse to take a right and lawful position on the issue of homosexuality. Consequently, they are in rebellion to the Lord, and we are losing the battle against the homosexual movement. It is interesting that most Christians regard homosexual acts so differently than they do other crimes. No Christian will shy away from agreeing that murder violates God's law and should be punished by the civil government. None will disagree with the statement that rape is a violation of God's law and should be punished by the civil authorities. Most will still agree that adultery is an unlawful act because it violates God's eternal statutes concerning marriage and thus should be proscribed by civil law and punished. I would hope that all Christians agree with laws which forbid a sister and a brother from marrying each other, no matter how sincere the couple may be in pledging to love and honor each other until parted by death. If questioned as to the origin of their position on all these unlawful acts, the majority would still point to the Bible, the law of God.

It is sheer hypocrisy of the worst sort (not to mention disobedient and self-defeating) for Christians to take the compromised stand that homosexuals should be granted full civil rights, just not special rights. Certainly all opinions and beliefs have an origin somewhere. From what source does this concept emanate? What religious doctrine, teaching, or intellectual discipline birthed the idea that open homosexuals should be accepted and treated as law-abiding citizens? Surely this modernistic myth within the body of Christ did not originate from the Word of God but rather from the mind of man, birthed in ungodly compromise, fueled by unholy fear, and steeped in political expediency. The hard truth is that if the civil government currently outlawed homosexual acts and a majority of the public supported such laws, so would a vast majority of the body of Christ, and Christian leaders would take that position publicly. Since an opposite situation is presently the status quo, most Christian and pro-family leaders go with that flow. All of this makes it painfully obvious that most of our leaders are looking to Caesar and the world rather than to God and His Word to formulate their position on this issue. Yet "what shall it profit a man, if he shall gain the whole world, and lose his own soul?"[22] Perhaps the full-civil-rights-but-just-no-special-rights policy makes for better public relations with the world and the secular press, but Christians who pursue such a policy would do well to remember Christ's warning: "Woe unto you, when all men shall speak well of you! For so did their fathers to the false prophets!"[23]

Those who insist on committing sodomy and other homosexual acts are sexual outlaws. They are criminals who should have every constitutional right that every other criminal has, including the right to due process of law and freedom from cruel and unusual punishment if convicted. They are criminals who need the gospel, not the false compassion and license which they are receiving from the majority of Christ's church and her leaders.

The outcome of the battle between the body of Christ and the new American Sodom depends entirely on how the Lord's people act and react rather than on the antics and strategies of the sodomites and their allies. If God's people will take an uncompromising, unrelenting, unapologetic, Biblical public stand against the homosexual nation in our midst, we will push the homosexual demon back into the closet for at least another generation or two; and perhaps we will see many homosexuals brought to Christ. If we continue to fight this battle with cowardly, carnal weapons, America is doomed to become another Sodom and Gomorrah. Perhaps it is time for Christians to take a good, long look into the eyes of their children and grandchildren and consider what sort of future they face if the body of Christ does not get its theology and its act together quickly and respond to the homosexual onslaught with uncompromising vigor, honor, and devotion to truth rather than with the compromise, cowardice, and disgrace which has thus far often marked our efforts. There can be no doubt that we will someday have to answer to the Lord for how we answer Sodom.

The words spoken by Joshua so long ago to the children of Israel are appropriate words with which to end this book:

> And if it seem evil unto you to serve the LORD, choose you this day whom ye will serve; whether the gods which your fathers served that were on the other side of the flood, or the gods of the Amorites, in whose land ye dwell: but as for me and my house, we will serve the LORD (Joshua 24:15).

May God stir His church and her leaders to take a truly righteous, implicitly compassionate, stirringly courageous stand on the issue of homosexuality. May we be a people who stand as an unyielding bulwark against the sodomite tide even as we reach out with the salvation message of the gospel to those committing homosexual acts. May our answer to Sodom be one which pleases our God rather than the gods of the Amorites.

Notes

Chapter 1: *Harbingers of Hell in the Halls of the Church*

1. "A Resolution on Civil Rights Without Discrimination as to Affectional or Sexual Preference," adopted by the Governing Board of the National Council of Churches of Christ in the USA (now known as the National Council of Churches), 6 March 1975.
2. "On Homosexuality and Christian Faith: A Madison Affirmation," appeared as an ad in the *Capital Times*, 11-12 October 1997, sec. A, p. 6.
3. Ibid.
4. Jeannine Aversa, "Believe It: Poll Finds Faith in God Is Rising," *Wisconsin State Journal*, 22 December 1997.
5. Ryan LaLonde, "McDonald Attends White House Hate Crimes Summit," *PFLAGpole*, Winter 1998, p. 6.
6. Public statement given by Rev. Dianne Reistroffer at a press conference held at the Wisconsin State Capitol, Madison, Wisconsin, 8 March 1996.
7. Ibid.
8. Interview with Dianne Reistroffer conducted by Katy Sai, WISC-TV 3 News, 6:00 P.M. edition, 8 March 1996.
9. "Voice of the People," *Capital Times,* 16-17 March 1996.
10. Patrick Henry, Remarks to the Second Virginia Convention, 23 March 1775; quoted in Catherine Millard, *The Rewriting of America's History* (Camp Hill, Pa.: Horizon House Publishers, 1991), p. 135.

Chapter 2: *Homosexuality: America's Sacred Sin*

1. Ralph Reed, *Active Faith: How Christians Are Changing the Soul of American Politics* (New York: Free Press, 1996), p. 264.
2. Ralph Reed, address given as part of the Wisconsin Union Directorate's Distinguished Lecture Series, Memorial Union Hall, Madison, Wis., 17 February 1998.
3. Romans 13:7.
4. Reed, *Active Faith,* p. 265.
5. Ibid., p. 266.
6. Federation of Parents and Friends of Lesbians and Gays, *Is Homosexuality a Sin?* (Washington, D.C.: P-FLAG, 1992), p. 3.
7. II Timothy 3:7.
8. Proverbs 1:7.
9. Romans 1:22.
10. P-FLAG, *Is Homosexuality a Sin?*, p. 8.

11. Ibid.
12. Ibid.
13. Ibid., p. 9.
14. Ibid.
15. Ibid.
16. Ibid., p. 11.
17. Ibid.
18. Ibid.
19. Terry Sanderson, "It's Time for Gay Christians to Give Up on the Churches and Walk Out for Good," *Wisconsin Light,* 31 July-13 August 1997, p. 11.
20. I Corinthians 6:9-11.
21. Leviticus 18:22, 20:13.
22. Romans 1:26.
23. Carla Barnhill, "A Gift of Grace," *Campus Life*, November-December 1997, p. 48.
24. Ibid., p. 50.
25. John 7:24.
26. Ezekiel 33:8.
27. Amos 5:15.
28. Ephesians 5:11.
29. I Timothy 3:15.
30. Matthew 28:19-20.
31. Barnhill, "A Gift of Grace," p. 50.
32. I John 1:9.
33. Romans 2:24.
34. Romans 2:1-11.
35. Matthew 7:15.
36. Matthew 23:15.
37. John 8:44.
38. Matthew 7:15.
39. Matthew 23:33.
40. Ibid.
41. Matthew 7:15.
42. Jonathan Edwards, "Sinners in the Hands of an Angry God," in *Beginnings of American Literature, Classics for Christians,* vol. 3, ed. Jan Anderson and Laurel Hicks (Pensacola: A Beka Book Publications, 1982), p. 160.
43. William Mac Donald, *Believer's Bible Commentary* (Nashville: Thomas Nelson Publishers, 1995), p. 155.
44. Charles H. Spurgeon, *Commenting and Commentaries* (New York: Sheldon and Co., 1876), p. 13.
45. Ibid.
46. Matthew Henry, *Commentary on the Whole Bible: Complete and Unabridged in One Volume* (n.p., Hendrickson Publishers, 1996), p. 46.
47. Ibid., p. 47.
48. Ibid., p. 172.
49. Ibid., p. 175.
50. Ibid., p. 368.
51. Ibid., p. 2,254.

52. Ibid., p. 2,461.
53. II Timothy 2:15.
54. Spurgeon, *Commenting and Commentaries,* p. 19.
55. Matthew Poole, *A Commentary on the Holy Bible,* 3 vols. (n.p., Hendrickson Publishers, n.d.), 1 : 44.
56. Ibid., 3 : 923.
57. Ibid., 1 : 44.
58. Ibid., 3 : 774; 1,005.
59. Ibid., 1 : 691; 3 : 923.
60. Ibid., 3 : 923.
61. Ibid., 3 : 482.
62. Ibid., 1 : 382.
63. Ibid., 3 : 482.
64. Ibid., 3 : 945.
65. John Vernon McGee, *Thru the Bible Commentary Series,* vol. 7: *Leviticus, Chapters 15-27* (Nashville: Thomas Nelson Publishers, 1991), p. 58.
66. Ibid.
67. Ibid., p. 59.
68. "Responding with Love and Truth," *Christian American,* July-August 1996, p. 45.

Chapter 3: *Serving Satan in the Name of God*

1. Interview with Tony Campolo conducted by Charlie Rose, PBS Television, 24 January 1997.
2. Tony Campolo, *Following Jesus Without Embarrassing God* (Dallas: Word Publishing, 1997), pp. 179-180.
3. Tony Campolo, *20 Hot Potatoes Christians Are Afraid to Touch* (Dallas: Word Publishing, 1988), pp. 111-113.
4. Ibid., pp. 109-110.
5. Ibid., pp. 118-119.
6. Campolo, *Following Jesus Without Embarrassing God,* p. 79.
7. Ibid., pp. 197-198.
8. Campolo, *20 Hot Potatoes,* p. 84.
9. Ibid., p. 85.
10. Peter Gomes, *The Good Book: Reading the Bible with Heart and Mind* (New York: William Morrow and Co., 1996).
11. "Embracing Our Cause: A Ritual of Commitment to Justice," *More Light Update,* June-July 1996, pp. 12-13.
12. Mary Jo Osterman, *Claiming the Promise: An Ecumenical Welcoming Bible Study Resource on Homosexuality* (Chicago: Reconciling Congregation Program, 1997), p. 2.
13. Ibid., p. 3.
14. Ibid.
15. Ibid.
16. Ibid.
17. Ibid, p. 48.
18. Ibid., p. 5.
19. Ibid.
20. Ibid.

21. Ibid., p. 6.
22. Ibid., p. 7.
23. Ibid.
24. Ibid., p. 8.
25. Ibid., p. 11.
26. Ibid., p. 20.
27. Ibid., p. 25.
28. Ibid.
29. Marie M. Fortune, "Doing Least Harm: An Ethical Standard and Five Relational Guidelines," adopted from *Love Does No Harm: Sexual Ethics for the Rest of Us* (New York: Continuum, 1995), pp. 33-39, quoted in Osterman, *Claiming the Promise,* p. 46.
30. Osterman, *Claiming the Promise,* p. 26.
31. Ibid., quote taken from inside of back cover.

Chapter 4: *High Rollers in a Cosmic Casino*

1. I Timothy 4:2.
2. Romans 3:6.
3. Revelation 16:7.
4. Judges 17:6.
5. "Letters from Readers," *Oconomowoc Focus,* 15 January 1998, sec. A, p. 3.
6. "There Is No Place for Dirty Politics," *Wisconsin Light,* 12-25 September 1996, p. 4.
7. Malachi 3:6.
8. Ezekiel 16:46-59; Matthew 10:15, 11:23-24; Luke 10:12.

Chapter 5: *Anything But Sin*

1. Wilfrid Sheed, "Gay in the Eyes of God," *Time,* 27 May 1996, p. 44.
2. I Timothy 3:15.
3. Ephesians 5:11.
4. Jude 3.
5. Harry C. Kiely, "A Plea for Compassion," *Gay Theological Journal* 1 (September-December 1997) : 27.
6. Lyn Jerde, "Reconciling Faith, Homosexuality," *Chippewa Herald Telegram,* 8 December 1996, sec. A, p. 5.
7. "Transgendered Association Launches Wisconsin Discrimination Survey," *Wisconsin Light,* 4-17 December 1997.
8. Ibid.
9. Susan Barber, "A Woman Scorned," *Eau Claire Leader Telegram,* 1 June 1997, sec. A, p. 2.
10. Tony Campolo, *20 Hot Potatoes Christians Are Afraid To Touch,* (Dallas: Word Publishing, 1988), p. 110.
11. Ibid., pp. 111-112.
12. Ibid., p. 113.
13. Ibid., pp. 116-117.
14. Joe Dallas, *A Strong Delusion* (Eugene, Oreg.: Harvest House Publishers, 1996), p. 219.
15. Don Thorsen, "Revelation and Homosexual Experience," *Christianity Today,* 11 November 1996, p. 34.

16. Ibid., p. 36.
17. Ibid., p. 38.
18. N. 2358, *The Catechism of the Catholic Church* (Liguori, Mo.: Liguori Publications, 1994), p. 566.
19. "Cardinal Ratzinger Comments on Textual Changes in Catechism," *The Wanderer,* 6 November 1997, p. 11.
20. National Conference of Catholic Bishops Committee on Marriage and Family, U.S. Catholic Conference, Inc., *Always Our Children: A Pastoral Message to Parents of Homosexual Children and Suggestions for Pastoral Ministers,* (Washington, D.C.: U.S. Catholic Conference, 1997).
21. "Catholic Bishops Affirm Being Gay Is Not a 'Choice,'" *Cabin Talk,* November 1997, p. 11.
22. Acts 2:37-38.

Chapter 6: *It's All Just a Big Mistake*

1. Campaign to End Homophobia, *Homophobia and Anti-Semitism: Making the Links* (Cambridge, Mass.: Campaign to End Homophobia, 1993).
2. Floss Whalen, "Was Personal Attack on Clergyman Necessary?" *Oconomowoc Enterprise,* 7 January 1998, sec. A, p. 4.
3. Al Geiersbach, "Don't Bother to Send in the Clowns, 'The Clown Show' is Already Here," *Wisconsin Light,* 10-23 April 1997, p. 6.
4. II Corinthians 6:7.
5. Galatians 1:8-9.
6. Evangelicals Concerned, *The Bible Is an Empty Closet* (New York: Evangelicals Concerned, n.d.).
7. Federation of Parents and Friends of Lesbians and Gays, *Is Homosexuality a Sin?* (Washington, D.C.: P-FLAG, 1992), p. 13.
8. Harry C. Kiely, "A Plea for Compassion," *Gay Theological Journal* 1 (September-December 1997) : 27.
9. Victor Paul Furnish, "What Does the Bible Say About Homosexuality?" in *Caught in the Crossfire: Helping Christians Debate Homosexuality,* ed. Sally B. Geis and Donald E. Messer (Nashville: Abingdon Press, 1994), pp. 57-58.
10. Virginia Ramey Mollenkott and Letha Scanzoni, *Is the Homosexual My Neighbor?* (San Francisco: Harper and Row, 1978), p. 54.
11. National Gay Pentecostal Alliance, *Homosexuality and the Bible* (Schenectady, N.Y.: Lighthouse Ministries, 1988), p. 2.
12. John 8:44.
13. Chris Glaser, "Illuminations 1998: Meditations for Lent," *More Light Update,* January-February 1998, p. 7.
14. William Federer, compiler, *America's God and Country: Encyclopedia of Quotations* (Coppell, Tex.: FAME Publishing), p. 311.

Chapter 7: *God vs. God?*

1. Acts 5:29.
2. Jude 3.
3. Ecclesiastes 1:9.

4. Tony Campolo, *20 Hot Potatoes Christians Are Afraid To Touch* (Dallas: Word Publishing, 1988), p. 115.
5. Nicole Gibeaut, "Alarmed by What's Done in the Name of Jesus," *Washington Blade,* August 1994, reprinted in *Tell Us,* November 1994, pp. 4-5.
6. Promotional flyer for the *Other Side,* 1998.
7. "Christians and Homosexuality: An Introduction," *Other Side: Christians and Homosexuality: Dancing Toward the Light,* 1994 Special Issue, p. 2.
8. Mark Olson, "Untangling the Web," *Other Side: Christians and Homosexuality: Dancing Toward the Light,* 1994 Special Issue, p. 18.
9. Ibid., p. 22.
10. Dianne Reistroffer, "Why We Stand with the GLBT Community," sermon preached at University United Methodist Church, Madison, Wis., 25 February 1996.
11. Shelly Birkelo, "Mom Learns to See Gift in Gay Son," *Janesville Gazette,* 22 April 1994, sec. B, p. 3.
12. Federation of Parents and Friends of Lesbians and Gays, *Is Homosexuality a Sin?* (Washington, D.C.: P-FLAG, 1992), p. 15.
13. Adam Chase Korbitz, "Jesus' Answers to Religious Right Found in Gospels," *Janesville Gazette,* 24 January 1997, sec. C, p. 1.
14. I Peter 2:22.
15. John 10:30; 17:11, 22.
16. Donald Eastman, *Homosexuality: Not a Sin, Not a Sickness: What the Bible Does and Does Not Say* (Los Angeles: Universal Fellowship of Metropolitan Community Churches, 1990), p. 3.
17. Nancy L. Wilson, *Homosexuality: Our Story Too: Lesbians and Gay Men in the Bible* (Los Angeles: Universal Fellowship of Metropolitan Community Churches, 1992), p. 6.
18. Ibid., p. 7.
19. Ibid.
20. John Linscheid, "A Thousand Trains to Heaven," *Other Side: Christians and Homosexuality: Dancing Toward the Light,* 1994 Special Issue, pp. 44-45.
21. Promotional flyer for the *Other Side,* 1998.
22. William Gordon, *The History of the Rise, Progress and Establishment of the United States of America, including An Account of the Late War,* 2d., 3 vols. (New York, 1794), 1 : 273-74, quoted in *Political Sermons of the American Founding Era,* 1730-1805, ed. Ellis Sandoz, (Indianapolis: Liberty Press, 1991), p. xv.

Chapter 8: *Shame on Who?*

1. "Same-Sex Marriage," *Wisconsin Light,* 13-26 March 1997, p. 4.
2. Informational brochure of the Stonewall Alliance for Youth, Long Beach, Calif.
3. Informational sheet distributed by Gays, Lesbians and Allies for Diversity in Education, Madison, Wis.
4. Ann Thompson Cook, "Who Is Killing Whom?," *Issue Paper 1 of Respect All Youth Project* (Washington, D.C.: Parents and Friends of Lesbians and Gays, 1991).
5. Susan Messina, compiler, *Lesbian, Gay and Bisexual Youth: At Risk and Undeserved* (Washington, D.C.: Center for Population Options, 1992).
6. Ibid.
7. Informational brochure of the National Youth Advocacy Coalition, Washington, D.C.

8. Promotional flyer on *Scared to Death: Gay Youth Suicide*, distributed by Lazarus Project, Hollywood, Cal.

9. William R. Wineke, "Gay Clergyman Decries 'Urge to Purge,'" *Wisconsin State Journal*, 7 April 1997, sec. B, p. 1.

10. We Are Family, "Consider the Children," *Plain Talk, Issue 2* (Charleston, S.C.: We Are Family), p. 1.

11. We Are Family, "The Last Acceptable Prejudice," *Plain Talk, Issue 2* (Charleston, S.C.: We Are Family), p. 5.

12. Ann Thompson Cook, "Who Is Killing Whom?," *Issue Paper 1 of Respect All Youth Project* (Washington, D.C.: Parents and Friends of Lesbians and Gays, 1991).

13. Ann Thompson Cook, "You Can Help," *Issue Paper 2 of Respect All Youth Project* (Washington, D.C.: Parents and Friends of Lesbians and Gays, 1991).

14. Jack Harrison, "Living Surrounded by Silence," *Christian Social Action*, February 1991, p. 15.

15. Shelly Birkelo, "Mom Learns to See Gift in Gay Son," *Janesville Gazette*, 22 April 1994, sec. B, p. 1.

16. Nancy Mayer, "Prayers for Bobby: A Mother's Change of Heart About Her Gay Son's Suicide," *Wisconsin State Journal*, 23 September 1995.

17. Peter LaBarbera, "Gay Youth Suicide: Myth Is Used to Promote Homosexual Agenda;" Americans For Truth About Homosexuality, P.O. Box 45252, Washington, D.C. 20026.

18. Ibid.

19. Paul Cameron, "Gay Suicide," *Family Research Report,* March-April 1998, p. 7; Family Research Institute, P.O. Box 62640, Colorado Springs, CO 80962.
Peter LaBarbera, "Gay Youth Suicide."

20. Julie Koepp, "Protesters Hit City," *Oconomowoc Press,* 18 December 1997, sec. A, p. 11.

21. Dianne Reistroffer, "Why We Stand with the GLBT Community," sermon preached at University United Methodist Church, Madison, Wis., 25 February 1996.

22. Romans 13:1-6.

23. Thomas E. Schmidt, *Straight and Narrow?: Compassion and Clarity in the Homosexuality Debate* (Downers Grove, Ill: InterVarsity Press, 1995), pp. 14-15.

24. Koepp, "Protesters Hit City," sec. A, p. 11

25. "Open Letter," *Stevens Point Journal,* 16 March 1998.

26. Tom Sine, *Cease Fire: Searching for Sanity in America's Culture Wars* (Grand Rapids: William B. Eerdmans Publishing Co., 1995), p. 37.

27. Ibid.

Chapter 9: *Deadly Deceptions*

1. Mary Jo Osterman, *Claiming the Promise: An Ecumenical Welcoming Bible Study Resource on Homosexuality* (Chicago: Reconciling Congregation Program, 1997), p.12.

2. II Corinthians 5:17.

3. Evangelicals Concerned, *The Bible Is an Empty Closet* (New York: Evangelicals Concerned, n.d.).

4. Universal Fellowship of Metropolitan Community Churches, *Homosexuality and the Bible Bad News or Good News?* (Los Angeles: UFMCC, 1994).

5. Donald Eastman, "Homosexuality: Not a Sin, Not a Sickness: What the Bible Does and Does Not Say," *Gay Theological Journal* 1 (September-December 1997) : 13-14.

6. Joseph C. Weber, "Does the Bible Condemn Homosexual Acts?" *Engage/Social Action,* 1975 May, pp. 28ff., reprinted and distributed by Lutherans Concerned.
7. Osterman, *Claiming the Promise,* p. 31.
8. Ibid.
9. Daniel A. Helminiak, *What the Bible Really Says About Homosexuality* (San Francisco: Alamo Square Press, 1994), p. 37.
10. Ibid., p. 39.
11. Ibid., p. 41.
12. Mark Olson, "Untangling the Web," *Other Side: Christians and Homosexuality: Dancing Toward the Light,* 1994 Special Issue, pp. 17-18.
13. Paul A. Tidemann, *Homosexuality and the Bible* (St. Paul: Wingspan, n.d.), pp. 2-3.
14. "Today's Mail: Christianity," *Wisconsin State Journal,* 8 March 1997.
15. Dianne Reistroffer, "Why We Stand with the GLBT Community," sermon preached at University United Methodist Church, Madison, Wis., 25 February 1996.
16. Wilfrid R. Koponen, *What Does the Bible Say About Homosexuality?* (New York: Integrity, n.d.), p. 3.
17. Tidemann, *Homosexuality and the Bible,* p. 3.
18. Isaiah 42:4, I Corinthians 9:21, I Timothy 1:8.
19. Eastman, "Homosexuality: Not a Sin, Not a Sickness," p. 14.
20. Ibid., p. 15.
21. Helminiak, *What the Bible Really Says About Homosexuality,* p. 45.
22. Evangelicals Concerned, *The Bible Is an Empty Closet.*
23. Dueteronomy 4:2, 12:32; Proverbs 30:5-6, Revelation 22:19.
24. Helminiak, *What the Bible Really Says About Homosexuality,* p. 65.
25. UFMCC, *Homosexuality and the Bible,* p. 6.
26. Eastman, "Homosexuality: Not a Sin, Not a Sickness," p. 15.
27. National Gay Pentecostal Alliance, *Homosexuality and the Bible* (Schenectady, N.Y.: Lighthouse Ministries, 1988), pp. 23-25.
28. II Timothy 3:16, I Peter 1:10-12, II Peter 1:20-21.
29. Isaiah 40:22.
30. Job 26:7.
31. I Corinthians 15:38-41.
32. Hebrews 11:3.
33. Hendrik Hart, "Romans Revisited," *Other Side: Christians and Homosexuality: Dancing Toward the Light,* 1994 Special Issue, p. 28.

Chapter 10: *Friendly Fire*

1. Joe Dallas, *A Strong Delusion* (Eugene, Oreg.: Harvest House Publishers, 1996), p. 148.
2. Chuck Colson, *Responding to the Gay Agenda,* "BreakPoint" radio series reprint (Washington, D.C.: Prison Fellowship Ministries, 1996), p. 15.
3. Interview with Billy Graham conducted by Hugh Downs, ABC, "20/20," 2 May 1997.
4. Romans 6:23.
5. Ezekiel 18:4.
6. Leviticus 18:22, 20:13; Deuteronomy 23:17-18.
7. Isaiah 59:11.
8. Genesis 2:24; Matthew 19:4-9; Mark 10:5-12; Ephesians 5:31.

9. Tony Campolo, *20 Hot Potatoes Christians Are Afraid to Touch* (Dallas: Word Publishing, 1988), pp. 109-110.
10. *Webster's Seventh New Collegiate Dictionary* (Springfield, Mass.: G. & C. Merriam, Co., 1971), p. 238.
11. Robert L. Mauro, "Will Buchanan Support Orthodox Rabbis' Stand Against Homosexual Exhibits?," *Wanderer,* 8 May 1997, p. 9.
12. Paul Cameron, *The Gay Nineties: What the Empirical Evidence Reveals About Homosexuality* (Franklin, Tenn.: Adroit Press, 1993), p. 46.
13. Scott Lively and Kevin Abrams, *The Pink Swastika: Homosexuality in the Nazi Party,* 3 ed. (Keiser, Oregon: Founders Publishing, Corp., 1997) p. 182.
14. Ibid., pp. 173-184.
15. Ibid., pp. 176-178.
16. Ibid., pp. 175-176.
17. Dean Merrill, *Sinners in the Hands of an Angry Church: Finding a Better Way to Influence Our Culture* (Grand Rapids: Zondervan Publishing House, 1997), p. 52.
18. Ibid., p. 53.
19. Ibid.
20. Ibid.
21. Chuck Colson, *Arguing Against Gay Marriage: How Not to Sound Homophobic,* "BreakPoint," 16 July 1996.
22. William Federer, compiler, *America's God and Country: Encyclopedia of Quotations* (Coppell, Tex.: FAME Publishing), p. 660.
23. Romans 1:16-17.
24. Federer, *America's God and Country,* pp. 647-648.
25. II Chronicles 7:14.
26. Isaiah 55:11.
27. Matthew 12:45.
28. Campolo, *20 Hot Potatoes,* pp. 109, 119.
29. Dallas, *A Strong Delusion,* p. 158.
30. Ibid., pp. 206-207.
31. Ibid., pp. 146-147.
32. Romans 14:13.
33. I Peter 2:9.

Chapter 11: *Answering Sodom*

1. I Samuel 17:47.
2. *Romer v. Evans,* 1996 WL 262293 (U.S.).
3. Anthony Kennedy, opinion, *Romer v. Evans,* 1996 WL 262293 (U.S.).
4. Antonin Scalia, dissent, *Romer v. Evans,* 1996 WL 262293 (U.S.).
5. Jack Nichols, "Father of Gay Activist Militancy Isn't Discouraged by Recent Losses," *Wisconsin Light,* February 26-March 11, 1998.
6. Ralph Reed, *Active Faith: How Christians Are Changing the Soul of American Politics* (New York: Free Press, 1996), pp. 265-266.
7. Byron White, opinion, *Bowers v. Hardwick,* 478 U.S. 186 (1986).
8. George Washington quoted in William Federer, compiler, *America's God and Country: Encyclopedia of Quotations* (Coppell, Tex.: FAME Publishing), p. 660.

9. William Blackstone, *Commentaries on the Laws of England,* vol. 4: *Of Public Wrongs,* 1769 (reprinted Chicago: University of Chicago Press, 1979), p. 215.

10. Ibid, p. 215-216.

11. Thomas Jefferson, *Notes on the State of Virigina* (Philadelphia: Matthew Carey, 1794), p. 211 as cited in David Barton, *Homosexuals and the Military: an Historical Perspective,* Wall Builders, P.O. Box 397, Aledo, TX 76086.

12. George Washington, *The Writings of George Washington,* John C. Fitzpatrick, editor (Washington: U.S. Government Printing Office, 1934), Vol. XI, pp. 83-84 as cited in Barton, *Homosexuals and the Military.*

13. Byron White, opinion, *Bowers v. Hardwick,* 478 U.S. 186 (1986).

14. *The Writings of James Madison,* (G. Hunt ed. 1900-10), p. 191, quoted in Stephen H. Galebach, "The Declaration of Independence and Original Intent," *Journal of Christian Jurisprudence,* vol. 6: *Reviving the American Republic: Laws of Nature and of Nature's God* (Virginia Beach: CBN University, 1987), p. 110.

15. John Quincy Adams, "The Jubilee of the Constitution," 30 April 1789 in *Journal of Christian Jurisprudence,* vol. 6: *Reviving the American Republic: Laws of Nature and of Nature's God* (Virginia Beach: CBN University, 1987), pp. 18-19.

16. Ibid, p. 21.

17. John Locke, quoting Hooker (Eccl. Pol., lib. iii, se. 9.) in *Of Civil Government,* XI:136n., 1689 (reprinted Chicago: Great Books Foundation, 1966), p. 83.

18. Blackstone, *Commentaries,* vol. 1: *Of the Rights of Persons,* 1765, p. 42.

19. Ibid., p. 39.

20. Ibid., p. 41.

21. Ibid., p. 42.

22. Mark 8:36.

23. Luke 6:26.